THE
ANCIENT
WORLD

THE
ANCIENT
WORLD

John Haywood

METRO BOOKS

NEW YORK

THE ANCIENT WORLD

The ancient world had several 'cradles' of civilization – Mesopotamia, Egypt, northern India, China, the Mediterranean and the Andes mountains and Central America. It was in these favourable areas, all with the rich natural resources to support dense populations, that history's most influential civilizations arose.

Roman republic
Through military and political innovation, the Roman republic expanded from a city state to become the greatest power of the ancient world.

The Maya
Surviving for 2,000 years, the warlike Maya civilization was the most long-lived and most accomplished of the Mesoamerican civilizations, noted for its achievements in astronomy and mathematics, literature, art and architecture. Its ruined temple pyramids and palaces, rising from the depths of the Central American rainforest, are among the most evocative monuments of the ancient world.

Atlantic Ocean

Pacific Ocean

The Inca
The Incas of the Peruvian Andes created the largest empire of the ancient Americas. Skilful metalworkers in gold, silver and bronze, the Inca was the only ancient American civilization to make extensive use of metal tools and weapons.

MAP KEY

- Sumer 3500–2004 BC
- Ancient Egypt 3100–1070 BC
- Ancient India 2600–185 BC
- Minoans and Mycenaeans 2000–1200 BC
- Ancient China 1766–206 BC
- Persian empire 700–329 BC
- Classical Greece 800–338 BC
- Roman republic 509–27 BC
- The Maya 600 BC–AD 1697
- The Inca AD 1000–1533

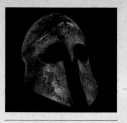

Classical Greece
Arguably the most creative of all ancient civilizations, Classical Greece laid the foundations of modern European civilization with its brilliant achievements in art, architecture, literature, politics, philosophy and the sciences.

Sumer
The Sumerians of ancient Mesopotamia were the pioneers of civilization, the first people to live in cities and the first to use writing. It was on Sumerian foundations that the great empires of Assyria and Babylon were built.

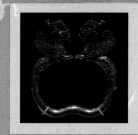

Persian empire
Persia was the world's first superpower. Persia's empire extended from India to the Mediterranean, incorporating elements of Mesopotamian, Indian, Greek and Egyptian civilizations to create a vast cultural melting pot.

Pacific Ocean

Minoans and Mycenaeans
The first civilizations of Europe, the Minoans and Mycenaeans left a rich and influential legacy of myths and legends, of the Trojan Wars, the quest for the Golden Fleece and the lost continent of Atlantis.

Ancient Egypt
The longest surviving of all civilizations, ancient Egypt was the first territorial kingdom, famed for its divine kings, vast pyramids and temples, colossal sculptures, mummies and its enigmatic hieroglyphic writing.

Ancient India
Ancient India was the birthplace of two of the world's most important and influential religions, Hinduism and Buddhism.

Ancient China
China's civilization rivals ancient Egypt's for longevity, descending in an unbroken tradition from its ancient roots in the Bronze Age over 3,000 years ago.

THIS book introduces ten of the most accomplished and influential of the world's ancient civilizations. Historians and archaeologists are agreed that the emergence of the ancient civilizations was one of the defining events of history, a dramatic step-change in the scale and pace of human development. Physically modern humans first appeared in sub-Saharan Africa over 100,000 years ago and slowly spread out to occupy almost every part of the world by the time the first civilizations appeared in Mesopotamia and Egypt just over 5,000 years ago. For most of that enormous period of time, technological and cultural change was almost imperceptibly slow. Since the emergence of the first civilizations, the pace of change has rarely slackened. Individual civilizations have failed for economic or environmental reasons, or because they were conquered by other civilizations. Some of their achievements have been lost, but always much has survived for their successors to build on. The great civilizations of the modern world, in the Americas, Europe, the Middle East, India and the Far East, all rest on ancient foundations.

Early writing
Cuneiform was one of the first forms of writing to be developed. The script gets its name, which means 'wedge-shaped', from the distinctive marks created by the reed stylus.

For something so important, 'civilization' has proved remarkably difficult to define. The word itself, first coined in the 18th century, derives ultimately from the Latin word *civilis*, meaning 'related to citizenship', as with 'civil law', for example. As commonly used, the word civilization came to imply moral qualities such as 'civility' and 'civilized' values and behaviour. A society which shows care and compassion towards the sick and elderly might be considered to be more civilized than one which did not, for example. Such definitions might seem simply to be common sense but on closer examination they all too often turn out to be ethnocentric value judgments. Many travellers have discovered to their embarrassment that what constitutes 'civilized' behaviour in their own culture is considered vulgar and 'barbaric' in another. Because of this, historians and archaeologists have sought to define civilization in objective terms that avoid value judgments by stressing the complexity of the organizational aspects of society. Although there is still no universally agreed definition, most historians and archaeologists would consider that a civilization must possess most or all of the following characteristics: settlement in cities; specialization of labour; concentration and redistribution of surplus food and other products; hierarchical class structure; government institutions; monumental public architecture and official art; long-distance trade; and writing, arithmetic, geometry and astronomy. This is a definition that the inhabitants of the ancient civilizations would have understood because, for most of them, it was living in a city, with all its diversity and complexity, that separated them from the barbarians.

Historians divide civilizations into two types: 'primary' civilizations, such as those of Mesopotamia, Egypt and the Indus Valley, which developed independently; and 'secondary' civilizations, such as those of Classical Greece and Rome, and the Maya and Inca civilizations in the Americas, which developed under the influence of neighbouring, older-established, civilizations.

Historians and archaeologists have proposed many theories to explain the emergence of civilizations. Some of these can be readily dismissed. Civilization did not emerge because of any mental changes in humans themselves, for example: humans attained their modern mental capacities at least 40,000 years ago and there is no convincing evidence that humans today are any more intelligent than their Stone Age ancestors. Perhaps surprisingly, technological advances were not a decisive factor either. For the first thousand years of its history, the ancient Egyptian civilization relied mostly on Stone Age technology and was unaware even of the existence of the wheel. Similarly, the ancient civilizations of the Americas relied on Stone Age technology right up until their conquest and destruction by the Spanish in the 16th century. This confirms the wisdom of defining civilization primarily in terms of social complexity. Given a large enough workforce, time and efficient organization, great things can be achieved even with the simplest tools. The pyramids were built with little more than stone hammers, soft copper chisels, wooden levers and ropes.

Certainly, the most important single factor in the emergence of civilization was agriculture. Agriculture broke the direct link between the natural productivity of the environment and the human population. Population growth among hunter-gatherer peoples was always constrained by the availability of wild foods. If there were too many mouths, starvation quickly reduced the population to a sustainable level. Farmers could accommodate a rising population by using the extra labour to bring more land into production and increase the food supply. Farming by itself did not make civilization inevitable, however. Most early farmers could produce little more food than they needed to feed themselves and their families. It was only where intensive agriculture developed, through innovations such as the plough or irrigation, that civilizations could develop. Intensive agriculture allowed farmers to produce more food than they and their families needed to survive. This surplus food became, and remains to this day, the basis of civilization and all its achievements. Societies with surplus food had labour to spare from the land, and the means to support it while it specialized full-time in other productive or cultural activities. These included a host of arts and crafts, trade, administration, teaching, medicine, religion, politics and – the darker side of civilization – organized warfare.

In most parts of the world, it is the emergence of the first civilizations that marks the boundary between prehistory and history. In most ancient civilizations (the Incas being an important exception) the needs of administering a complex society efficiently led to the development of writing. At first, writing was used only for record keeping, but its potential as a means of preserving and accurately transmitting knowledge from one generation to the next gradually became apparent. In this way, one of the greatest achievements of the ancient civilizations was the invention of history itself.

Massive monuments
Using little more than Stone Age tools, the ancient Egyptians were able to build enormous monuments, including the Great Pyramids at Giza and the Sphinx.

SUMER

FOR the ancient Mesopotamians, the world began when the gods created the first city. They believed that gods created humans almost as an afterthought, solely that they might have subjects to worship them and take care of their cities. The Mesopotamians could not imagine a world without cities. They understood that social organization was the foundation of civilization, and it was in the cities of Mesopotamia that civilization as we know it began. Writing, bureaucracy, mathematics, astrology, glass, the wheel (both for transport and making pottery), irrigation, the plough and the sail are among the inventions that were first developed by the Mesopotamians. Their civilization survived for about 3,000 years (roughly 3500–500 BC), exercising a powerful influence on neighbouring cultures. The founders of this civilization are known today as the Sumerians.

Northern Mesopotamia was a part of the 'Fertile Crescent', a great arc of territory extending through the Middle East, running through Israel, Lebanon, western Syria, southern Turkey and the Zagros Mountains between Iraq and Iran. In this region, the world's first farming communities began to develop at the end of the last Ice Age, some 10,000 years ago. Today, after millennia of intensive cultivation and over-grazing, much of the Fertile Crescent is reduced to semi-desert, but even in its original natural state its soils were never outstandingly fertile. There are no great alluvial plains to compare with those in southern Mesopotamia. What really made this area so favourable to the early development of farming was, firstly, that it had sufficient rainfall to support dry farming (farming without artificial irrigation), and, secondly, that it was very rich in plants and animals that were suitable for domestication. These included wild strains of plants, such as wheat, barley, onions, peas, lentils and date palms, and wild animals, such as cattle, goats, sheep, asses and pigs.

THE FERTILE CRESCENT

Because of its rich resources of wild foods, the Fertile Crescent supported a relatively dense population of semi-nomadic hunter-gatherers during the last Ice Age. As the Ice Age came to an end approximately 10,000 years ago, the climate of the Near East became drier, reducing the availability of wild foods. The hunter-gatherers living in the region responded to these changes by deliberately planting the seeds of their favourite food plants close to their campsites to improve the security of their food supply. They also began to control and manage herds of wild cattle, sheep and goats, achieving this by penning them up and selectively slaughtering young male animals while releasing females of breeding age. In herd animals, only dominant males get to mate, so large numbers of young males can be taken without depleting the breeding stock. From these simple beginnings there followed a long process of selective breeding to produce fully domesticated crops and farm animals best suited to supplying grain, meat, milk and skins for clothing and shelter. The need for vessels to store and prepare food spurred the development of pottery technology.

Previous page:
Warrior king
The victorious army of the king of Ur (shown larger than the other figures in the middle of the top row) returns from a successful campaign in this scene from the 'war side' of the Standard of Ur, made c. 2600–2400 BC. The standard, a wooden box decorated with shell and lapis lazuli set in bitumen, was probably part of a musical instrument.

DOMESTICATION

Cultivating wild plants and penning up wild animals is only the first stage of the transition to dependence on agriculture. The next stage is the domestication of wild plants and animals by selective breeding to improve their usefulness. Wild cereals found in the Near East have small grains (the seeds) that are difficult to harvest because they break off the ear of the plant and scatter on the ground as soon as they are ripe. All animal and plant species show a degree of variability, however. Some individual wild cereal plants would have had larger than average grains and tougher ears that scattered less readily when ripe. By selectively planting seeds from these plants, early farmers in the Near East bred high-yielding strains of cereal with ears that did not break up during harvesting. This selection process has now gone so far that domesticated wheat and barley are almost totally dependent on humans to propagate them as they are unable to scatter their own seeds. Early farmers in other parts of the world, such as the Far East, Mesoamerica and the Andes, independently discovered the principles of selective breeding. Globally, far fewer animals than plants have proved suitable for domestication, either because they are too nervous of humans, too aggressive, or because they compete with humans for the same food. Grazing animals that instinctively live in herds and follow a leader, like sheep, goats and cattle, proved most suitable for domestication. This is because they are easily managed and can convert grass and leaves, which humans cannot eat, into meat and milk. In the Near East, farmers bred selectively for characteristics that made animals easier to manage, such as docility and smaller body size.

Animals for the feast
A bullock and goats from the 'peace side' of the Standard of Ur. In contrast to the 'war side' this face of the standard features scenes of feasting and celebration. It portrays a parade of animals, including fish, cattle, sheep and goats, in front of seated figures who are being entertained by musicians.

In the Fertile Crescent, the transition from hunting and gathering to complete reliance on agriculture and settlement in permanent villages took around 2,000 years and, once complete, there could be no going back. With hunter-gatherers, population is limited by the natural productivity of the environment. If the population rises to an unsustainable level, starvation soon restores the natural balance. Hunter-gatherers who survived into the modern age often took extreme measures to limit population growth, for example, by killing or abandoning unwanted babies. Farming broke this link, though perhaps not permanently. Even simple subsistence farming can support a much denser population than hunting and gathering. The human population began to rise, and, as it did so, it inevitably became more reliant on farming for its food supply. However, more mouths also meant more hands, enabling more land to be brought into cultivation and worked more intensively, so increasing the food supply even more. More people also meant more brainpower and the pace of cultural and technological change began to increase too.

'When you are about to cultivate your field, keep a close eye on the opening of the dikes and ditches, so that when you flood your field the water will not rise too high in it. When you have drained it of water, watch the field's moist soil so that it will remain fertile for you.'

Sumerian farmers' almanac

Except for brief pauses resulting from plagues and famines, the global population has risen inexorably ever since the introduction of agriculture, aided by ever more efficient farming methods and technology.

As the population in the Fertile Crescent grew, settlers moved out of established villages to create new villages on virgin land. As the ever-growing numbers of farmers encroached on their hunting grounds, the remaining hunter-gatherers in the region were forced to take up farming too in order to survive. By around 6000 BC, the farming way of life had become widespread in the Near East, but only in areas with sufficient rainfall for dry farming. Around 5900 BC, farmers in the foothills of the Zagros mountains began to dig canals to carry water from rivers to their fields to irrigate them during the dry season. This was the key development that allowed farmers to settle in Sumer and unlock the tremendous fertility of its alluvial soils.

PRELUDE TO CIVILIZATION

The period of the farming settlement of Sumer is known as the Ubaid (c.5900–4200 BC), after the archaeological site of Tell al-Ubaid, not far from modern Nasiriyah, the scene of the first major battle of the US-led invasion of Iraq in 2003. *Tells* are the most distinctive archaeological sites of the Near East. *Tell* is the Arabic word for 'mound'. Historically, the most important building material across the Middle East was mud brick or adobe: it is still widely used today. Mud bricks are made simply by filling a wooden mould with a mixture of compacted mud and chopped straw. The mould is removed and the brick is left to dry in the sun. Thin mud serves as mortar between the bricks. Provided they are protected by a roof, walls of mud brick are surprisingly durable, especially in areas with dry climates, but eventually they begin to crumble to dust. When this happens, rather than repair the building, it is easier to knock the whole structure down, level the site and build a new one on top of the remains of the old. Over centuries and millennia of occupation, thick layers of debris build up as a result of repeated rebuilding, raising the sites of villages, towns and cities above the surrounding countryside, sometimes by as much as 46 metres (150 ft). Excavating a *tell* is akin to taking apart a Russian doll, as successive occupation layers are removed to reveal still earlier ones below.

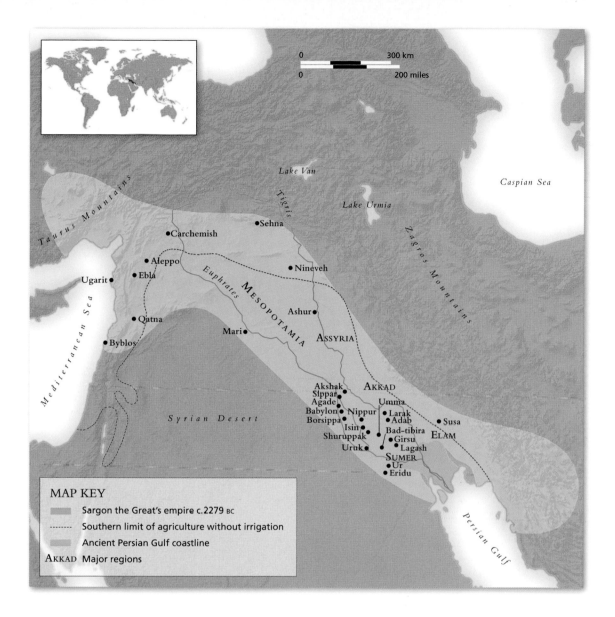

MAP KEY

- Sargon the Great's empire c.2279 BC
- ----- Southern limit of agriculture without irrigation
- Ancient Persian Gulf coastline
- AKKAD Major regions

Once the principle was understood, irrigating the Sumerian plains was not technically difficult. Like other great rivers, such as the Mississippi in the United States, the Tigris and Euphrates have built up high banks, called levees, so that the river beds are actually higher than the surrounding countryside. Irrigation canals dug from the rivers into the surrounding countryside were simply fed by gravity. Productivity was further increased by the introduction of heat-tolerant strains of wheat and barley, and by the use of draught animals, such as donkeys and oxen, which were harnessed to the newly invented *ard* or scratch plough. Though it was little more than a pointed wooden digging stick adapted to be drawn by animals, the *ard* enabled one person to cultivate a larger area more intensively than was possible with hand tools alone. Thanks to these developments, Mesopotamian farmers could reliably produce more food than they needed to support themselves and their families.

Offering a prayer
A small bronze and gold statue of a kneeling man, known as the 'worshipper of Larsa'. This piece was created for an inhabitant of the city of Larsa and dedicated to the Sumerian god Amurru.

Creating and maintaining irrigation systems was a labour-intensive task, beyond the capabilities of individual families. Irrigation canals silted up and needed to be dug out frequently, there was flood damage to be repaired, and if, as often happened, rivers changed their courses, new canals to be built. Labour needed to be organized and fed, while food supplies needed to be collected and redistributed as rations. Disputes over access to water needed to be resolved. It was the need for a central body to manage these essential tasks that many archaeologists have identified as beginning the process of state formation in Sumer. Another factor may have been long-distance trade. Apart from its soils, Sumer lacked natural resources. Everyday essentials such as timber, stone and copper for toolmaking, as well as luxuries, such as precious metals and semi-precious stones, had to be imported in exchange for surplus food and fine wheel-thrown pottery. The people who controlled the distribution of these imported goods would have accrued considerable power.

THE RISE OF THE ZIGGURAT

The population of Sumer increased rapidly. By 5000 BC, many of the Sumerians' farming villages were growing into small towns, each typically centred on a temple complex. The largest of these, with a population of around 5,000 people, was Eridu. Now called Tell Abu Shahrein, it is a typical multi-layered *tell* site rising around 23 metres (75 ft) above the surrounding plain. Eridu was sited right at the edge of the alluvial plain, close to the marshes on the east and the Arabian desert to the south. This position provided the people of Eridu with access to three different types of environment: rough grazing land in the desert; fish and wildfowl in the marshes; and fertile farmland. A small shrine built at Eridu early in the Ubaid period established the pattern for all later Mesopotamian temples. Though little more than 9.3 square metres (100 sq ft), the shrine possessed an ornamental facade, an offering table and an altar for a statue of the god, in this case the water-god Enki. The shrine was rebuilt several times, each new building being more elaborate than the last. By the close of the Ubaid period, the shrine had grown into a large temple complex built on top of a 1-metre (3-ft) tall platform, incorporating the debris of its predecessors. Over the centuries, the platforms of such temples grew taller until, by c.2100 BC, they evolved into ancient Mesopotamia's most distinctive monument, the ziggurat. Most of Eridu's people worked on the land, but there was a small community of craftworkers who maintained the temple. A distant memory of Eridu's early pre-eminence inspired later Mesopotamian myths, which hold that it was the place of creation, the first city to emerge from the *abzu* – the primeval water-world.

Mud brick
Sun-dried and partly kiln-fired brick from Ubaid. First made
c.3200–2800 BC, bricks baked in this way were more
durable and water resistant than sun-dried mud bricks.

The prominence of temples in Eridu and towns like it
suggests that their rulers combined secular and spiritual
authority in a way that was common in the ancient
world. The farmers of the plains were always vulnerable
to flooding and unpredictable changes to the course of
the rivers on whose waters they were totally reliant.
Eridu was completely abandoned for short periods
for this very reason. Sumerians came to believe
that they were at the mercy of capricious gods.
The most famous of the Mesopotamian myths
is that of the flood that the gods sent to
destroy humanity because they had tired
of their constant chattering. This was the
prototype for the later Biblical story of
Noah's flood. The Mesopotamian myth has its
own Noah, a wise man called Utnapishtim who
built an ark, and loaded it with his family and 'the
seed of all living things', after being warned about the flood
by Ea, the god of wisdom. Under these circumstances of constant
insecurity, any leader who was believed to be able to intercede with the
gods on behalf of his followers might easily have used his religious authority to
gain control over irrigation works and the collection and redistribution of food
surpluses and trade goods, making them extremely powerful.

WHEN DID IT HAPPEN?

Ancient Mesopotamians used a calendar based on a year
of 12 lunar months (28–29 days each). Each month
began with the first sighting of the crescent of the new
moon. The first month of the year was *nisannu*, which
fell in March or April. Because the lunar year had only
354 days, it slipped out of line with the seasons by 11
days every year. As many Mesopotamian festivals were
linked to events in the agricultural cycle, a 13th month
was intercalated every few years to stop the lunar year
falling too far behind the solar year. The ancient
Egyptians used a similar, but not identical, calendar.

Both the Mesopotamians and the Egyptians lacked fixed
points, such as the birth of Christ in the Christian
calendar, for dating events. Events were normally dated
with reference to the accession of the reigning king.
Remarkably complete king lists survive for both

Mesopotamia and ancient Egypt going right back into
the third millennium BC, but the lengths of their reigns
are not always known. This means that, though the
relative chronology of recorded events is known,
historians are faced with great difficulties in establishing
an absolute chronology. Because of these uncertainties,
historians have calculated several different absolute
chronologies for both ancient Mesopotamia and ancient
Egypt, which can be confusing for general readers.
There are four chronologies in use by historians of
ancient Mesopotamia, all of them calculated from
observations of the planet Venus recorded in the eighth
year of the reign of king Ammisaduqa of Babylon. These
fix the date of the king's accession to either 1702 BC
('high'), 1646 BC ('middle'), 1582 BC ('low') or 1550 BC
('ultra low'). The most widely used, and the one used
here, is the 'middle' chronology.

The final steps towards urbanization and state formation took place in the Uruk period (4200–3100 BC), which is named for Sumer's oldest and largest city. All Sumerian cities grew out of earlier settlements of the Ubaid period and preserved the same basic plan, having temple complexes at their centres. Most Sumerian cities in the Uruk period had a population of between 2,000 and 8,000 people, but Uruk had over 10,000, and, by 2700 BC, this had risen to over 50,000. The demands of ruling such large communities led to the growth of organized government.

THE SUMERIAN CIVILIZATION

Every Sumerian city had its own independent government based in the temple precinct, which was an administrative and economic centre as well as a place of worship. The Sumerians were polytheists, but each city had its own patron god who was believed actually to dwell in the temple. It was essential to serve the god well: if he or she became dissatisfied and left, the city would fall. The temples were run as households, with the god as titular head, but with an official, called the *en*, as effective ruler. The *en* was usually a man, but they could be female, in which case she had the title *nin*. *En* is often translated as 'chief priest', but the post was probably more akin to that of the god's earthly administrator as well as being a spiritual intercessor. The city, its people and its lands were seen as being the property of the god. Food produced on the land was brought to the temple, either as offerings to the gods or as tribute from dependent villages in the surrounding countryside, where it was stored and redistributed to the temple community. Members of the community included farmers, gardeners, craftworkers, labourers, merchants, priests, administrators, bakers, brewers and others who prepared the community's food rations. Pots of a standard size were used to measure the rations, and these varied in size according to the status of the individual they were given to. The temple also organized labour for public works, including the building and maintenance of irrigation canals and temples on a far larger scale than had been possible before. Construction of the temple of Anu at Uruk, for example, took an estimated 65 million man hours to complete.

Foreign trade
A murex seashell imported to Sumeria from the Persian Gulf or the Red Sea, inscribed with the name of Rimush, king of Akkad (ruled 2278–2270 BC). Shell was an important decorative material in Sumerian times.

Any food not needed for rations was stored against famines or traded for imported raw materials. The distribution of these imported raw materials was also controlled by the temple. Early Mesopotamian cities did not need markets, shops or currency. Sumeria's trade links were far-ranging. Timber, silver, lead and copper came from the Anatolian mountains; shells and more timber came from Lebanon; copper from Cyprus; alabaster and diorite (for sculpture), and gold from Egypt; pearls and shells from Bahrein; stone for building from Arabia; and lapis lazuli and tin from Afghanistan. Later in Sumerian history, trade links were established with the Indus valley, a source of copper. The Sumerians used donkeys as pack animals and

'Young man, because you hated not my words, neglected them not, may you complete the scribal art from beginning to end.'

Sumerian teacher to his pupil c.2000 BC

were the first people known to have made extensive use of wheeled vehicles. Their main transport routes, however, were the great rivers. Model boats from Sumeria are the earliest evidence for the use of the sail.

KEEPING A RECORD

It was to manage this complex economic system efficiently that writing was invented. The earliest examples of writing come from Uruk itself and date to around 3300 BC, but it must have been invented earlier, because it was already a complete system with over 700 symbols. This early writing was based on pictographs which were inscribed on tablets of moist clay. The invention of writing marks the end of Mesopotamian prehistory. Writing allowed people to record their beliefs, myths, values, traditions and history for posterity, but this did not happen at once. Literacy was confined to a very small circle of high-status bureaucrats who, for nearly 1,000 years after it was invented, used writing almost exclusively for bookkeeping: lists, receipts, accounts, labels and arithmetical calculations of rations and other supplies. Inscribed tablets were dried and stored in archives on wooden shelves. Clay writing tablets are extremely durable and tens of thousands of them have survived from all periods of ancient Mesopotamian history. Sumerian bureaucrats were just as obsessed with 'paperwork' as their modern successors – for example, at Ur the death of a single sheep has been found recorded in triplicate on clay tablets. The needs of detailed administration also drove the earliest developments in advanced mathematics and the measurement of time.

Building token
Bronze statuette of a king of Ur carrying building material in a basket on his head. Sumerian kings placed such statuettes in the foundations of new temples to remind the gods of their piety.

The Uruk period also saw the appearance of a new art form, official propaganda. This took the form of standardized representations of the *ens* interceding with the gods on behalf of their people. This art was combined with monumental architecture to project an impression of the power and authority of the ruling class.

CYLINDER SEALS

The Sumerian pictographic script probably developed from an earlier recording system that used clay tokens of different shapes to stand for different quantities of commodities, such as grain or sheep. The shapes of the written symbols for counting are similar to the shapes of the tokens, making it likely that the script grew out of the token system with the addition of pictographic symbols. The tokens were stored in hollow clay containers. The lids of the containers were marked with the number and type of tokens within by impressing the clay with the shape of the tokens while it was still wet. Eventually, it was realized that the information on the lid was sufficient and the tokens fell out of use. The token system was used alongside cylinder seals. One of the most distinctive Mesopotamian artefacts, these were small cylinders of stone, glass or metal that were carved with unique designs. When the cylinder seals were rolled in wet clay, they formed a continuous design in relief. These designs are an important source of information about religious iconography, myths and daily life in ancient Mesopotamia. Cylinder seals were used to seal storage vessels and documents to indicate authenticity

Cylinder seal
Limestone cylinder seal carved with a design showing a herd of cattle and farm buildings.

or ownership. They were first made around 3400 BC and continued to be used for about 3,000 years. The seals were designed to be worn around the neck on a string or as a pendant on a swivel.

THE INVENTION OF BRONZE

If writing was a cultural revolution, the invention c.3900 BC of bronze, an alloy of copper and tin or arsenic, was a technological revolution. Ornaments and small tools, such as needles, were made by hammering native copper and gold as early as 7000 BC. Around 6200 BC, metalworkers in Anatolia discovered how to extract copper from ore by smelting it in adapted pottery kilns, in which hand- or foot-operated bellows were used to raise the temperature sufficiently to melt copper, and cast it in simple stone moulds. Copper was too soft for it to replace stone tools in everyday use, however, and it was only with the invention of bronze that the Stone Age truly came to an end. Bronze is much harder than pure copper and keeps an edge better. Though more costly, tools and weapons made of bronze are less likely to break than those made out of stone, are more easily re-sharpened, and, when worn out, can be melted down and recast.

A related advance in metallurgy was the invention c.3600 BC of the *cire perdue*, or 'lost wax', method of casting, which allowed complex three-dimensional shapes to be cast in metals such as bronze, gold, silver and lead. First a model of the object was made in wax. This was then covered in clay, which was heated to a temperature high enough to melt the wax so that it ran out of the mould. Molten metal was then poured into the mould, which was broken open to reveal the completed object. The most common objects cast were farm and carpentry tools and weapons. These important developments probably originated in the metal ore mining areas bordering Mesopotamia, perhaps Anatolia or Iran, but their use was very quickly adopted by the Mesopotamians.

Seal imprint
When rolled into wet clay, the cylinder seal leaves a never-ending imprint. In this case, the resulting image left in the clay is a farming scene complete with cattle and buildings.

WRITING

The meaning of most Sumerian pictographs is clear. The symbol for barley is a simplified picture of an ear of barley, while the symbol for 'to walk' is a foot. More complex ideas were expressed by combining signs. For instance, the combination of a head and a bowl meant 'to eat'. As the system developed, the symbols became more abstract and were inscribed using a rectangular-ended reed stylus that made wedge-shaped impressions from which the script gets its name, cuneiform ('wedge-shaped').

In cuneiform, a sign could also stand for the phonetic value of the word so that it could be combined with other signs to make other words. If this system were used in English, the sign for 'man' could be combined with the sign for 'age' to make another word 'manage'. Syllable signs were also introduced so that cuneiform was able to record all elements of human speech. Written from left to right, cuneiform was used not only by the Sumerians, but also by the Assyrians, Babylonians, Elamites and Persians, among other peoples, remaining in use for nearly 3,000 years. From around 600 BC, cuneiform was gradually replaced by the Aramean alphabet. This was not only simpler to learn than cuneiform, it was also more suitable for writing on parchment, which gradually replaced clay tablets. The last known cuneiform inscriptions date to the first century AD.

The first European scholar to speculate about the meaning of cuneiform was the English historian Thomas Herbert (1606–1682), who concluded that the signs represented words and syllables. In the early 19th century, Danish, French and German scholars reconstructed the phonetic values of Persian cuneiform symbols after correctly guessing from their positions in inscriptions that certain combinations of symbols represented the names of historically known kings. The final key to deciphering the cuneiform script was the discovery of a trilingual inscription, in Old Persian, Akkadian ('Babylonian') and Elamite, that was carved on a cliff face at Bisitun in Iran in the fifth century BC. This was to cuneiform what the Rosetta Stone was to the interpretation of Egyptian hieroglyphs. Using his knowledge of modern Persian, the British historian Henry Rawlinson (1810–1895) deciphered the Old Persian part of the inscription in 1838. This allowed him to go on and translate the Babylonian and Elamite parts. Bilingual inscriptions in Akkadian and Sumerian enabled Sumerian cuneiform to be deciphered by 1879. By this time, archaeologists had recovered tens of thousands of inscribed clay tablets from ancient Mesopotamian cities: the task of translating and recording them all is still far from complete.

Wedge writing
A developed cuneiform inscription. The script gets its name, which means 'wedge shaped', from the distinctive marks created by the reed stylus.

The Sumerian civilization entered a new and troubled phase in the Early Dynastic period (2900–2334 BC). Massive defensive walls were built around the cities, bronze weapons were produced in increased quantities, and representations of war began to feature prominently in official art, with rulers being shown trampling on their defeated enemies. Competition for resources resulting from continuing population growth was the likely cause of conflicts between the Sumerian cities. At the same time, there is evidence of major social change. The gap between rich and poor widened and slaves – probably captives taken in war – are mentioned in records for the first time. Rulers adopted new titles. Some are called *sangu* ('accountant'), suggesting that bureaucrats had achieved equal status with the *ensis*. Others were called *lugal* or *sharru* ('king'). These may well have been temporary war leaders who had been chosen by the *ens* in times of emergency, but who had usurped power and established hereditary dynasties.

Silver offering
A silver vase dedicated by king Entemena of Lagash (ruled c.2400 BC), son of the conqueror Eannatum, to his city's patron deity, the warrior god Ningursu.

AN AGE OF KINGS

The new rulers built opulent palaces next to their cities' temples to show their subjects that they ruled with the support of the gods. Kings took over much of the spiritual authority of the *ensis*, personally participating in a calendar of ceremonies, the correct performance of which was believed to be essential for the welfare of their people. Kings and members of the ruling classes erected statues of themselves in the temples. These represented them in a position of continuous prayer so that both other worshippers and the gods would be sure to recognize their piety. Kings expected to continue to enjoy their regal status in the afterlife. They and their families were given magnificent burials, such as those excavated at the Royal Cemetery of Ur, accompanied by luxury goods appropriate to their status: gold, silver and copper tableware, gold headdresses, jewellery, armour and weapons, statues of gold and lapis lazuli, gaming boards and musical instruments. There is inconclusive evidence that retainers were sometimes sacrificed to accompany rulers in death. Most Sumerians were buried beneath the floors of their family homes with more modest grave goods.

To their military and religious leadership, Sumerian kings added a third source of authority: law. The earliest known law code is that of Urukagina, king of Lagash (ruled 2360 BC). Though the code itself has not survived, much of its content can be reconstructed from references in other documents. Urukagina appears to have been concerned to establish clear rights for the poor to limit their exploitation by the rich in what was an increasingly unequal society. He decreed that the rich must use silver when buying from the poor and that they could not compel them to sell land, livestock, grain or other food if they did not wish to. Poor families who had become indentured to the rich because of debt were freed. Widows and orphans were exempted from taxes and the city paid the funeral expenses of the poor, including the cost of the ritual offerings of food and drink for the journey of the dead

> 'King Urukagina amnestied the people of Lagash ... and set them free. He made a covenant with Ningursu that a man of power must not commit an injustice against an orphan or a widow.'

Law code of Urukagina of Lagash (ruled 2360 BC)

into the underworld. Other measures limited the powers of palace officials to charge commissions on a wide range of economic activities. Urukagina's laws were addressed to the city god Ningursu. Justice was a way to please the gods, and the gods in turn supported the just king. Urukagina placed a great deal of emphasis on the need to make plain, in writing, the offence for which someone was being punished. For example, the convicted thief was stoned to death with stones on which a record of his crimes had been inscribed.

STRUGGLING CITIES

In the early Dynastic, the cities of Kish, Uruk and Ur vied constantly for supremacy. Around 2500 BC, king Mesilim of Kish began a trend towards regional empire when he was accepted as the nominal overlord of Sumeria by the other city states. Around a century later, king Eannatum of Lagash overthrew the hegemony of Kish. Eannatum's influence extended well beyond Sumer, but his empire did not outlive him. The age of independent city states was finally brought to an end by king Lugalzagesi of Umma, who conquered all of Sumer. By this time, Sumer no longer existed in splendid isolation. New city states had arisen under Sumerian influence throughout Mesopotamia and in neighbouring Elam, now part of southern Iran.

Praying statue
Limestone bust of an unidentified king of Uruk. Well-to-do Sumerians placed statuettes of themselves in the act of praying in the temple of their city's god as a sign of their piety.

In 2334 BC, Akkad displaced Sumer as the main centre of Mesopotamian civilization. Akkad was the district of central Mesopotamia around the city of Agade, whose king Sargon (ruled 2334–2279 BC) founded the first great empire of the Middle East. The Akkadians adopted Sumerian culture wholesale, worshipping many of the same gods (though they often knew them by slightly different names), and sharing the same art, architecture, political ideology and writing system. The Akkadians, however, were not closely related to the Sumerians. They spoke a Semitic language, related to Hebrew and Arabic, and were descended from peoples who had migrated into Mesopotamia from Arabia in the fourth millennium BC.

Around 2334 BC, Sargon became king of Kish in the far north of Sumer. Sargon came from a humble background: he was the son of a date grower who entered the service of Ur–Zababa, the king of Kish. It is likely that Sargon overthrew his employer in a coup because his name means 'the king is legitimate'. Later legends supplied Sargon with a suitable royal pedigree. He was really the illegitimate child of a royal priestess who set her baby adrift on the Euphrates river in a basket to avoid being shamed. Sargon was saved by the royal gardener of Kish who brought him up as his own son and secured employment for him in the royal household. Later Biblical writers would appropriate this legend for the story of Moses.

POLITICAL INTRIGUE

The Mesopotamians recognized the ebb and flow of political fortune, believing that the gods permitted one dynasty to achieve dominance for a time, only to cast it down when they tired of it. Sargon won the love of Ishtar (Sumerian Inanna), the Mesopotamian goddess of sex and war, and with her help he became king – exactly how is not known, because this part of the legend has been lost. Ishtar would not have been disappointed with her protégé. Sargon overthrew Lugalzegesi of Lagash, destroying his armies in two pitched battles, and took over Sumer. Sargon appointed Akkadian governors to many Sumerian cities and appointed his daughter Enheduanna as high priestess of the temple of Inanna at Ur. The hymns Enheduanna wrote to the goddess have survived. In his subsequent career, Sargon conquered a vast swathe of territory extending across the Middle East from the Persian Gulf to the Mediterranean Sea. He also turned the minor town of

Agade into a new capital for his empire. The site of Agade has never been found, but is thought to have been about 30 miles (48 km) southwest of modern Baghdad.

Sargon's son Rimush (ruled 2278–2270 BC) put down rebellions which broke out after his father's death. Rimush was murdered in a palace conspiracy and replaced by his brother Manishtushu (ruled 2269–2255 BC), who extended the empire into southern Iran. The empire reached its height under Sargon's grandson Naram-Sin (ruled 2254–2218 BC). Earlier Mesopotamian kings claimed to rule as agents of the gods. Naram-Sin abandoned this tradition, declaring himself to be a god and adopting the title 'king of the four quarters, king of the universe'. According to tradition, Naram-Sin's pride offended Enlil, the god who bestowed kingly authority, who sent hordes of Gutian tribesmen from the Zagros mountains to ravage Mesopotamia, causing the empire of Agade to collapse. In reality, the empire struggled on against the Gutians for another generation under Naram-Sin's son Shar-Kali-Shari (ruled 2217–2193 BC), but his death was followed by 80 years of political anarchy. Kings came and went in such rapid succession that a Sumerian chronicler asked 'Who was king? Who was not king?' In 2153 BC, Agade was conquered by Uruk and never recovered any political importance.

Wall of spears
This scene of the 'Vulture Stele' of king Eannatum shows a phalanx of Sumerian infantrymen behind a wall of shields. The king is shown below, leading his troops in a battle wagon.

ENVIRONMENTAL DISASTER

Mesopotamia lacks defendable frontiers and was always vulnerable to invasion by tribes from the Zagros mountains and desert nomads. The empire's ability to resist the Gutians may have been undermined by an environmental disaster. A Sumerian poem, 'The Curse of Agade', describes a great famine brought on by a long drought: 'For the first time since cities were built, the fields produced no grain ... He who slept on the roof, died on the roof. He who slept in the house had no burial, the people flailed at themselves in hunger.' Archaeological evidence supports the poem's account. Excavations of the Akkadian city of Sehna (now called Tell Leilan) have shown that it was completely abandoned c.2200 BC following the onset of a drought so severe that even the earthworms died and the city was buried in wind-blown sand from the barren fields.

THE FIRST ARMIES

With the rise of kingdoms and empires came the first formally organized armies. Most of the evidence for the nature of Sumerian armies comes from battle scenes in art and from weapons buried in high status graves, such as that of Meskalamdug, who ruled Ur c.2600 BC. Meskalamdug's gold helmet and ornate gold dagger demonstrate that martial display was very important to Sumerian kings. In art, Sumerian war leaders are shown riding over their enemies in four-wheeled war wagons drawn by asses. As these could have been neither manoeuvrable nor fast, their main function was probably high status transport to the battlefield. Most Sumerian soldiers were infantrymen armed with bronze-tipped spears, daggers and axes. For protection, they wore a bronze or leather helmet, a metal-studded leather cloak and carried a body-length rectangular shield. In battle, the soldiers formed a wall of overlapping shields which bristled with spears. On other occasions soldiers may have dispensed with their shields so that they could use a weapon in each hand. Representations of the bow are rare, but documentary evidence refers to the production of bronze arrow heads in very large quantities, demonstrating the importance of archery. The production and distribution of weapons was controlled by palace officials. Swords, metal armour and horse-drawn chariots were not used in warfare until the middle of the second millennium BC.

Ur-Nammu (ruled 2112–2095 BC), founder of the Third Dynasty of Ur, finally ended the anarchy caused by the fall of Agade. Like Sargon, Ur-Nammu came from an obscure background. He entered the service of king Utuhegal of Uruk, who appointed him governor of Ur. When Utuhegal was accidentally drowned, Ur-Nammu made himself king of Ur. A competent soldier, one of Ur-Nammu's first achievements was to conquer the city of Lagash, which had often allied itself with the Gutians. However, his reign was not marked by the overt militarism that was so typical of the Agade dynasty. Though Ur-Nammu created a sphere of influence that encompassed all of Sumer and Akkad, diplomacy, marriage alliances and religious influence played a greater part in this undertaking than war. Ur-Nammu commissioned many building projects, including the great ziggurat he raised in honour of the goddess Inanna at Ur, and was an active legislator: his law code is the oldest one to have survived.

FURTHER DECLINE

Ur-Nammu's successors faced the same border problems that Agade had faced. The empire of the Third Dynasty collapsed in 2004 BC when Ur itself was captured and sacked by the Elamites after a long siege. 'Elam, like a swelling flood wave, left only the spirits of the dead' lamented a Sumerian poet. The fall of Ur ended forever Sumer's dominance. In the century that followed, Amorites, semitic-speaking nomads from Arabia, infiltrated Mesopotamia, overthrowing native ruling dynasties and seizing power themselves. The most successful Amorite dynasties were those established in the Akkadian city of Babylon (1895 BC) and at Ashur in Assyria (1813 BC) in northern Mesopotamia. These became rival imperial powers who dominated Mesopotamia until it was conquered by the Persians in 539 BC. Sumerian died out as a spoken language around 1800 BC, replaced by Akkadian, but such was its prestige that it survived as a literary language until the first century BC. The same was true of the rest of the Sumerian cultural heritage. By the time of the famous law-maker Hammurabi (ruled 1792–1750 BC), cultural leadership of Mesopotamia had passed to the Babylonians, whose achievements in mathematics, astronomy and literature were built on a solid Sumerian foundation. It was through Babylon that the achievements of Mesopotamian civilization were communicated to the wider world: they were particularly important in the early development of Classical Greek civilization.

Standard weight
A basalt half-mina weight – about 248 grams (8.75 oz) – used in the temple of the Moon-god Nanna, whose crescent Moon symbol is above the dedication by king Shulgi (ruled 2094–2047 BC).

The decline of Sumer is generally thought to have been due to environmental factors. Long-term irrigation on the poorly drained plain led to waterlogging of the soils. As the water evaporated under the hot sun, it left behind residues of mineral salts which damaged the soil's fertility and reduced crop yields. This was not a sudden catastrophe, but a gradual process that continued for centuries. Farmers in Akkad and northern Mesopotamia, where higher rainfall made them less reliant on irrigation, did not suffer from these problems to the same extent. New salt-tolerant strains of wheat and greater reliance on date palms, which are tolerant of saline groundwater, staved off agricultural collapse, but Sumer slowly lagged behind as it became less able than the north to support dense urban populations. Well before the time of Christ, most Sumerian cities had been abandoned and the fields that had once supported them had reverted to desert.

Ziggurats, imposing stepped pyramids with temples on their summits, are the most distinctive monuments of the ancient Near East. Ziggurats (from ancient Akkadian *ziqqurratu*) contained no internal chambers and were not used for burials like Egyptian and Mesoamerican pyramids.

Ziggurats developed from the Sumerian practice of building temples on platforms to raise them above the ground. It is generally thought that they were stairways to heaven to allow priests to get closer to the gods, who it was believed took up residence in the temples. The oldest known ziggurats, at Ur, Eridu, Nippur and Uruk in Sumeria, date from the reign of Ur-Nammu of the Third Dynasty of Ur, but there may have been earlier ones because representations of stepped buildings are known in Sumerian art from around 2500 BC. In Sumer and Akkad, ziggurats were free-standing structures; access to the summit shrine was by either a triple external stairway or a spiral ramp. The most famous ziggurat was that of the god Marduk at Babylon. Known to the Babylonians as *Etemananki* ('the house that is the foundation of Heaven and Earth') it has been immortalized in Judaeo-Christian mythology as the Tower of Babel. In Assyria, most ziggurats were not free-standing, but formed part of larger temple complexes. Ziggurat building died out after Mesopotamia was conquered by the Persians in the sixth century BC.

Ziggurats were built of mud brick that was strengthened with courses of straw mixed with bitumen. The exteriors were clad in baked brick and painted. Time and weather have since reduced most ziggurats to undistinguished mounds of mud. The 30-metre (100-ft) tall ziggurat of Ur gives the best impression of their grandeur. This was partially restored by Saddam Hussein, using bricks stamped with his name.

Ziggurat at Agargouf
Excavated between 1943 and 1945, the ziggurat at Agargouf in Iraq is unusually well preserved. It stands 52 metres (170 ft) tall and, like the ziggurat at Ur, was partially restored by Saddam Hussein in the 1970s.

ANCIENT EGYPT

EGYPT was the first territorial kingdom, the first recognizably national state. The modern study of ancient Egypt began in a dramatic way. When Napoleon Bonaparte invaded Egypt in 1798, he took with him a team of antiquarians. At that time, all that was known of ancient Egypt was based on Bible stories, ill-informed ancient Greek writers and travellers' tales. The astonishing archaeological discoveries made by Napoleon's scholars caused a sensation in Europe and interest in ancient Egypt has never flagged since. Egypt's legacy of awesome architecture and colossal statuary has proved perennially fascinating. So too has their enigmatic hieroglyphic writing, esoteric religion and their obsession with preserving the bodies of their dead by mummification, thanks to which a great many ancient Egyptians, including several pharaohs, are still with us.

Right: Philae Island
Located in Aswan in southern Egypt, Philae comprises two small islands in the Nile. The smaller island is the site of an ancient Egyptian temple complex.

Egypt, said the ancient Greek historian Herodotus, is 'the gift of the Nile'. The Nile's annual cycle dominated the lives of ancient Egyptians: Egypt has too little rainfall to support farming and without its life-giving waters their civilization simply could not have existed. From the First Cataract, the rapids that traditionally marked the southern border of Egypt, the Nile flows in a narrow valley for nearly 500 miles (800 km) until it divides into dozens of channels in the Delta before flowing into the Mediterranean Sea. As far as the ancients were concerned, the Nile's flood plain was Egypt.

FLOODING THE LAND
Though very confined, the Nile flood plain was one of the ancient world's most favourable farming environments. The Egyptian year began when the Nile flooded at the beginning of August, following the summer rains in the East African highlands. During the flood, no one could work on the land, so in this period kings conscripted peasant farmers to work on their building projects. As the river level fell in the autumn, the flood plain was left moist and fertilized with fresh silt ready for ploughing and sowing. The crops grew through Egypt's warm, dry winter and ripened in the spring before the next cycle of flooding began. The fertility of the soil was effectively inexhaustible and good harvests could be got year after year. Canals and ditches spread the flood waters to the very edges of the valley, maximizing the cultivable area, but the large-scale irrigation systems and flood defences used in Mesopotamia were unnecessary. In comparison to Mesopotamia, where the rivers flooded violently and unpredictably, the Nile valley was a stable and benign environment. However, if the floods did fail, then there would be famine throughout the land. Egyptians watched with nervous anticipation for the dawn rising of the bright star they called Sothis (which we call Sirius). They believed the appearance of this star brought with it the flooding of the Nile. Much of the authority of Egyptian kings derived from the belief that they were divine and had the power to control the flood. A succession of low floods could undermine royal authority and bring down a dynasty because it would appear that the king had lost the favour of the gods.

Previous page:
The Great Pyramids
The pyramids were originally covered with a smooth white limestone casing, but this was stripped off during the Middle Ages for the buildings of Cairo – today it remains only on the tip of the 143-metre (470-ft) pyramid of Khafre.

The Nile was also Egypt's main highway. In Egypt, the prevailing winds blow from north to south, so ships can travel upstream under sail and make the return journey downstream with the flow of the river. Heavy loads of grain and building stone could be transported easily and economically over long distances. The Nile also linked Egypt with Nubia (roughly modern Sudan), an important source of slaves, ivory and gold. From the mouths of the Nile, sea routes connected Egypt to Lebanon, the source of timber, a commodity Egypt lacked almost completely. Because Egypt was basically a long thin strip of cultivable land, it did not lend itself so well to the growth of towns as the broad Mesopotamian plain. It was not until very late in ancient Egypt's history that it had cities that compared in size to Mesopotamia's. Most Egyptians lived in farming villages on the edge of the flood plain, close to their fields. The transition between the intensively cultivated valley and the sparsely populated deserts on either side was sudden and stark. The deserts were the source of gold, metal ores, gems and stone for building, sculpture and tool making, and of rough grazing that supported nomadic pastoralists. The deserts were also important because they isolated Egypt from contact with other civilizations, protecting it from invasions. Though it often suffered raids by desert tribes, Egyptian civilization was some 1,500 years old before it suffered a major invasion.

Isolation contributed to Egypt's astonishing cultural conservatism. No other civilization in world history has shown the same degree of continuity in its traditions of art, religion and rulership for such a long period. It was not until around 1600 BC that bronze tools and wheeled vehicles were used in Egypt, even though by then they had been used in the Near East for nearly 2,000 years. The *shadouf*, a simple water-lifting device that was widely used in the region until recently, was ancient Egypt's only significant technological invention. This lack of technological innovation confirms that civilization is first and foremost defined by the complexity of its social organization rather than by its technology. The Great Pyramids of Giza were built with much the same technology that was available to the Stone Age tribes who, around the same time, erected the stone circle at Stonehenge in southern England. The difference in scale of the monuments is the measure of the difference in the scale and organization of the societies that built them.

THE ORIGINS OF ANCIENT EGYPT

The formative period of Egyptian civilization, known as the Predynastic period, began with the settlement of the Nile valley by farming peoples around 5000 BC. The first settlers were probably refugees from the Sahara. Unlikely as it seems today, it was in the Sahara that Africa's first farming societies developed. Immediately after the end of the Ice Age, the Sahara was a wildlife-rich savanna, while the Nile valley was a tangled swamp that was unattractive to human settlement. Early settlers in the Sahara lived around the shores of the many lakes that dotted the savanna, living by fishing, hunting and gathering, and, from around 7000 BC, by growing cereals and herding cattle. Between around 5000 BC and 3500 BC, climate change turned the Sahara into a desert, forcing most of the people to leave. The same climate change dried out the Nile valley and Delta,

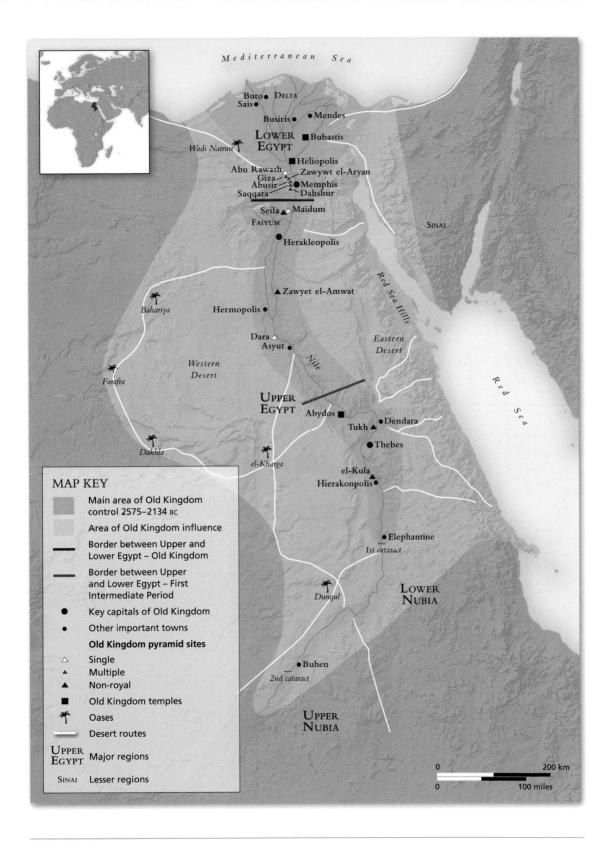

Mediterranean Sea

Buto ●
Sais ●
● DELTA
Busiris ● ● Mendes

LOWER EGYPT
■ Bubastis

Wadi Natrun

■ Heliopolis

Abu Rawash △
Giza ▲
Abusir ▲ Zawywt el-Aryan
Saqqara ▲ ● Memphis
  ▲ Dahshur

Seila △ Maidum ▲
FAIYUM

● Herakleopolis

▲ Zawyet el-Amwat

Bahariya
Hermopolis ●

Dara △
Asyut ●

Western Desert

Red Sea Hills

Eastern Desert

Nile

UPPER EGYPT
Abydos ■
Tukh ▲ ● Dendara
● Thebes

Red Sea

Farafra

Dakhla

el-Kharga

el-Kula
Hierakonpolis ● ▲

● Elephantine
1st cataract

SINAI

Dunqul

LOWER NUBIA

● Buhen
2nd cataract

UPPER NUBIA

MAP KEY

Main area of Old Kingdom control 2575–2134 BC

Area of Old Kingdom influence

▬ Border between Upper and Lower Egypt – Old Kingdom

▬ Border between Upper and Lower Egypt – First Intermediate Period

● Key capitals of Old Kingdom

● Other important towns

Old Kingdom pyramid sites

△ Single

▲ Multiple

▲ Non-royal

■ Old Kingdom temples

🌴 Oases

▬ Desert routes

UPPER EGYPT Major regions

SINAI Lesser regions

0 _____ 200 km
0 _____ 100 miles

making it attractive to farming settlement. The valley was densely populated by the mid fourth millennium BC and chiefdoms and towns had begun to develop. Competition between these chiefdoms in the narrow Nile valley was intense and, by c.3100 BC, they had been amalgamated into two kingdoms of Upper (southern) and Lower (northern) Egypt. Around 3000 BC, Narmer, the king of Upper Egypt, marched north and conquered Lower Egypt, unifying the country for the first time.

Commemorative palettes and other objects made to commemorate Narmer's victory portray the king as an incarnation of the falcon god Horus, showing that the ideology of divine kingship that was such a defining characteristic of Egyptian civilization was already formed. These objects also carry some of the earliest known examples of hieroglyphic writing. Excavations at Hierakonpolis, the capital of Upper Egypt, have provided evidence for the emergence of other typical features of Egyptian civilization. Burials in the city's cemeteries show that mummification was already practised. An industrial complex in the city had a brewery capable of brewing 1,400 litres (300 gallons) of beer a day and 13 pottery kilns, suggesting that the centralized control of food supplies and craft production that was a feature of government in historical times had also developed by this time.

SHADOWY RULERS

Narmer's achievement was insecure, and it was only in the Early Dynastic Period (c.2920–2650 BC), the period of Egypt's first two historical dynasties, that Egypt emerged as a stable territorial kingdom. The kings of the Early Dynastic are shadowy figures, known mainly from fragmentary annals and brief inscriptions. Later Egyptian tradition regarded Hor-Aha, who took the ruling name Men ('established') or Menes, as the founder of the first dynasty. Recently discovered king lists in the tombs of the first dynasty kings Den and Qa'a suggest Hor-Aha was the son of Narmer. Hor-Aha was the founder of Memphis. Sited at a strategically important location near modern Cairo where the narrow Nile valley began to spread out into the Delta, Memphis was the capital of Egypt for most of the next 900 years.

The kings of the first and second dynasties faced tensions between Upper and Lower Egypt, and these sometimes resulted in war. It was probably as a result of one of these wars that the first dynasty was brought down c.2770 BC, because the name of the first king of the second dynasty, Hetepsekhemwy, means 'peaceful in respect of the two powers'.

Hawk-headed god
Statue of the sky-god Horus at the temple of Horus at Edfu. In mythology, Horus' struggle with the evil god Set symbolized the unification of Egypt by the kings of Upper Egypt.

The second dynasty also seems to have suffered its share of disputed successions and renewed tension between north and south. During the reign of Khasekhemy, the last king of the dynasty, a force of northern rebels almost captured Hierakonpolis before it was defeated. An inscription on a stone vase dating to his reign claims that over 47,000 of the northerners were killed in battle. However, it was not only military success that consolidated the unity of the kingdom. The Early Dynastic kings created an effective administration for the kingdom and successfully used the cult of divine kingship to legitimize their authority in both halves of their kingdom. The subsequent history of Egypt is marked by a clear pattern of three periods of strong royal government, called 'kingdoms' by historians, divided by periods of weak government and division, known as 'intermediate periods'.

THE OLD KINGDOM (2649–2134 BC)

The development of divine kingship, writing and a civil service made possible a huge increase in the power of the monarchy during the Old Kingdom period. The great pyramids that were built during this period are only the most obvious evidence of the absolute power that Egyptian kings wielded over their subjects. The Old Kingdom is reckoned to have begun with the accession of Sanakhte (ruled c.2649–2630 BC), the founder of the third dynasty (2649–2575 BC). A considerable body of religious

HIEROGLYPHS

Egyptian hieroglyphic writing developed between 3200 and 3000 BC from motifs used to decorate pottery. There is no evidence of Sumerian influence, so it is likely that the Egyptians invented writing independently. There were two main types of hieroglyph. Some were logograms which represented words or concepts. Others represented consonants which could be used to spell out words like characters in an alphabet. A third class of hieroglyph was used as determinatives to define the grammatical function of a word (a bit like case endings in an inflected language like German or Latin). Altogether, there were about 800 different hieroglyphs.

Hieroglyphic (meaning 'sacred carving') was used for monumental and religious inscriptions and other formal writing. During the third dynasty, a simplified form of writing was developed called hieratic ('priestly'), which was used for religious texts and official documents. It was more suitable for writing quickly on paper made from the papyrus reed. In time, the spoken language of Egypt diverged from the formal language of hieroglyphic and hieratic. A third script, demotic ('popular'), came into use for the spoken language and was used for business documents, private letters and popular literature. Training as a scribe was the foundation for any career in government, the priesthood or the military.

In the Roman period, hieroglyphs were gradually replaced by the Coptic alphabet, a version of the Greek alphabet adapted to the sounds of the Egyptian spoken language.

The last known hieroglyphic inscription dates to AD 396. After understanding of hieroglyphic died out, it was thought that the mysterious symbols were a secret writing system used to convey esoteric magical information. The discovery of the Rosetta Stone, a trilingual inscription in Greek, demotic and hieroglyphic, by Napoleon's expedition in 1799 allowed scholars to begin deciphering hieroglyphic. The task was finally completed by French classical scholar and philologist Jean-François Champollion (1790–1832) between 1822 and 1824.

Picture words
A hieroglyphic inscription from a New Kingdom period temple at Thebes. Writing in hieroglyphs was time-consuming and laborious, so simplified scripts were introduced for writing everyday documents.

First pyramid
Designed by the vizier Imhotep, the 62-metre (203-ft) step-pyramid of king Djoser (ruled c.2630–2611 BC) at Saqqara was the first pyramid to be built. Like the Great Pyramids, its original cladding of white limestone was stripped in the Middle Ages.

literature has survived from the Old Kingdom, including the famous 'Pyramid Texts', but other historical sources are few and brief. Surprisingly little is known about the reigns even of the builders of the three greatest pyramids at Giza.

EFFICIENT BUREAUCRACY

During the Old Kingdom, the authority of the kings (the title pharaoh was not used until the New Kingdom) did not extend far beyond the Nile valley but, then, it did not need to. Control of the most productive agricultural area of the ancient world made the kings fabulously wealthy. What Egypt could not provide for itself was obtained by state-organized expeditions to Nubia, the eastern desert, Sinai and Lebanon. Private trade was limited to opportunistic bartering between individuals. The Old Kingdom was governed by efficient central and local bureaucracies. The kingdom was the king's property and he had the right to commandeer whatever labour, property or supplies he wished to use and for whatever purpose. The central bureaucracy was simply an extension of the royal household. The senior official was the *tjaty*, or vizier, who supervised the administration of justice and taxation. Below the vizier were chancellors, quartermasters and other officials supported by a staff of scribes trained in mathematics, measurement, astronomy and writing, who kept the records and made the calculations on which the administration depended. No form of currency was used in the Old Kingdom. Officials were paid with grants of royal land, together with its cultivators. On the death of the official, the land reverted to the crown.

For local government, Egypt was divided into 42 districts. Historians usually call these *nomes*, after the ancient Greek practice, but the original Egyptian name was *sepat*. Provincial governors, or *nomarchs*, were selected from the royal or noble families and had their own staffs of administrators and scribes. One of the most important responsibilities of the nomarchs was the organization of irrigation works and the restoration of landmarks and field boundaries washed away by the Nile floods. The *nomes* remained the basis of Egyptian local government until late Roman times.

DIVINE RULERS

The king was believed to be an incarnation of Horus, who was the son of the Sun-god Ra. As a living god, the king's power was, in theory and often enough in practice, absolute. Only he had the power to command the Nile flood. He was held to be immortal and after his death his soul rejoined the gods. Mummification preserved the king's corpse for eternity and his tomb became a place of worship. Only the king was guaranteed an afterlife but, as a god, he could allow his loyal subjects to join him. In this way, the ideology of divine kingship welded the people of Egypt into a community of interest that was willing to invest enormous amounts of labour and wealth in

THE 'PYRAMID TEXTS'

The oldest known religious texts in the world, the 'Pyramid Texts' were carved on the walls of the royal tombs and sarcophagi in the pyramids at Saqqara c.2400–2300 BC. The texts are spells to protect and reanimate the king's body after death and help him ascend to heaven. Exclusively for the use of the king, the 'Pyramid Texts' later evolved into the 'Book of the Dead', which guided all Egyptians to the afterlife.

building royal tombs. All who contributed to the construction of these tombs gained the assurance that they too would enjoy an afterlife, though, of course, it would be one appropriate to their status in this life.

THE PYRAMID BUILDERS

Predynastic and Early Dynastic kings, and members of the elite, were buried in low rectangular flat-roofed buildings called *mastabas* ('benches'), which were constructed from a mixture of mud brick and stone. Royal *mastabas* became steadily more elaborate. The mastaba of king Khasekhemy at Abydos was 68 metres (223 ft) long by 40 metres (130 ft) wide and was divided into 58 chambers for grave goods. One of the few royal tombs not to be robbed in antiquity, Khasekhemy's tomb contained vast quantities of copper tools and tableware, stone tools, stone vessels with gold fittings, semi-precious stones, basketwork and pottery vessels filled with grain and fruit. The practice of building pyramids as royal tombs began in the reign of the second king of the third dynasty, Djoser (ruled c.2630–2611 BC). Djoser's pyramid, the Step Pyramid of Saqqara, near Memphis, was masterminded by his vizier Imhotep, the first architect whose name is known to history. Djoser's pyramid began as a very large *mastaba* which Imhotep progressively heightened by the addition of six stepped platforms. The pyramid was part of a walled compound which included a mortuary chapel, where food and prayers were offered for the well-being of the dead king. Uniquely, the compound included a complex where the king could celebrate the *sed* festival. Celebrated in the 30th year of a king's reign, the *sed* was a ritual race run by the king to show he still had the vigour to rule. Djoser probably never used the complex as he died in the 19th year of his reign. Imhotep survived his king by a few years. Later traditions credited him with systematizing and simplifying hieroglyphic script and with outstanding medical knowledge. By the 13th century BC, Imhotep was regarded as a god in his own right, an honour which has not been extended to many bureaucrats.

EARLY PYRAMIDS

The transition to building true pyramids began in the reign of Huni (ruled c.2599–2575 BC), the last king of the third dynasty. His pyramid, at Maidum, was built on poor foundations and soon collapsed. Snofru (ruled c.2575–2551 BC), the first king of the fourth dynasty (2575–2465 BC), made a more successful effort with the so-called bent pyramid of Dahshur. This was started at too steep an angle and became unstable when it was only half complete. The peak had to be added at a shallower angle. The lessons learned on Snofru's pyramid enabled his successors, Khufu (Cheops) (ruled c.2575–2528 BC), Khafre (ruled c.2520–2494 BC) and Menkaure (ruled c.2490–2472 BC) to bring pyramid building to its magnificent peak with the three great pyramids at Giza. Reaching 146 metres (479 ft) tall, Khufu's Great Pyramid is the tallest, overtopping his grandson Khafre's by just 3 metres (9 ft). Menkaure's pyramid was a more modest affair, only 66 metres (215 ft) tall, a sign that the giant pyramids of his predecessors had strained the kingdom's resources. At the foot of the pyramids were the kings' mortuary temples and small subsidiary pyramids for members of the royal family. Also close by were dozens of *mastaba* tombs belonging to nobles and senior bureaucrats, and even low-born craftsmen and artists. Most of these tombs were gifts of the kings to reward the loyal service of these civil servants and craftsmen. Associated with Khafre's pyramid is the enigmatic Sphinx, one of the world's largest and oldest monumental sculptures, though it is not

Ancient riddle
The sphinx, a mythological creature with a human head and the body of a lion, originated in the Middle East. In Egypt, carvings of sphinxes were commonly used as temple guardians. Kings were sometimes shown as sphinxes to associate them with the lion-headed warrior goddess Sekhmet. The largest, the Great Sphinx at Giza, is believed to show king Khafre.

'The pyramids are feared by time, although everything else in our present world fears time.'

Umara al-Yamani, Arab historian, C.AD 1300

absolutely certain that he built it. There have been many theories about how the pyramids were built, some of them involving aliens or lost Ice Age civilizations for which no credible evidence exists. It is generally agreed that the first stage was to construct a step pyramid. This gave the pyramid a firm base. The steps were then filled in with packing blocks, and a casing of smooth white limestone completed the transformation into a true pyramid. Khafre's pyramid alone still has some of its original casing: the rest was stripped for the buildings of Cairo in the Middle Ages. It is estimated that about 2.5 million blocks were used to build Khufu's pyramid alone, each averaging about 2.5 tonnes in weight. The real problem has been explaining how the heavy stone building blocks were moved into place. At this time, the Egyptians did not know of the wheel, cranes or pulleys, or bronze tools. The blocks were shaped using stone hammers and soft copper chisels, and had to be moved using only sleds and levers. Most theories assumed some sort of ramp must have been built outside the pyramid, but to keep a constant gradient as the pyramid grew in height, its length and the width of its base would have had to be constantly increased. This would have required almost as much material as the pyramids themselves, and what was done with it all afterwards? Recent investigations of the interior of Khufu's pyramid have provided evidence that the blocks were actually moved into place by a ramp which spirals its way up inside the pyramid. L-shaped chambers allowed the blocks to be turned round the pyramid's corners. After completion of the pyramid, the ramps were closed off with stone blocks.

WILLING WORKERS

Contrary to popular belief, the pyramids were not built by slaves – slavery was not an important institution in Old Kingdom Egypt – but by professional craftsmen who lived in purpose-built villages near the building site. Conscripted peasants provided most of the muscle for hauling the blocks into position. The workforce for the Great Pyramid is estimated at about 6,000 craftsmen and 20,000 labourers. Feeding and housing these workers for years on end was a considerable drain on resources, but the cost of a pyramid did not end with its completion. A pyramid was intended to provide for the well-being of the king for all eternity. Pyramids were closely associated with the cult of Ra and it is thought that their flared shape represents the rays of the Sun, which the deceased king used as a stairway to the gods: the ancient Egyptian word for pyramid is *mer*, meaning 'place of ascension'. In later pyramids, the walls of the burial chamber were inscribed with religious texts and spells, known as the 'Pyramid Texts', intended to ensure a safe journey for the king's soul. Once the king's mummy was interred, the tomb was filled with all the luxuries necessary for a comfortable afterlife, then sealed off and concealed. The considerable wealth that was lost to Egypt in this way was eventually returned to circulation by looters who, despite all precautions, robbed most of the pyramid tombs in antiquity. Royal land was granted to the mortuary temple to support its priests and craftsmen, and provide regular offerings for the king and his dependents to enjoy in the afterlife. These grants, which were necessarily permanent, steadily diminished the resources available to living kings.

Signs of declining royal authority appear under the fifth dynasty (2465–2323 BC). The position of *nomarch* became hereditary and gradually drifted out of royal control. *Nomarchs* were able to use the resources of the provinces to enrich themselves, as shown by the proliferation of lavishly decorated tombs built privately by the nobility. Extracts from the 'Pyramid Texts', which were supposed to be exclusively for the king's benefit, were copied onto the walls of these tombs. The nobles no longer depended on royal favour either in this life or the next. The ideology of Egyptian kingship was slowly unravelling. Royal authority declined even further under the sixth dynasty (2323–2150 BC). Bodyguards murdered Teti, the first king of the dynasty, and a plot to murder his successor Pepi I was narrowly foiled. The Old Kingdom was finally brought down by a period of low Nile floods, which began late in the very long reign of Pepi II (ruled c.2246–2152 BC). Relief carvings of emaciated people and animals graphically depict the famine and starvation that followed the poor floods. The monarchy's manifest failure to bring about the return of the annual flood destroyed whatever remained of its authority. Pepi's son Merenre II was murdered only a year after his accession, following which central government collapsed. Merenre's burial place is unknown, as there was no time to build a pyramid for him.

Boat of the dead
Discovered in a pit at the foot of the Great Pyramid of Khufu at Giza, this is the world's oldest intact ship. The ship was probably a ritual vessel, a 'solar barge' intended to carry the king across the heavens with the Sun-god Ra.

RELIGION

Because the king was the intermediary between his people and the gods, there was no clear boundary between secular and religious matters in ancient Egypt. Inscriptions in temples and tombs tell us a great deal about Egypt's official state religion and the beliefs about death, burial and the afterlife.

Official worship was conducted in temples, which were treated as the palaces of the resident gods. The most sacred part of a temple was the sanctuary or shrine containing the cult statue of the god who was worshipped there. The chief priest tended the statue in much the same way that servants tended the king. Every day, the statue was washed, dressed, perfumed and symbolically fed with offerings of food and drink. The public were deliberately excluded from these rituals. During festivals, the cult statues were taken out of their temples so that the gods could speak with the people, but even then they were kept hidden from sight in a shrine, which was carried on a symbolic boat. Cult statues sometimes went on journeys. During the annual 'Festival of the Good Meetings', Hathor, the goddess of women, love and fertility, was taken from her temple at Dendara to visit her husband, the sky-god Horus, at his temple at Edfu 80 miles (130 km) away.

Excluded from the temples, the common people worshipped at local shrines, where they prayed, made offerings and left oracular questions. Private prayer in the home was also practised. Popular religion shaded off into magic, for example in the widespread use of protective amulets, love charms and spells to cure sickness.

Egyptian religion had no systematic theology and many different versions of its myths are known. Most of Egypt's 2,000 or so gods were associated with a particular aspect of life or nature, such as Ra with the Sun, Thoth with writing, Ptah with crafts and Taweret with pregnancy. Egyptian gods fell into two classes:

local gods whose worship was associated with a particular town or area, and universal gods, whose worship was not associated with any one place. Gods could change status, such as Amun, originally a local god of Thebes who became the universal ruler of the gods during the Middle Kingdom. Egyptians portrayed their gods in human form or as humans with animals' heads, but they did not believe that this is what they actually looked like. To foreigners, the most striking aspect of Egyptian religion was the worship of animals. The most famous was the Apis, the sacred bull of Ptah, who was worshipped at Memphis.

Imposing entrance
The temple of Horus at Edfu. Egyptian temples were entered through a monumental gateway flanked by tapering towers called pylons. The pylon was modelled on the hieroglyph for 'horizon', which was two hills between which the Sun rose and set. The pylons, therefore, symbolized death and rebirth.

Coffin
Mummies were protected
by several layers of coffins,
which could be richly
decorated with religious
texts and spells to help the
deceased navigate the
underworld safely.

Following the fall of the Old Kingdom, Egypt suffered over a century of political instability and warfare, known as the First Intermediate Period (2150–2040 BC). Lower Egypt and the northern half of Upper Egypt came under the control of a succession of 17 short-lived kings who made their capital at Herakleopolis. Another dynasty, descended from a family of *nomarchs*, established a rival state at Thebes in southern Upper Egypt. The Herakleopolitan kingdom was in most respects a continuation of the late Old Kingdom, with a weak crown and strong *nomarchs* who ruled as local warlords. The Theban kings, however, suppressed the *nomarchs* in the area under their control and imposed a strong centralized government. In 2040 BC, King Mentuhotep II (ruled 2061–2010 BC) of Thebes conquered Lower Egypt and united the country once again.

THE MIDDLE KINGDOM (2040–c.1640 BC)

The reunification of Egypt marks the beginning of the Middle Kingdom, the second of Egypt's ages of imperial greatness. The most serious problem facing Middle Kingdom rulers was how to restore the prestige of the monarchy. The problems that brought down the Old Kingdom undermined belief in the divinity of the king. Egyptians no longer believed that he alone was guaranteed an afterlife. During late Old Kingdom times, worship of Osiris, the god of fertility and ruler of the underworld, had become popular. The followers of Osiris were pretty much guaranteed a blissful afterlife in the 'Field of Reeds', a lush paradise that lay beyond the western horizon, so long as they were not irredeemably wicked. Osiris did not expect moral perfection. All that was needed was to follow the correct burial practices and to possess the right spells for the soul to complete the journey through the underworld safely.

Kings adopted various measures to rebuild their authority. Exploiting the new religious beliefs, the kings identified themselves with Osiris, with whom they would be united in the afterlife. The minor Theban god Amun was identified with the Sun-god Ra and promoted as a national cult. The kings actively encouraged the production of a large body of literature, including poetry, hymns, religious teachings, prophecy and lively moral tales, which presented kingship in a favourable light. Royal statuary was used in a similar way to create an image of the king as the careworn 'good shepherd', taking upon himself the burden of providing for his

The Egyptians practised mummification, the artificial preservation of the bodies of people and sacred animals, such as cats and ibises, in the belief that this was essential if the soul was to enjoy an afterlife. It is believed that the practice was inspired by the natural preservation of bodies by desiccation when buried in desert graves.

The mummification process varied, but always included the removal of all the internal organs, including the brain, which was pulled out through the nose. The body was then dehydrated using a natural chemical called natron. The body cavity was then packed with fragrant substances, such as cinnamon and myrrh, and with resin-soaked linen cloth and sawdust. The mummy was wrapped in layers of linen bandages. Protective amulets were placed between each layer. Finally, the mummy was placed in one or more human-shaped coffins. Depending on the status of the deceased, these could be elaborately decorated. The internal organs were stored in containers called canopic jars and these were placed in the tomb along with the mummy.

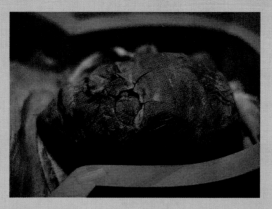

Head of a mummy
Embalmers removed the brain through the deceased's nose and threw it away: it was thought not to be an important organ.

Religious texts and scenes of the good life were painted on tomb walls in the belief that they could be activated in the afterlife. Grave goods and models of houses, boats, farm animals, soldiers and so on were placed in tombs for the same reasons. From the Middle Kingdom on, small figurines carrying farm implements were also placed in tombs. Called *ushabti*, these were a replacement for the deceased if they were called upon to do any work in the afterlife.

The word 'mummy' comes from the Arabic word *mumiyah* ('bitumen'). It was widely believed that mummies were prepared using bitumen, which was supposed to have healing powers. Cemeteries were plundered for mummies to be ground into medicinal powder. The trade in mummy powder continued until the 18th century. Today, mummies are studied for evidence about the health, appearance and diet of ancient Egyptians.

people's welfare. To prevent succession disputes, kings began appointing their successors during their own lifetimes. Pyramid building, which had ceased after Pepi II's death, was resumed, but Middle Kingdom rulers did it on the cheap. Outwardly, their pyramids must have looked nearly as impressive as those of the Old Kingdom, but their white limestone casings covered a core made of cheap mud brick or masonry recovered from ruined temples. The problem of the over-mighty *nomarchs* was solved by transferring their powers to town mayors, making them irrelevant.

FOREIGN INVADERS

Middle Kingdom rulers faced more serious border problems than their Old Kingdom predecessors. Well organized chiefdoms and small kingdoms had developed in Nubia and the Levant, so the desert borders were less secure. Middle Kingdom rulers adopted an aggressive foreign policy. Senwosret I (ruled 1971–1926 BC) conquered Lower Nubia and its rich gold fields, and established a fortified frontier around the second cataract of the Nile. Strong fortifications also defended the isthmus of Suez against invasions from the Near East via Sinai. Senwosret III (ruled 1878–1841 BC) forced the native rulers of the Levant to become vassals of Egypt. The Middle Kingdom reached its peak under Amenemhet III (ruled 1844–1797 BC), but after his death, it declined rapidly. Over 70 kings are recorded in the next 160 years, none of whom reigned longer than 14 years. Pyramid building also came to an end, this time for good.

Egypt's neighbours took advantage of its weakness. Around 1700 BC, the Upper Nubian kingdom of Kush drove the Egyptians out of Lower Nubia. Then, around 1640 BC, the Hyksos, invaders from Canaan, took control of Lower Egypt. Upper Egypt retained its independence under a native dynasty based at Thebes, which eventually reunited Egypt during the reign of king Ahmose I (ruled 1550–1525 BC). This period of disunity and foreign rule is known as the Second Intermediate Period (c.1640–1532 BC). Compared with its neighbours in the Near East, Middle Kingdom Egypt was technologically backwards. The influence of the Hyksos resulted in the introduction of many innovations. These included wheeled vehicles and bronze working, an improved potter's wheel and the vertical loom, new crops and domestic animals, including the horse and zebu (Asian hump-backed cow), and new musical instruments and fashions in dance and clothing. The nature of warfare changed dramatically with the introduction of the horse-drawn war chariot and new weapons, such as the scimitar and the powerful composite bow. In their turn, the Hyksos rulers adopted the trappings of Egyptian kingship, government and religion.

Mighty ruler
Alabaster statuette of Amenemhet III (ruled c.1844–1797 BC), the greatest ruler of the Middle Kingdom. Amenemhet's tomb in his pyramid at Hawara was protected with a variety of traps for unwary looters, but was still robbed in antiquity.

Using their military technology against them, Seqenenre II (died 1555 BC) began the long struggle to expel the Hyksos. Examination of his mummy has shown that he died violently in battle – he suffered an axe blow to the head and was finished off with a knife wound to the neck. The war was continued by his successor Kamose (ruled 1555–1550 BC) and concluded by Ahmose I after he led a great war fleet into the Delta and captured the Hyksos capital at Avaris in 1532 BC.

THE NEW KINGDOM (1532–1070 BC)

The expulsion of the Hyksos ushered in Egypt's last and greatest period as an imperial power, the New Kingdom (1532–1070 BC). The Hyksos invasion left the Egyptians painfully aware that their borders were no longer secure. From the beginning, New Kingdom rulers followed an aggressively expansionist policy abroad and at home adopted the imagery of military kingship that had long been common in Mesopotamia. It was also under the New Kingdom that Egyptian kings first adopted the title 'pharaoh'. Meaning literally 'great palace', this was a sign of the central role played in government by the royal household and of the complete identification of the king with the state.

Most of Egypt's imperial expansion was achieved by two exceptional warrior pharaohs, Tuthmose I (ruled 1504–1492 BC) and his grandson Tuthmose III (ruled 1479–1425 BC). In a reign of constant military activity, Tuthmose I campaigned as far south as the Fifth Cataract of the Nile, deep inside modern Sudan, and as far north as Carchemish in Syria. The Egyptians were amazed by their first sight of the Euphrates river. Most had never seen a river flowing south before and it therefore seemed to be flowing 'uphill' and against nature. Tuthmose III inherited the throne as a child under the regency of his domineering step-mother, Hatshepsut. In the sixth year of his reign, Hatshepsut seized power and ruled as pharaoh. Family descent was measured through the maternal line in ancient Egypt, but it was rare for a woman actually to rule. Hatshepsut's death in 1458 BC freed Tuthmose to rule in his own right. In the remaining 33 years of his reign, he led at least 17 military campaigns, conquering

Sinai, Canaan, Lebanon, Syria, Lower and Upper Nubia and Kush. Tuthmose's first victory, the battle of Megiddo in c.1456 BC, is notable as the earliest battle in recorded history for which a detailed account survives, including the tactics used and the numbers of casualties and captives.

FOREIGN POLICY

The conquests of Tuthmose I and Tuthmose III created a comfortable buffer zone for Egypt in the north against the militaristic Mesopotamian empires, and gave it control of Nubia's vast mineral wealth. In the Levant, the Egyptians emulated the Mesopotamian empires and ruled through local vassal kings, but Nubia was subjected to full colonial government. Nubian gold funded lavish diplomacy, conducted through gift exchange, marriage alliance and letters, to maintain good relations with the Mesopotamian powers. Dealing with foreign rulers as equals was a novel experience for the pharaohs, but Egypt's prestige had never been higher. Envoys arrived from Babylonia, Assyria, the Hittite empire, Minoan Crete and Mycenaean Greece to lay exotic gifts at pharaoh's feet.

The pharaohs generally held conservative attitudes to kingship. In official art, they deliberately emphasized continuity of tradition as a way to legitimize their power. The pharaohs rejuvenated the ideology of divine monarchy. The success of the Theban kings in expelling the Hyksos raised the status of their patron Amun. He came to be

First aid
The Smith Papyrus is the only surviving part of an Egyptian handbook on trauma surgery. One of the earliest surgical texts in the world, the papyrus was written in the 16th century BC. Among other treatments, it recommends using honey and mouldy bread to cure infections.

seen as the ruler of the gods. The pharaoh was the earthly embodiment of Amun, conceived by a sacred marriage between the god and the queen mother that was ritually re-enacted annually in the Opet festival at Thebes. The pharaohs rebuilt the temple of Amun at Karnak, outside the royal capital at Thebes, on a lavish scale: its priests became wealthy and politically influential.

A NEW RELIGION

Recognizing it as a potential threat to royal authority, Amenhotep III (ruled 1391–1353 BC) tried to curb the power of the priesthood of Amun. His son Amenhotep IV (ruled 1353–1335 BC) went even further and abolished it. A radical religious reformer, Amenhotep tried to replace Egypt's traditional polytheism with a monotheistic cult of the Aten, or Sun disc. Amenhotep changed his name, which meant 'Amun is satisfied' to Akhenaten ('he who is pleasing to the Aten') and founded a new capital, dedicated to the cult, called Akhetaten ('horizon of the Aten'). The cult of the Aten was a religion without mysteries. Akhenaten was the son of the Aten and the sole intermediary between it and the people, who depended, rather as they had in Old Kingdom times, entirely on the pharaoh's intercession if their souls were to enjoy an afterlife. Accompanying the new religion was a new informal, naturalistic form of official art, often showing intimate scenes of the pharaoh's family life. Akhenaten's attempted religious revolution ultimately failed to win popular support and after his death Akhetaten (now called el-Amarna) was abandoned.

Image-conscious pharaoh
During his 76-year long reign, Ramesses II, 'the Great', ensured that he would be remembered as a mighty ruler by commissioning an extraordinarily large number of colossal statues of himself.

Orthodoxy was formally restored during the reign of Akhenaten's son, the boy pharaoh Tutankhamun (ruled 1333–1323 BC). Tutankhamun spent the whole of his reign under the domination of the vizier Ay and the general Horemheb. His present-day fame rests entirely on the spectacular treasures discovered in his tomb when it was excavated in 1922.

A SHRINKING EMPIRE

In the period of instability after Akhenaten's death, Egypt lost control of the Levant to the Hittite empire and attempts by Sethos I (ruled 1305–1290 BC) and his son Ramesses II (ruled 1290–1224 BC) to restore the situation met with only partial success. A brilliant self-publicist, Ramesses claimed a great victory over the Hittites at the battle of Kadesh (Syria) in 1285 BC, but, as the Hittites still controlled the area after the battle, the outcome was probably less favourable. A peace treaty ended the war in 1256 BC: remarkably both Egyptian and Hittite copies of the treaty still survive. Around 1200 BC, the entire eastern Mediterranean and Near East was disrupted by a series of migrations. The Sea Peoples, a coalition of various migrating peoples who came from all parts of the Mediterranean, fell upon Egypt. Ramesses III (ruled 1194–1163 BC) decisively defeated them in the Delta, but he could not prevent them settling in Palestine.

Ramesses III was Egypt's last great pharaoh. The authority of his successors was steadily undermined by the priesthood of Amun, which had become hereditary and was totally out of royal control. The temple of Amun at Thebes dominated the Egyptian economy: it owned around a quarter of Egypt's land, 90 per cent of its shipping, and it controlled about 80 per cent of all craft production. During the reign of Ramesses XI (ruled 1100–1070 BC), the last king of the New Kingdom, Herihor, the high priest of Amun, became the independent ruler of all of Upper Egypt. The status of the monarchy was so low that almost all the royal tombs in the Valley of the Kings were robbed at this time. Egypt's empire in the Levant and Nubia was lost. After Ramesses' death in 1070 BC, royal authority collapsed entirely.

A BROKEN REED

During the Third Intermediate Period (1070–712 BC), weak pharaohs struggled to assert their authority over the priesthood. They failed, and the period ended in a civil war which split the country into half a dozen petty kingdoms. These were easily conquered by the revived Nubian kingdom of Kush. The Hebrew prophet Isaiah described Egypt at this time as 'a broken reed'. The Nubian conquest began the Late Period (712–332 BC), a period of foreign rule interspersed with native revivals. After Alexander the Great conquered Egypt in 332 BC, the country remained under foreign rulers. Egyptian civilization survived at first, sustained by its religion and the statesmanship of Greek and Roman rulers, who used the trappings of traditional Egyptian kingship to make themselves more acceptable to their subjects. Only when Christianity destroyed its religious basis in the fourth century AD did ancient Egyptian civilization finally begin to die out. The indigenous Egyptian language became extinct after the seventh century AD, and Egypt is now culturally and linguistically an Arab country.

'Now, as for Pharaoh [Ramesses XI] – life, prosperity and health! – how will he ever get to this land? And as for Pharaoh – life, prosperity and health! – whose master is he anyway?'

Private letter of general Piankh expressing his contempt for Ramesses XI (c.1075 BC)

ANCIENT INDIA

INDIA is the birthplace of two of the world's great religions, Hinduism and Buddhism. Today, nearly half the world's population live in countries whose cultural development has been influenced by one or both of these religions. Apart from India itself, these countries include China, Tibet, Nepal, Japan, Sri Lanka, Burma, Thailand, Cambodia, Vietnam, Laos and Indonesia. The influence of ancient India was not just limited to its religions. Indian mathematicians were the first in the Old World to discover the mathematical value of zero, and gave the world quadratic equations and the now universally used system of 'Arabic' numerals. The alphabets of Tibet, Mongolia and all of the Southeast Asian languages are of Indian origin. Yet despite their wide-ranging influence, the early civilizations of the Indian subcontinent are the least well known of any of the ancient civilizations.

Red pottery
Fragment of a large pottery vessel from Harappa (c.2500 BC). Red pottery with red and black slip-painted decorations is characteristic of the Indus valley civilization.

Indian civilization had two beginnings, the first in Pakistan's Indus river valley c.2600 BC, and a second over a thousand years later in the Ganges river valley in India. The relationship between these two civilizations is a controversial one. The Indus civilization was literate, but its unique script has so far defied translation. As a consequence the identity, language and beliefs of the Indus people remain mysterious. Did they contribute to the later Gangetic civilization, or was the Indus civilization essentially a false start? Later Hindu traditions certainly gave no clues that the Indus civilization ever existed and it was only rediscovered by archaeologists working for the British Raj in the 1920s.

THE INDUS VALLEY CIVILIZATION

The Indus river gave India both its name and its first civilization: ironically its course, and the ruins of the ancient cities that depended on it, now lie mostly in Pakistan. The Indus civilization superficially resembled the Mesopotamian civilization in that it developed on the fertile but arid flood plain of a great and unpredictable river, where intensive agriculture and the need for irrigation and flood defences led to the rise of a well-ordered urban society. In other respects, the Indus civilization defies expectations – to all appearances, it was a peaceful, almost classless society lacking even an organized religion. As in Mesopotamia, farming first began not on the flood plain itself, but on the edges of nearby mountains – in this case, in Baluchistan. Farming began with the domestication of the zebu, a native Indian species of cattle which has a distinctive hump on its shoulders, by indigenous hunting communities around 6000–5500 BC. Wheat, barley and dates, all probably introduced from the Middle East, were also grown. The earliest evidence for the domestication of the cotton plant has also been found at ancient settlements in Baluchistan. By around 5000 BC, there is evidence for breeding sheep and goats, and the use of pottery.

From around 4000 BC, farmers from Baluchistan began to colonize the Indus valley flood plain, always settling close to rivers. The Indus river is fed mainly by summer monsoon rains falling on the Himalaya mountains far to the north. The central and southern parts of the river's flood plain receive little more than 20 centimetres (8 in) of rain a year, making it a very marginal area for dry farming. Once the fertility of the alluvial soil was unlocked by irrigation, the flood plain could sustain a dense human population. The flood plain was deficient in other resources, however. As a result there was considerable interaction between the people of the plain and the highlanders. Highland people brought their flocks to winter on the plain and they traded copper, gold, chert (for stone tools), semi-precious stones, such as lapis lazuli and carnelian, and timber for grain and other foodstuffs.

By 3000 BC, some large settlements had grown up on the flood plain. Excavations of towns such as Kot Diji, Kalibangan and Harappa (from which the Indus civilization gets its alternative name, the Harappan civilization) reveal that they possessed massive mud-brick defensive walls and streets laid out in a grid pattern. The appearance of high quality, wheel-thrown pottery is evidence of a degree of craft specialization. These developments were the prelude to the emergence of the fully developed Indus civilization around 2600 BC. The final transition may have resulted from the establishment of trade links to Sumeria. Copper was the Indus civilization's main export and the trade was on a substantial scale: Sumerian writing tablets record delivery of one shipment of over 6.5 tonnes. It is also likely that much of the semi-precious lapis lazuli that was used in Sumeria came via the Indus valley from a remote Indus trading colony at Shorthugai on the Amudarya river in northern Afghanistan. This was close to the mines in the Pamir mountains, which at that time was the only known source of the stone.

MASS STANDARDIZATION

The outstanding characteristic of the Indus civilization is an astonishing, almost obsessive, degree of standardization of artefacts, writing, weights and measures, urban planning and settlement hierarchy. Even pots and everyday tools of stone, copper and bronze conformed to standard patterns. This cultural uniformity extended over a vast area of almost 200,000 square miles (500,000 sq km), stretching from the

Pages 52–53:
Epic carvings
Intricate carvings from the exterior of the Temple of Keshava at Somnathpur in Karnataka built around AD 1268.

Chariot driver
Bronze model of a two-wheeled cart drawn by two oxen from Harappa (c. 2200 BC).

TIMELINE

c.4000 BC
Farmers from Baluchistan colonize
the Indus river valley

c.2600 BC
Cities develop in the Indus valley
flood plain

c.2350 BC
Trade links established between
the Indus and Mesopotamia

c.1900 BC
Indus cities decline and are
gradually abandoned

c.1600 BC
The Vedic migrate to India
from Central Asia

1400–1000 BC
Composition of the *Rigveda*,
the earliest text of Hinduism

c.900 BC
Tribal kingdoms develop on the
Ganges river flood plain

c.700 BC
Emergence of the *Mahajanapadas*,
or 'great realms', on the
Ganges plain

c.599–527 BC
Life of Mahavira, founder of the
Jain religion

c.563–483 BC
Life of Gautama the Buddha

c.549–491 BC
Magadha becomes the leading
Mahajanapada under king Bimbisara

c.340 BC
Magadha conquers the Ganges plain

326 BC
Alexander the Great invades the
Indus valley

321 BC
Chandragupta, founder of the
Mauryan empire, seizes power
in Maghada

305 BC
Chandragupta conquers the
Indus valley

268–233 BC
Mauryan empire reaches its
greatest extent under Ashoka

240 BC
The Third Buddhist Council defines
the doctrines of Buddhism

185 BC
The Mauryan empire
is overthrown

Makran coast in the west to the upper part of the Ganges plain in the east, and from Gujerat in the south right up to the Hindu Kush mountains lying to the north.

The civilization had a clearly defined hierarchy of settlements, divided into four tiers. The first tier consisted of three cities of almost equal size, Mohenjo-daro, Harappa and Dholavira, which each covered more than 100 hectares (250 acres) and probably had populations of 30,000–40,000 people. Though not identical, these cities were planned according to similar principles, including internal divisions into walled enclosures to house different social classes and craft activities, a grid pattern of streets, 'citadels' with public buildings and granaries, and massive mud-brick defensive walls. Extensive use was made of baked bricks for building. Streets were built wide enough to accommodate bullock carts, which were widely used by the Indus people. Two other large cities are known, Rakhigarhi and Ganweriwala, but they have not yet been extensively excavated and their layout is not known.

The second tier of settlement consists of 32 smaller planned sites, generally covering less than 20 hectares (50 acres). Kalibangan was, for example, a miniature version of Mohenjo-daro, while Lothal was a fortified industrial centre where local semi-precious stones were collected and processed. Lothal, situated close to the Gulf of Khambhat, was also a port with an artificial dock: evidence has been discovered there of trade links to Mesopotamia. The third tier consisted of small walled sites with an area of 2–4 hectares (5–10 acres), and the fourth of small farming villages, of which about 15,000 have been discovered so far. These small settlements show rather more cultural diversity and adaptation to local conditions than the larger settlements.

WORKING WITH WATER

The Indus people were skilled hydraulic engineers. Some sites, such as Mohenjo-daro and Dholavira, had public baths. At Dholavira there were 16 stone-lined reservoirs, the oldest in the world, for storing either rainwater or water diverted from rivers along channels. Almost every domestic compound at Mohenjo-daro was provided with a toilet, connected to a system of brick-lined sewers running under the streets. The sewers were covered with stone slabs which could easily be removed for maintenance. It is unclear if the concern for hygiene was motivated by health reasons or for ritual purity.

'The Meluhhaites, the men of the black land, bring to Naram-Sin of Agade all kinds of exotic wares.'

The Curse of Agade c.2000 BC

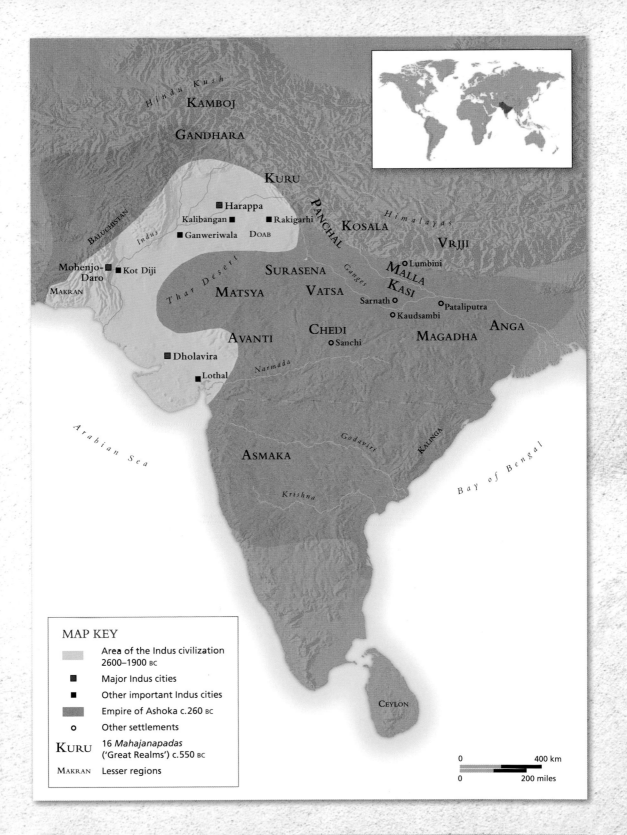

KAMBOJ

Hindu Kush

GANDHARA

KURU

■ Harappa

Kalibangan ■

Rakigarhi ■

PANCHAL

KOSALA

Himalayas

VRJJI

Ganweriwala ■

DOAB

Mohenjo-
Daro   ■ Kot Diji

Indus

Baluchistan

SURASENA

MAKRAN

Thar Desert

MATSYA

VATSA

MALLA

KASI

○ Lumbini

Sarnath ○

○ Pataliputra

AVANTI

CHEDI

○ Kaudsambi

Dholavira ■

○ Sanchi

MAGADHA

ANGA

■ Lothal

Narmada

Arabian Sea

ASMAKA

Godavari

KALINGA

Bay of Bengal

Krishna

CEYLON

MAP KEY

Area of the Indus civilization
2600–1900 BC

■ Major Indus cities

■ Other important Indus cities

Empire of Ashoka c.260 BC

○ Other settlements

KURU   16 *Mahajanapadas*
('Great Realms') c.550 BC

MAKRAN   Lesser regions

0 ———— 400 km

0 ———— 200 miles

Harappa ruins
The foundations of
domestic dwellings in
a residential quarter of
Harappa. The Indus
valley people made
extensive use of baked
brick in their buildings.

The Sumerians referred to the Indus valley as *Meluhha* and the people who lived there as *Meluhhaites*. What they called themselves is unknown and is likely to remain so unless their writing system can be deciphered. Most scholars believe that the Indus people were probably related to the Dravidian-speaking peoples of southern India (such as the Tamils, for example). Isolated groups of Dravidian speakers in central and northern India demonstrate that these languages were once spoken all over the Indian subcontinent. One of these groups, the Brahui people of Baluchistan, in Pakistan, are thought by many to be direct descendents of the Indus people.

A SOCIETY OF EQUALS

The social organization of the Indus civilization is also mysterious. Even in the absence of writing, the existence of state-level organization can be inferred from archaeological evidence of palaces, monumental artwork, representations of organized war, specialized weapons, prestige objects and richly furnished elite burials, for example. Such evidence is completely lacking for the Indus civilization. There are no rich burials, no evidence of martial display, very few weapons, no palaces and no prestige objects. Yet the uniformity of Indus culture and the orderly planning of the cities could only credibly have come

DECODING THE INDUS SCRIPT

Inscriptions in the Indus script have been found on tools, jewellery and pottery, but the majority of them are on soapstone stamp seals. About 1,700 of these beautiful and distinctive artefacts have been found, each carved with a depiction of a real or mythological animal as well as a short inscription. The seals were used to stamp clay seals on shipments of goods as symbols of ownership. The Indus script has around 400 different signs. Most attempts to decipher the script have been based on the assumption that the Indus people spoke a Dravidian language. However, attempts to use early forms of living Dravidian languages, such as Tamil, as a model for deciphering the Indus script have been unsuccessful. It is possible that the Indus language was unrelated to any modern language.

Indus valley seals
Two of the most common animals shown on seals are the zebu (the distinctive Indian humped cow), and the 'unicorn'.

The decipherment of the Indus script is made more difficult by the brevity of the inscriptions; most contain an average of only five symbols. There is general agreement that the numerals for ones and tens have been identified, and that the script was written right to left. It is also likely to have been logo-syllaballic – some symbols (logograms) represent whole words, while others represent individual phonetic syllables. The key to deciphering ancient Egyptian hieroglyphs was the discovery of the Rosetta Stone, which carried a trilingual inscription, in hieroglyphic, demotic and Greek. Unless some Indus equivalent is discovered, for example, in the Indus script and Mesopotamian cuneiform, then it is highly likely that the Indus civilization will remain essentially unknown and prehistoric.

about under the direction of strong governing authorities. A social elite must surely have existed, but it is archaeologically invisible. One possibility is that the Indus elite was a priestly class that rejected the accumulation and display of wealth for religious reasons. However, no temples or other evidence of organized religion have ever been discovered in any of the Indus cities. Alternatively, the elite may deliberately have hidden their wealth in order to promote a public ideal of social egalitarianism.

The Indus civilization's political structure is equally uncertain. The obsessive standardization that characterises the Indus civilization is persuasive evidence that it was united under a single powerful government. If so, this would have been by far the largest state of its age anywhere in the world. However, this empire of the Indus has no obvious capital. The five pre-eminent Indus cities were all of roughly equal size and status and are therefore more likely to be the capitals of independent kingdoms or city states. Perhaps the kingdoms formed some Bronze Age equivalent of the European Union, which imposed standardization to promote internal trade? In this, as in so much else, the Indus civilization offers more questions than answers.

THE END OF THE INDUS CIVILIZATION

Around 1900 BC, most of the characteristics of the Indus civilization disappeared. The cities and towns were abandoned, writing and standardized weights and measures fell out of use, and standardized artefacts were replaced by a variety of local traditions. The collapse of the civilization was at first explained as the result of an invasion. This now seems to be unlikely. Although the larger settlements were abandoned, life in the Indus farming villages carried on much as normal, with no sharp break in cultural continuity as might be expected if the civilization had been overrun by invaders. Many Indus traditions continued, especially in the north of the region, for example in the so-called Cemetery H and Ochre Coloured Pottery cultures, which extended across the Doab (the area between the upper Indus and upper Ganges river basins).

More recent attempts to explain the collapse have sought economic and environmental factors which caused a reversion to a simpler level of social and economic organization. As was the case in Sumeria, a build up of salt in the soil, and a resulting loss of fertility, resulting from poor irrigation techniques may have led to a decline in agricultural production. Another factor may have been radical changes in the course of the Indus and its tributaries, one of which, the Saraswati, completely dried up in ancient times. Neither of these factors seem sufficient to have caused the complete collapse of the civilization, though, so a truly convincing explanation remains to be found.

REBIRTH ON THE GANGES

The true end of Indian prehistory is marked by the emergence of the early Hindu civilization on the Ganges river basin in the early first millennium BC. This civilization is closely associated with the *arya* ('noble'), nomadic peoples from Central Asia who had migrated across the Hindu Kush mountains into the Indian subcontinent. They spoke an early form of Sanskrit, an Indo–European language closely related to the language spoken by the ancient Iranians, with whom they shared a common origin. Though long extinct in everyday use, Sanskrit is the language of the Hindu scriptures and survives today as a liturgical language. Spoken Sanskrit gradually diverged from the scriptural form, giving rise to a number of *Prakrits* (vernaculars) which evolved into many modern languages, including Hindi, the official language of modern India.

There are no truly historical accounts of the *arya*'s migration but a mythic record of their wanderings and wars with the native *dasa* ('slaves') is preserved in the *Rigveda*. The most ancient of the

Agni
Agni was the Vedic fire god and remains an important deity in modern Hinduism. His name means 'fire' in Sanskrit and is cognate with the Latin word *ignis*, which is the root of the English word 'ignite'.

THE ARYAN MYTH

The people of the *Rigveda* have no name. When referring to themselves they describe themselves as the *arya*. In classical Sanskrit this means 'noble' or 'pure', but in the *Rigveda* it is simply self-referential, meaning 'ourselves', 'we'. The practice of calling the people of the *Rigveda* 'the aryans' was begun by European scholars in the early 19th century. Pretty soon aryan became a synonym for the ancient Indo-Europeans in general.

Probably the greatest intellectual revolution of the 19th century came from the publication of Darwin's *On the Origin of Species* in 1859, which founded the science of evolutionary biology. Darwin tactfully said little about human evolution, but others were not so reluctant. Darwin's doctrine of 'survival of the fittest' chimed with the spirit of an age of imperialism. It was easy for Europeans to believe that they dominated the world because they were fitter than other humans.

Ethnologists, such as the Comte de Gobineau (1816–1882), propagated the notion of an aryan 'master race'. The aryan race spoke Indo-European languages and was responsible for all progress in human history. It was innately superior to all other races. European colonialists took comfort from these ideas. The British could claim to be saving India from the decadence which had resulted from its aryan conquerors interbreeding with the racially inferior natives.

Supporters of aryanism regarded the Nordic and Germanic peoples as the purest aryans. Adolf Hitler and the Nazis used this idea to justify their policy of exterminating the non-aryan Jews and Gypsies, and enslaving other 'inferior' races. The Nazi excesses left aryanism morally bankrupt and the collapse of the European empires after World War II made European claims to superiority ring hollow. Anthropologists and geneticists have comprehensively debunked aryanism's pseudo-scientific basis. Because of its acquired racist overtones, however, many historians are now reluctant to use the term 'aryan', even to describe the peoples of the *Rigveda*.

Hindu scriptures, the *Rigveda* ('the knowledge of verses') is a collection of over 1,000 hymns and liturgies that were chanted by priests during rituals and sacrifices. The *Rigveda* portrays the *arya* as tribal peoples, nomadic pastoralists whose lives revolved around their herds of cattle and horses. They travelled in wagons and fought in two-horsed chariots, not for land, but to seize their enemies' herds. The *arya* did not practise arable farming or build permanent dwellings, and they were illiterate: their language had no words for plough, furrow, mortar or writing. Vedic beliefs varied significantly from classical Hinduism. The most important Vedic gods were the storm god Indra, the fire god Agni, Varuna, the guardian of cosmic order, and the Sun god Surya. Some of the major gods of classical Hinduism held only minor significance, such as Vishnu, then a solar deity, or were absent altogether, like Shiva. The most important ritual was the soma sacrifice. Soma was a hallucinogenic drink prepared from an unknown plant, some of which was offered as a libation to the gods, the remainder being drunk by the priests. Cattle and, more rarely, humans were sacrificed. The *Rigveda* describes how the gods divided society into four varnas or classes; the *Brahmin* (priests), *Kshatriya* (warriors), *Vaishya* (commoners) and *Shudras* (servants). These formed the basis for the development of the Hindu caste system.

LAND OF THE SEVEN RIVERS

It is not possible to say with any great certainty when the *arya* arrived in India. The *Rigveda* was not committed to writing until around 300 BC at the earliest, but comparisons with other early written forms of Indo-European languages, such as Old Iranian Avestan, led linguists to conclude that it was originally composed between 1400 and 1000 BC. The geographical horizons of the *Rigveda* are narrowly confined to the upper Indus valley, which it calls the 'Land of the Seven Rivers'. The Ganges is only mentioned once and there are no references to either the Indus cities or to places in Central Asia. This suggests that the *arya* arrived long after the Indus civilization had fallen, but also so long before the *Rigveda* was composed that any folk memory of Central Asia had been lost. For this reason, most scholars believe that the *arya* arrived sometime around 1600 BC. This was about the time of the emergence of the Gandharan grave culture which emerged in northern Pakistan. This culture

Avatar
This stone sculpture from a temple at Ekambesvara depicts Matsya (the Fish), the first avatar of Vishnu. As Matsya, Vishnu retrieved the Vedas from the demon Hayagriva, who had stolen them, and saved Manu, the first human, from a global deluge.

is the earliest in the entire Indian subcontinent that is known to have used horses and also to have practised cremation, the usual funeral practice of Hinduism.

In the centuries following the composition of the *Rigveda*, northern India was gradually aryanized. This probably occurred through a combination of further eastward migrations of *arya*, and through the adoption, voluntary or otherwise, by the native peoples of their language, caste system and religious beliefs. How much of the post-Indus traditions of the native peoples the *arya* absorbed in return is unknown, but some aspects of classical Hinduism, such as ritual bathing, appear to have precedents in Indus times. The eastward drift of the *arya* is manifested in later Hindu scriptures, such as the *Brahmanas* and *Upanisads* (composed around 900 BC), whose geographical horizons are centred on the Doab and the upper Ganges basin. This creeping aryanization is associated with the spread of two types of pottery that appeared around 1000 BC: Painted Grey Ware pottery, which is found across northern India from the Doab to the middle Ganges, and Black-and-Red Ware, which spread south of the Ganges into central India. The Painted Grey Ware is of particular importance because its appearance marks the beginning of iron working in India.

Kausambi coin
A cast copper coin from Kausambi, made in the first century BC. The first coins were issued in northern India c.400 BC, but in southern India they were not used until the early centuries AD.

THE GREAT REALMS

By the ninth century BC, dozens of small tribal kingdoms and aristocratic tribal republics, known as *janapadas*, had developed on the Ganges plain and south as far as the Godavari river in central India. Competition for power was intense and, by c.700 BC, the *janapadas* had coalesced to form 16 *Mahajanapadas* or 'great realms'. By c.400 BC, the number had been reduced to only half a dozen. The most powerful of these was Magadha (present day Bihar), which achieved a dominant position in the sixth century BC under its expansionist king Bimbisara (ruled c.543–491 BC). Bimbisara's success owed as much to astute marriage alliances as to force. The conflicts of this period are reflected in the vast Hindu mythological epic, the *Mahabharata* (composed c.400 BC).

A revival of urban life accompanied the rise of the *Mahajanapadas*. Each kingdom had its fortified capital. Kausambi, the capital of the kingdom of Vatsa, was typical with an area of 50 hectares (120 acres) enclosed within its walls. Not only was Kausambi smaller than any of the Indus cities, but it also lacked their monumental public buildings. Only perishable materials such as timber and earth were used for building. Durable baked brick, so ubiquitous in the Indus cities, was not used on the Ganges plain until the second century BC. Kausambi stood at the head of a four-tier hierarchy of settlements. The second tier was composed of provincial towns, which were centres for local administration and manufacturing luxury goods. The third rank settlements were manufacturing centres producing iron and stone tools and pottery. The lowest tier of settlements were small farming villages. To serve the needs of increasingly complex administration and tax gathering, writing came back into use

KINGS OF MAGADHA

The kingdom of Magadha, centred on the lower Ganges flood plain, was the greatest of the *Mahajanapadas* and it twice dominated India, first under the Mauryan dynasty, and a second time under the Guptas, whose rule was regarded as a 'golden age' of Hindu culture. Magadha declined after the Guptas and fell to the Muslims in the 12th century AD.

Brihadratha dynasty (semi-legendary)

Pradyota dynasty
c.799–684 BC

Haryanka dynasty
c.543–413 BC

Shishunga dynasty
c.413–343 BC

Nanda dynasty
c.343–321 BC

Mauryan dynasty
c.321–185 BC

Shunga dynasty
c.185–73 BC

Kanva dynasty
c.73–26 BC

Minor dynasties
25 BC–AD 240

Gupta dynasty
c.AD 240–550

The longest work of literature in the world, the *Mahabharata* was composed around the middle of the first millennium BC. The epic tells the story of a feud between two groups of royal cousins, the wicked Kauravas who tricked the virtuous Pandavas out of their kingdom in a crooked dice game, and of the war of annihilation that followed. To help the Pandavas, the great god Vishnu takes human form as his avatar Krishna, to see that justice prevails. The climax of the conflict is the battle of Kurukshetra (near Delhi) in which all of the Kauravas are slain and of the victorious army only five Pandava brothers and Krishna survive. Krishna dies soon after when a hunter, mistaking him for a deer, shoots him with an arrow in his one vulnerable spot, his foot. The traditional date for the war is 1302 BC, but most historians believe that it took place several centuries later. The story was probably originally the property of the *Kshatriya* class of rulers and

warriors, who revered the new deity Krishna. The epic served as a way to spread knowledge of the god. Over the centuries, the *Brahmins* took control of the cult of Krishna and greatly expanded the narrative to include long didactic passages, descriptions of places of pilgrimage and many other myths and legends. In its final form, reached around AD 400, the *Mahabharata* is about eight times the combined length of Homer's epics, the *Iliad* and the *Odyssey*. Historians regard the *Mahabharata* as a major source of information about the development of Hinduism in the first millennium BC. Its religious significance for Hindus is as a text about *dharma*, or moral law.

Royal battle
Kichaka, the king of Matsya, fighting with the Pandava Bhima, whose wife Draupadi he coveted. Bhima eventually slew Kichaka.

in the sixth century but it used an adaptation of the Semitic alphabetic scripts used in the Near East, not the ancient Indus script that had previously been used. Coinage came into use in the fifth century BC as a form of portable wealth.

RICE AND IRON

Several factors contributed to the rise of the *Mahajanapadas*. One was a shift from wheat to rice cultivation on the Ganges flood plain, which took advantage of the river's annual monsoon floods. Constructing irrigation channels and paddy fields to retain the waters of the Ganges' monsoon floods required an enormous communal effort. This by itself would have promoted a high degree of social organization. The effort was worthwhile because rice yields a substantially greater surplus than other cereals. These surpluses could sustain a growing population and increasing numbers of specialist workers. The availability of iron tools contributed to increased agricultural productivity by making it easier to clear the land and work fields. Iron weapons may have led to an intensification of warfare, promoting the growth of states for more effective defence (or offence, of course). In particular, warfare empowered the leaders of the *Kshatriya* caste, the rajas, who emerged as dynastic rulers. Finally, the rising population and agricultural surpluses stimulated growth in regional trade, which in turn stimulated urbanization. By the sixth century BC, a long-distance trade route, the *Uttarapatha* ('North Road'), linked most of the capitals of the *Mahajanapadas* with the Bay of Bengal in the southeast and the Kabul valley in the northwest.

AN AGE OF FAITHS

The age of the *Mahajanapadas* was a time of intense religious turmoil, seeing major developments in Hinduism and the foundation of two new religions. Hinduism is a continuously evolving religious tradition and no particular event or individual can be associated with its foundation. However, it was during this period that Hinduism gained its defining concepts of *dharma* and *karma*. *Dharma* ('righteousness') forms the basis of Hindu religious and moral law. *Dharma* became the subject of the *dharmasutras* ('righteousness threads'), collections of maxims dealing with the rules of caste, religious duty, and the relationship between the individual and the rest of society and the state. *Karma* existed in Vedic times as a concept of ritual action. By the sixth century BC, *karma* had become linked to belief in reincarnation. The soul was trapped in a cycle of rebirth – *samsara* – moving from body to body as determined by *karma*, the moral force of the individual's actions. The range of *samsara* extended from insects to divine beings. The individual's rank in the hierarchy of life was determined by the quality of his or her previous life. This both justified the social order and gave an incentive to live a good life.

At the same time, the chief gods of the Vedic period declined in importance. Vishnu grew in stature, becoming the great preserver of the universe. Vishnu's avatar (incarnation) Krishna become an object of popular worship, probably because his role in the *Mahabharata* gave him great appeal to the warrior *Kshatriya* class. Rudra, a minor Vedic god associated with death, disease and healing evolved into the powerful and ambivalent god Shiva, who possessed both benevolent and destructive characteristics. The worship of Vishnu and Shiva became central to the two main theistic movements that developed in Hinduism, Vaishnavism and Shaivism, but this development still lay some centuries in the future.

ELEPHANTS

Elephants have played an important part in Indian life since the earliest historical times. The Indian elephant, which is smaller than the African elephant, was probably domesticated by the time of the Indus valley civilization, and it commonly appears on its stamp seals. The Vedic *arya* were impressed by their first encounters with elephants and in the *Rigveda*, the angry storm-god Indra is compared to a maddened elephant. The huge grey shape of the elephant also symbolized the approach of the dark clouds of the life-giving monsoon rains. Indra's own elephant was called Abhranu, 'the one who binds the clouds'.

Domesticated elephants were used for heavy transport and lifting, as prestige transport and for hunting and war. In war, elephants were used as platforms for archers and spearmen, and as a shock weapon to break up enemy formations. The use of war elephants spread to the Mediterranean world as a result of Alexander the Great's encounters with them during his invasion of the Indus valley in 326 BC. They were also later adopted in Southeast Asia.

'To save a family, abandon a man;
to save a village, abandon a family;
to save a country, abandon a village;
to save the soul, abandon the world.'

Mahabharata (The Book of the Assembly Hall)

SHIVA

Shiva and Parvati
Shiva with his wife Parvati, the Hindu mother goddess, and their children – Ganesh, the god of beginnings and obstacles, and Skanda (Kartikeya), the god of war.

Hindu belief holds that the universe is populated by a multitude of gods. These gods share a common godhead, but are essentially human in their behaviour, having relationships with female deities and fathering children. Like humans, the gods often possess contradictory qualities, none more so than the powerful and ambivalent god Shiva. Shiva had many names. He was Mahadeva ('the Great God'), Bhairava ('the Terror'), Hara ('the Ravisher'), and Kala ('Death'). Shiva embodies all of life, in all of its many aspects, so whatever Shiva is, he is also its opposite.

Shiva is both ascetic and sexually voracious, not only with his consort Parvati, but also with many other women too. He was worshipped in the form of a *linga*, a phallic symbol, which some historians believe may be derived from a pre-Vedic fertility cult. Shiva is also Yogesvara, the chaste prince of ascetics, who meditates on Mount Kailas, the centre of the universe, with unkempt hair and his body smeared in ashes. In this aspect, Shiva stood for the mastery of vital forces. Shiva saved the world by drinking poison that threatened to engulf it, but as 'king of dancers' he will dance the *Tandava* dance which destroys the world, and he is supreme lord of the universe.

Shiva has four arms, wears a girdle made of skulls and has a third eye in the middle of his forehead with which he can destroy anything he looks at. He is often featured wearing a crescent moon on his head, a snake around his neck, sitting on a tiger skin (an honour reserved for the most accomplished Hindus) and armed with his favoured weapon, the trident. According to legend, the sacred river Ganges is said to flow from his hair. The city of Varanasi is thought to have been held special by Shiva, and it has become one of the holiest pilgrimage sites in India.

Unlike Vishnu, Shiva rarely intervenes in human affairs, but he is not entirely remote from human concerns, being a father of three children, including the war god Skanda, and the elephant-headed Ganesh, the god of favourable beginnings.

Dancing Ganesh
Ganesh was born with a human head. Shiva beheaded Ganesh when he prevented his father from entering his mother's house. Parvati demanded Shiva restore Ganesh to life. When his original head could not be found, Shiva replaced it with an elephant's head.

Statue of Shiva
Bronze statue depicting Shiva as Nataraja, the Lord of Dance. Shiva is closely associated with sacred music and dance, such as the powerful *Tandava* dance and the graceful *Lasya* dance.

The Buddha
A first to second century
AD Gandharan sculpture
depicting Gautama's
Great Departure from his
luxurious life in his family's
palace, the first step on
his road to Enlightenment.

Hinduism, as it was practised in this period, was highly ritualistic. The main source of religious authority was the *Brahmin*, or priest class, who were the guardians of scripture and law, which at this time was still committed to memory and transmitted orally. On account of their ritual purity, the *Brahmins* were able to perform intercessionary sacrifices on behalf of the lower castes. Although the slaughter of milk cows was abolished in the *Mahabharata*, animal and even human sacrifice continued to be part of Hinduism into the Middle Ages. Early Hindus performed their rituals outdoors and, like the Indus people before them, did not build temples to their gods.

CHALLENGING AUTHORITY

The ritualistic nature of early Hinduism was unsatisfactory to individuals who sought a more spiritual religious experience. Because of the doctrine of reincarnation, which linked all animals and humans in the same cycle of rebirth, unnecessary killing became unacceptable to many. The religious authority of the *Brahmins* was challenged by 'renouncers' who abandoned ritual, wealth and family for the life of a wandering mendicant. Their radical teachings attracted the support of the emerging mercantile class, who, despite their wealth, belonged to the lower castes. The most successful of the renouncers were Mahavira and Siddhartha Gautama, the Buddha.

Mahavira was the founder of the Jain religion. Traditionally, he is said to have lived c.599–527 BC, but many scholars believe that this is up to a century too early. Mahavira was born to a wealthy family, but at the age of 30 he adopted a life of extreme asceticism and meditation, renouncing all possessions and living on alms. He went naked and did not even own a bowl for food or drinking water. To avoid sinful acts, Mahavira developed the doctrine of *ahimsa*, or non-violence, which forbids the killing or injuring of any animal life. Mahavira would not even brush insects off his body to prevent them from biting him. Followers of Jainism are strong advocates of vegetarianism, and Jain monks take extreme precautions against causing accidental injury to living things, including wearing a cloth over the mouth to avoid accidentally swallowing anything. To help them in their quest for salvation, Mahavira's followers took five vows, to renounce killing, speaking untruths, greed, sexual pleasure and all attachments to the world. Jainism is too demanding to have attracted a mass following – today there are only about three million Jains – but its principle of *ahimsa* has been

Mauryan coins
A silver coin of the
Mauryan empire, punched
with royal symbols of the
elephant and the Sun as
signs of authenticity.

extremely influential in Hindu and Buddhist thought. In modern times, the principle was applied to political action by Mahatma Gandhi (1869–1948), who led a campaign of non-violent resistance to British rule in India that culminated in Indian Independence in 1947.

THE LIFE OF BUDDHA

The life of Gautama the Buddha resembles Mahavira's in many ways, but his advocacy of moderation gave his teachings a wider appeal. The historical Buddha is elusive because none of the traditions about his life and teachings were committed to writing for several hundred years after his death. Scholars disagree about when he actually lived: the traditional dates are c.563–483 BC, but some think it was up to a century later.

Gautama was born at Lumbini on the northern edge of the Ganges plain, in what is now Nepal, to a princely family of the *Kshatriya* caste. According to tradition, Gautama had a sheltered upbringing and he was an adult before he ventured outside his father's palace and witnessed human suffering for the first time. Overcome with sorrow, Gautama decided to renounce the world and, aged 29, he left his wife and newborn son and became a religious ascetic, living on alms. Early in his wanderings he met king Bimbisara of Magadha, who became his patron.

For six years, Gautama sought a way for the soul to escape the endless cycle of death and rebirth. He joined other ascetics, practised mortification of the flesh and nearly fasted to death before concluding that extreme asceticism was not the way to liberate the soul. He sought instead a 'middle path' between luxury and asceticism. Meditating under a tree one night, Gautama finally attained enlightenment and became the Buddha (the 'enlightened' or 'awakened one'). Buddha preached his first sermon at Sarnath, outlining the doctrine of the Four Noble Truths: the fact of suffering; that suffering has a cause; that suffering can be ended; and that it can be ended by following the Eightfold Path. The Eightfold Path was a course of behaviour by which the soul could escape from *saṃsara* and attain *nirvana* ('becoming extinguished'), the cessation of suffering and liberation from the cycle of rebirth. Buddha converted his former ascetic companions as monks and accepted both male and female lay disciples. Buddha's ministry continued for 45 years: when he died, aged 80, his body was cremated. By this time, Buddha's disciples were spreading his teachings throughout India.

THE MAURYAN EMPIRE

The age of the *Mahajanapadas* was brought to an end by the short-lived Nanda dynasty, which came to power in Magadha in 343 BC. The founder of the dynasty, Mahapadma, was the son of a barber and a courtesan who used a successful military career as a springboard to usurp the throne. Mahapadma's low social origins rankled and he led his kingdom in a war against the *Kshatriya* caste. As all kings were *Kshatriyas*, this was an attack on the whole social order of the *Mahajanapadas*. Mahapadma's armies conquered the

Mauryan statue
Mauryan statuette of a dancing boy, second century BC.

whole of the Ganges plain and advanced through central India as far south as the Godavari river. Mahapadma was succeeded by an uncertain number of his sons, the last of whom to rule was Dhanananda. Dhanananda was king when Alexander the Great's army invaded the Indus valley in 326 BC. The prospect of fighting Dhanananda's army of 20,000 cavalry, 200,000 infantry, 2,000 chariots and 3,000 war elephants was too much for Alexander's war-weary men and they mutinied, forcing the would-be world conqueror to turn back.

OVERTHROWING THE NANDAS

Despite their military achievements, the Nandas were resented for their avarice and high taxes, and in 321 BC they were overthrown by one of their generals, Chandragupta Maurya (ruled 321–c.293 BC). Chandragupta's origins are obscure, but he was a commander on Magadha's northwest border at the time of Alexander's invasion: he fought against Greek outposts in the area and may have met Alexander. Chandragupta continued the expansionist policies of the Nandas and, by 311 BC, had extended his kingdom to the Indus. This brought him into conflict with Seleucos, one of the generals who had seized power in Alexander's empire after his death. In 305 BC, Chandragupta triumphed and was ceded control of the whole Indus valley in return for a gift of 500 war elephants, which Seleucos used to good effect against his rival generals.

Chandragupta was an able administrator as well as a good soldier. The efficient central bureaucracy he created controlled economic activity and commissioned road building, irrigation and other works. He imposed a harsh penal code on his people. In about 293 BC, Chandragupta abdicated in favour of his son Bindusara (ruled c.293–268 BC) and became a Jain monk. He died around 286 BC. Bindusara made extensive conquests in central India, pushing the empire's frontier south of the Kaveri river. The Mauryan empire was brought to its greatest extent by Bindusara's son Ashoka (ruled 268–233 BC), one of India's most remarkable rulers. Following his bloody conquest of Kalinga (an important source of war elephants) in 261 BC, Ashoka suffered a deep crisis of remorse for the suffering he had caused and was said to have converted to Buddhism.

Sanchi stupa north gate
The four gateways were built in AD 70 by the Satavahana king Satakani. The gate, constructed to imitate wooden structures, is carved with scenes from the Buddha's life.

ASHOKA AND BUDDHISM

Ashoka publicly renounced military conquest and sought to rule by moral authority alone. He adopted a principle that he described as 'conquest by *dharma*', that is by applying the Buddhist principles of right conduct and non-violence in all aspects of public life. To publicize his aims, Ashoka went on preaching tours and ordered edicts on morality and compassion to be carved on to rock faces and stone pillars throughout his empire. Over 30 of these have survived, providing historians with their most important source of information about Ashoka's aspirations for his empire. In one edict Ashoka declared 'All men are my children. As on behalf of my own children, I desire that they be provided by me with complete welfare and happiness in this world, and in the other world also, even so is my desire on behalf of all men.' The edicts encouraged Ashoka's subjects to practise *dharma* by becoming vegetarians, by being honest, truthful, compassionate, merciful, benevolent and considerate to others, and by avoiding extravagance or acquisitiveness. Ashoka appointed special '*dharma* ministers' who were responsible for promoting the welfare of the common people.

The earliest Buddhist monuments are *stupas*, the earliest of which date from the time of Ashoka. *Stupas* are commemorative monuments built to house sacred relics of the Buddha. Early *stupas* had a hemispherical form which was derived from pre-Buddhist burial mounds. The finest is the great *stupa* at Sanchi (third century BC), which consists of a circular base supporting a massive stone dome (the 'egg' or 'womb') on the summit of which is a small umbrella structure. The building is encircled with a stone fence, pierced by four gateways, which are decorated with relief sculptures portraying scenes of the Buddha's life.

The concept of the *stupa* spread throughout the Buddhist world, evolving into many different forms, such as the bell-shaped *stupas* of Sri Lanka, the vast terraced temple of Borobodur in Java, and the pagodas of China and Japan. Veneration of the Buddha was performed by walking around the *stupa* in a clockwise direction.

Sanchi *Stupa* from the East Gate
The *stupa* was commissioned by the Mauryan emperor Ashoka in the third century BC and remained an important place of pilgrimage until the 12th century AD.

Ashoka never explicitly mentioned Buddhism in his edicts, and he allowed complete religious freedom in his empire. Nevertheless, he worked hard to promote Buddhism in other ways, transforming it from a minor Indian sect into a world religion. He also sent missions to southern India, Ceylon, Indonesia, the Greek states of western Asia and the nomads of Central Asia. Ashoka was a generous patron of Buddhist monasteries and shrines. Some of the first monumental *stupas* – hemispherical structures built to house relics of the Buddha – date to Ashoka's reign. The majority of Ashoka's subjects did not convert to Buddhism and Hinduism later made such a strong comeback that Buddhism was virtually extinct in its homeland by the Middle Ages. By that time, however, the religion had put down deep roots in the other regions whose conversion had been begun by Ashoka.

ASHOKA'S LEGACY

Ashoka's public idealism was leavened with pragmatism. He moderated Chandragupta's penal code, but retained the death penalty and maintained a secret police force. Nor did he disband his army. Modern scholars dispute the sincerity of Ashoka's conversion to Buddhism, seeing his emphasis on *dharma* as an attempt to appeal across the boundaries of caste and religion and create a common social identity among his subjects. If Ashoka promoted *dharma* to hold his empire together, it was a failure. The Mauryan empire began to break up into independent states almost as soon as Ashoka was dead, and the dynasty itself was overthrown in 185 BC. No native dynasty would ever again rule so much of India, but the ideal of a pan-Indian empire was not forgotten.

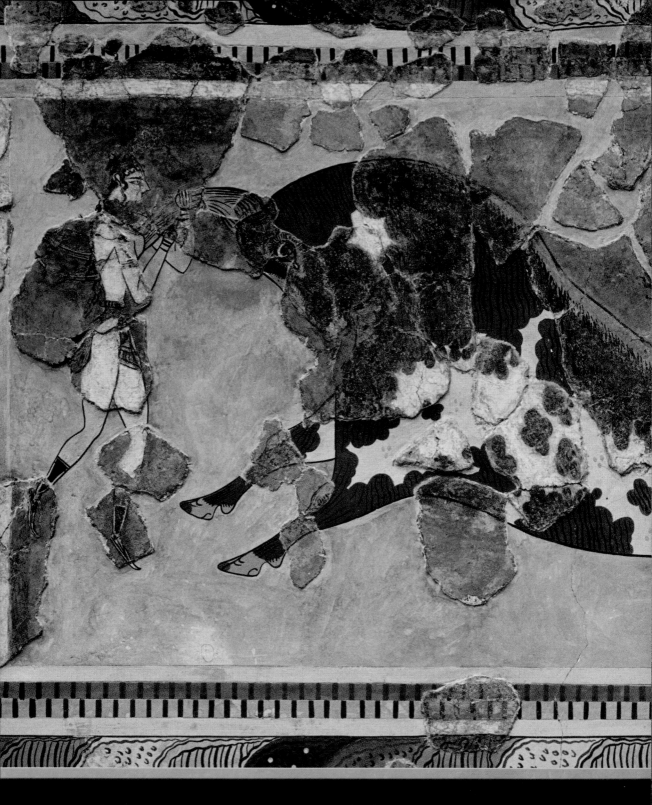

MINOANS AND MYCENAEANS

N O ancient civilizations have left such a legacy of myth and legend as the Minoans and Mycenaeans of the Aegean Bronze Age. The first European civilization, the Minoans originated on the island of Crete around 2000 BC. Four hundred years later, the Mycenaean civilization developed in southern Greece. The Mycenaeans were expansionist; they conquered the Minoans and founded colonies throughout the Aegean, on the coast of Anatolia and as far away as Cyprus. Then, around 1200 BC, this flourishing civilization suddenly collapsed as a wave of destruction swept over Greece. During the long 'dark ages' which followed, true historical memories of the Aegean Bronze Age faded. By the time of the Classical Greek civilization, it was remembered as a heroic age when legendary warriors fought the Trojans, slew the Minotaur and stole the Golden Fleece.

Copper ingot
Copper ox-hide ingots (so-called because of their shape) were widely distributed around the eastern Mediterranean during the Bronze Age. The protruding corners were probably there to make the ingots easier to carry. Analysis of the metal content indicates that most ox-hide ingots were made on Cyprus, which had important copper mines in the Bronze Age.

The existence of the Minoan civilization was completely unsuspected until 1900, when the British archaeologist Arthur Evans (1851–1941) excavated the site of Knossos and discovered a vast and lavishly decorated Bronze Age palace. Evans named the civilization he had discovered the Minoan, after Minos, a mythological king of Crete. The Minoan civilization was one of the first not to develop on the flood plain of a great river. Crete is a rugged, mountainous island with a typical Mediterranean climate of hot, dry summers and mild winters with moderate rainfall. Apart from the small Plain of Messara in the south, the island has no plains with fertile soils and no large rivers to provide a reliable source of water for irrigation. The Minoans developed a system of intensive farming based on the so-called 'Mediterranean Triad' of wheat, olives and vines. Olives and vines grew well on Crete's rugged, scrubby mountain slopes and produced two valuable and easily stored and transported commodities – oil and wine. The Minoans traded these goods overseas for commodities that Crete lacked, such as copper, tin and ivory. This allowed the limited areas of fertile valley land to be dedicated to the intensive cultivation of wheat. Flocks of sheep, kept on Crete's extensive mountain pastures, produced meat, milk and wool. The wool sustained a textile industry that exported cloth as far afield as Egypt. Fishing was also an important activity. In these ways, the Minoans maximized the productivity of their environment. Other craftwork produced by the Minoans, including ornamental metalwork, painted pottery and dyes (a red dye made from the murex shellfish, and a yellow dye made from the saffron crocus) were exported to supplement the main trade in oil, wine and cloth.

THE FOUR PALACES

By 2000 BC, Crete's growing prosperity and dense population led to the development of four small kingdoms centred on magnificent palace complexes at Knossos, Phaistos, Mallia and Khania. The largest, at Knossos, covered 1 hectare (2.5 acres). There were also a number of smaller palaces, thought to have been subordinate power centres. Though not identical, the palaces had many common features. None of them had defences. All were built around a central courtyard and included residential areas, spaces for entertainments and shrines for the performance of religious rituals. They were decorated with brightly painted frescoes. The palaces also incorporated extensive workshops, granaries and storerooms crammed with huge *pithoi* (storage jars for wine, oil and perhaps other commodities). The palaces were multi-storied buildings: the palace at Knossos may have been five stories high. The complex layout of the palaces may have given rise to the later Greek legend of the Labyrinth, the underground maze at Knossos where king Minos kept the Minotaur, a half-human, half-bull monster.

THE DEVELOPMENT OF WRITING

The workshops and storerooms show that the palaces were centres where craft production was controlled and where surplus food from the surrounding countryside was collected and stored, either for redistribution as rations for craftworkers or for export. The need to manage this system led to the development of writing, on clay tablets, and stamp seals. The earliest form of writing used was a form of hieroglyphic that may have been inspired by contacts with Egypt. Around 1700 BC, hieroglyphic was superseded by a script based on syllabic symbols, known as Linear A. A third script is known from a single example, a clay disc discovered at Phaistos in 1908. This was made by

TIMELINE

c.2000 BC
Origins of the Minoan civilization: first palaces built on Crete, hieroglyphic writing comes into use

c.1700 BC
Linear A script comes into use

c.1700 BC
Knossos becomes the dominant Minoan centre

c.1650 BC
Origins of the Greek Mycenaean civilization: city states ruled by kings develop in mainland Greece

c.1628 BC
Volcanic eruption of Thera destroys the Minoan city of Akrotiri

c.1450 BC
Mycenaean Greeks invade and conquer Crete

1260–1240 BC
Troy destroyed by fire

c.1200 BC
All major Mycenaean cities destroyed by unknown invaders: beginning of the Greek dark ages

1184 BC
Traditional date of the Trojan War

Pages 72–73: Bull jumpers
One of several small frescoes from the Minoan palace at Knossos showing a bull-jumping ritual or competition (c.1450–1375 BC).

Minoan jar
Pithoi were large pottery jars, often as tall as a man, used for storing oil, wine and grain. Despite their utilitarian nature, they were usually richly decorated.

Minoan palace
Part of a reconstructed
arcade from the palace
at Knossos, the largest
of the Minoan palaces.
The colours have been
deduced from traces of
paint left on fallen plaster
and masonry.

pressing pre-formed hieroglyphic seals into the wet clay in a clockwise succession, spiralling in to the centre of the disc. Because it is not known what language the Minoans spoke, none of the Minoan scripts has been deciphered. Analysis of early Cretan place names indicates that the Minoans did not speak an Indo-European language, so, whatever their origins, they were not Greeks.

The nature of rulership in Minoan Crete is very uncertain because there are no representations in art or sculpture of any figures that can unambiguously be identified as rulers. Religious iconography is, in contrast, common. Figurines of bare-breasted women clutching snakes, double-headed axes, representations of bulls and of a bull-jumping ritual or contest, and 'horns of consecration' (symbolic bull horns) appear in a range of contexts. The exact beliefs associated with these representations are uncertain. The importance of the bull to the Minoans is reflected in the legend of the Minotaur, while the female figurines are thought to represent a mother goddess. Though the palaces contain shrines, the Minoans did not build temples to their gods. Caves and mountain tops remote from human settlement were the most important ritual sites. The palaces were visually aligned on sacred places in the landscape, the palace of Knossos being aligned on the sacred peak of Mount Iouchtas, for example. Archaeological investigation on Crete has concentrated on the palaces and sacred sites and very little is known about the living conditions of the common people. The workers who served the needs of the rulers lived in towns that grew up around the palaces. The largest of these towns, at Knossos, covered about 75 hectares (185 acres) and had a population of around 12,000.

Dolphin fresco
Partially restored fresco from the palace of Knossos. Minoan painters were highly skilled and delighted in scenes from nature.

WAVE OF DESTRUCTION

Around 1700 BC, most of the Cretan palaces were destroyed by fire, probably as the result of wars between the Minoan kingdoms (though some archaeologists put the destruction down to earthquakes). All the palaces were subsequently rebuilt, but only Knossos regained its former splendour. Knossos would seem, therefore, to have taken over the whole of Crete and to have reduced the other palace states to the status of tributaries. This marked the beginning of the Minoan civilization's greatest period of artistic achievement, producing pottery and frescoes of superb quality. Minoan art emphasized dynamic movement, bright colours and patterns, and a delight in nature.

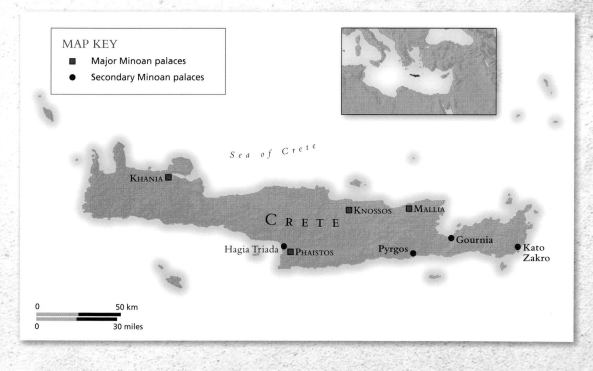

MAP KEY
■ Major Minoan palaces
● Secondary Minoan palaces

Sea of Crete

KHANIA ■

C R E T E

■ KNOSSOS   ■ MALLIA

● Gournia

Hagia Triada ● ■ PHAISTOS   Pyrgos ●   ● Kato Zakro

0 — 50 km
0 — 30 miles

The influence of Knossos spread well beyond Crete. Minoan colonies were established on the Aegean islands of Cythera, Thera, Melos, Rhodes and Kea, and on the Anatolian coast at Miletos. There was also a Minoan quarter at the Egyptian city of Avaris in the Delta. The Minoans may have paid tribute to the pharaohs for this privilege. Tomb paintings at Thebes, dating to c.1500 BC, depict processions of men, described as *Keftiu*, wearing Minoan-style clothes, sandals and hairstyles, offering gifts to pharaoh.

MINOAN SHIPS

Depictions of Minoan ships in art and on stamp seals show that they were long and narrow, and were driven by a single square sail and by up to 30 oarsmen. So far only one Minoan shipwreck has ever been discovered. Although all the wood of the ship, discovered of Pseira in Crete in 2009, had decayed long ago, its size was estimated at around 11–15 metres (35–50 ft) long from the distribution of its cargo of over 200 pottery wine jars which still lay on the seabed. The ship is estimated to have sunk between around 1800 and 1700 BC.

Minoan cultural influence on mainland Greece increased in this period and, if there is any historical basis to the later Greek legends associated with king Minos of Knossos, some parts may even become tributaries of Crete. According to the legends, Minos commanded a great fleet which he used to rule over the Aegean, sweeping it clean of the pirates who preyed on trade. He defeated Athens in a war and imposed a nine-yearly tribute of seven boys and seven girls, who he fed to his pet monster in the Labyrinth, the Minotaur. Evidence has, in fact, been found at Knossos and other sites that the Minoans did indeed practise child sacrifice. The legendary hero Theseus freed Athens from the tribute. Taking the place of one of the boys, he entered the Labyrinth and slew the Minotaur, escaping with the aid of Minos' daughter Ariadne, who had fallen in love with him.

MINOAN POMPEII

In c.1628 BC, the volcanic island of Thera (modern Santorini) exploded with a force four times greater than that of Krakatoa in 1883, devastating large parts of the Minoan world. Tsunamis destroyed coastal settlements and earthquakes associated with the

Preserved in ash
A heavily restored fresco showing two boys boxing from the Minoan city of Akrotiri on Thera. The fresco has survived because it was buried in ash from a volcanic eruption.

'Out in the dark blue sea is a land called Crete, a rich and beautiful land, densely populated and boasting 90 cities ... The greatest of these is called Knossos, and there, for nine years, king Minos ruled and enjoyed the friendship of almighty Zeus.'

Homer, *The Odyssey* (seventh to eighth century BC)

eruption caused widespread damage to buildings. Ash falls in eastern Crete, the Aegean islands and in Anatolia may have damaged agriculture. Perhaps more damaging was the dust thrown into the upper atmosphere by the eruption, which caused a short period of climatic cooling that interfered with plant growth across the northern hemisphere. About two-thirds of Thera was destroyed by the explosion, leaving a huge caldera which was flooded by the sea. The Minoan city of Akrotiri on the surviving eastern part of the island was buried under a 61-metre (200-ft) thick layer of volcanic ash and lava. As at Pompeii, the ash preserved the buildings it buried. Excavations carried out in the 1960s and 1970s discovered perfectly preserved frescoes on the walls of houses which still stood to their original height. Unlike Pompeii, no bodies were found and few artifacts, suggesting that the inhabitants had some forewarning of the eruption and fled, taking their belongings with them.

The eruption at Thera did not do any lasting damage to the Minoan civilization, which continued to flourish for nearly 200 years. In c.1450 BC, another spasm of destruction swept over Crete. Nearly all the island's known palaces, towns and country villas were destroyed or damaged by fire, and some were permanently abandoned. Only at Knossos was the damage limited. New burial customs, new art forms and a new script were introduced, all evidence that a foreign ruling dynasty had

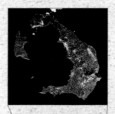

Volcanic remains
The eruption of Thera blasted away the entire centre of the island, creating a deep lagoon. At the centre of the lagoon, a new volcanic cone is slowly growing.

ATLANTIS

The story of Atlantis was first recorded in two works by the Athenian philosopher Plato (470–399 BC), the *Critias* and the *Timaeus*. In the *Timaeus*, Plato describes how priests told the story of Atlantis to the Athenian law-giver Solon (c.630–560 BC) during a visit to Egypt. Atlantis, they said, was a large island, bigger than Libya and Asia Minor combined, that lay to the west of the Pillars of Hercules (the Straits of Gibraltar) in the Atlantic Ocean. The sea-god Poseidon carved the capital city of Atlantis out of a mountain. The city consisted of three concentric rings, each separated by a ring of water. Tunnels cut through the rings allowed ships to sail into the heart of the city. Fortified gateways protected every entrance to the city and a stone wall surrounded each of the city's rings. Brass, tin and orichalcum, a precious metal found only in Atlantis, covered the walls. A palace and citadel lay on an island at the centre of the third ring of water. Canals linked the city to the sea and inland to an intensively farmed plain irrigated by a chequer pattern of canals. Atlantis grew rich and powerful under its rulers. About 9,000 years before Solon's time, the priests said, the Atlanteans went to war, enslaving all the lands of the Mediterranean until they

were defeated by the Athenians. The gods decided to punish the Atlanteans for their arrogance and, in one night, Atlantis was destroyed by earthquakes and swallowed up by the sea.

The story of Atlantis was not taken very seriously in ancient times. Most commentators believed that Plato invented the story for didactic purposes: most modern historians are inclined to agree. After the fall of the Roman empire, Atlantis was largely forgotten about in western Europe until the revival of interest in Greek philosophy in the 12th century. Such was scholars' respect for Plato, the story of Atlantis was believed to be true. Many locations have been proposed for Atlantis, the hypothesis that the story was inspired by memories of the devastation caused by the massive volcanic eruption on the island of Thera (modern Santorini) in 1628 BC being the most plausible. Detailed surveying of the ocean floor has found no evidence of any large sunken landmass in the Atlantic and the modern understanding of plate tectonics makes it most improbable that any such a landmass could have existed in recent geological time.

Tomb entrance
The so-called Treasury of Atreus at Mycenae is the largest and best preserved Mycenaean *tholos* ('beehive') tomb. These stone-vaulted underground tombs get their name because they are shaped like a beehive. Atreus was a legendary king of Mycenae.

taken over at Knossos, most likely as the result of invasion and conquest, bringing the Minoan civilization to an end. The Minoans survived as an underclass under the new rulers: their descendants were probably the people described by Greeks of the Classical age as *Eteocretans* ('True Cretans'), who seem to have died out some time around the third century BC.

THE MYCENAEANS

The new rulers at Knossos were Mycenaean Greeks from the mainland. The identity of the invaders is known for certain because of the discovery at Knossos of an archive of clay tablets inscribed with the new script, known as Linear B. Inscriptions in Linear B have been found at Knossos, and two other sites on Crete, and at several Mycenaean sites on the mainland. The script is clearly adapted from Linear A and for decades after its discovery in 1900 Linear B was assumed to record a form of the Minoan language.

CRACKING THE CODE

In 1952, Michael Ventris – one of Britain's top code-breakers in World War II – followed a hunch and discovered to everyone's surprise that the script in fact recorded an early form of Greek. Greek is a member of the widespread Indo-European family of languages, which also includes English, that were introduced into Europe by migrants who arrived from west-central Asia in the third millennium BC. The Greek language probably evolved in the Balkans from earlier Indo-European languages and was introduced to Greece by ancestors of the Mycenaeans c.2000 BC. Several thousand Linear B tablets have now been discovered and translated: most of the documents deal with palace administration. Others concern religion and reveal that the Mycenaeans already worshipped several of the Greek gods of Classical times, including Zeus, Athena, Apollo and Poseidon.

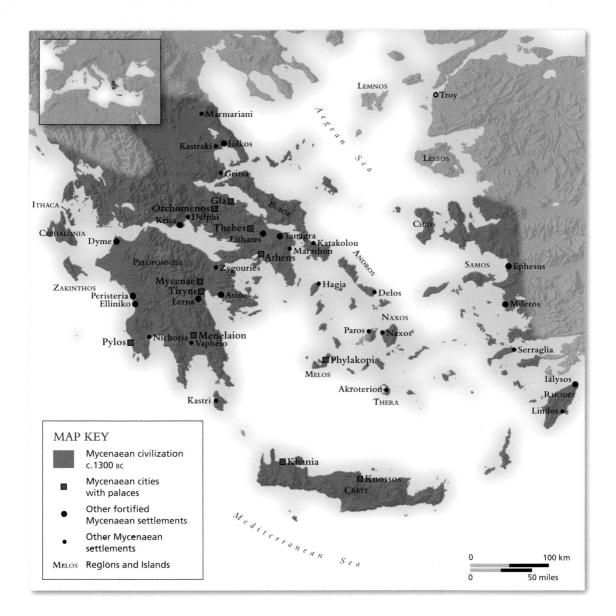

The Mycenaeans take their name from Mycenae, a hilltop citadel in the Peloponnese which features in Homer's epics as the capital of king Agamemnon, the leader of the Greeks in the Trojan War. The Mycenaeans probably called themselves Achaeans – at least that is the name (*Akhaivoi*) Homer used to describe the Greeks who fought at Troy. The earliest evidence for the emergence of the civilization comes from a series of richly furnished shaft graves at Mycenae, dating from between 1650 BC and 1550 BC. Excavated by the pioneering German archaeologist Heinrich Schliemann in the 1870s, the finds from these graves, including gold vessels and weapons, and a number of gold death-masks, revealed the Mycenaeans as a wealthy, warlike and aristocratic society. From around 1500 BC, the Mycenaean elite were buried in impressive communal *tholos* ('beehive') tombs, so-called because their shape resembles that of a traditional beehive. Built of masonry, with vaulted roofs and impressive entrance passages, *tholos* tombs were buried under earth mounds. These were probably as richly furnished with grave goods as the shaft graves but, being so conspicuous, all but one were looted in antiquity. The exception is at Vapheio, near Sparta, where looters failed to notice two burials in cists under the floor of the tomb. When excavated, the burials were found to contain gemstones and artifacts of gold, silver, bronze, lead, amber and crystal. There were also two magnificent Minoan gold cups, decorated with scenes of hunting and taming wild bulls. Most Mycenaeans were buried in communal tombs which remained in use for generations.

INDEPENDENT CITIES

Mycenaean Greece was a land of small fortified cities, each one an independent power centre ruled by a *wanax* (king) with the support of a landowning warrior aristocracy. Most Mycenaean settlements were built on natural strongholds. Mycenaean Athens was built on the rock of the Acropolis; Mycenae itself was built on a steep hill overlooking a strategic pass leading from the Isthmus of Corinth into the Peloponnese; nearby Tiryns on a long low limestone outcrop; and Pylos on a steep-sided peninsula surrounded by sea on three sides. Strong walls and well-protected bastioned gateways supplemented the natural defences. Many Mycenaean cities are known to have had suburbs outside the walls, but they were still generally smaller than Minoan cities. With a total area of around 30 hectares (75 acres), Mycenae was less than half the size of Knossos. Each city had its palace, the residence of its king, and these too were smaller than their Minoan equivalents. The seat of power itself is thought to have been the *megaron*, a three-roomed oblong structure consisting of a columned porch leading into an antechamber and then into a columned audience hall with a central hearth. Kings combined secular and religious authority and it was here that they presided over ceremonial feasts and religious rituals as well as conducting official state business. Minoan-style frescoes decorated the walls of the *megarons* at Mycenae and the so-called Palace of Nestor (a Homeric hero) at Pylos. Storerooms, archives and workshops show that Mycenaean palaces functioned, like Minoan palaces, as centres for the control of crafts, and for the collection and redistribution of food and goods.

Dagger blade
Mycenaean dagger blade with an inlaid gold dolphin design found in a grave at Prosymna. The dagger's wooden handle has decayed long ago, but the rivets that fastened it to the blade remain.

The number and size of the kingdoms of Mycenaean Greece is not known for certain. Book Two of Homer's *Iliad* contains the 'Catalogue of Ships', a detailed survey of the places ruled by the heroes of the Trojan War and the number of ships and men they provided for the Greek army. The historical value of the catalogue has been much debated, but it possibly records the political geography of Greece in late Mycenaean times. According to the catalogue, Greece was divided into around 20 independent kingdoms, but the king of Mycenae was recognized as having a poorly defined primacy over the other kings. Clay tablets discovered at Pylos provide some details of the administration of a Mycenaean kingdom. The senior official below the king of Pylos was the *lawageta* ('leader of the people') who had military, naval and religious responsibilities. Administration of the palace was in the hands of four 'collectors'. Careful records were kept of royal resources, especially the numbers of livestock. Pylos controlled most of the modern province of Messenia, 900 square miles (2,300 sq km). The kingdom was divided into two provinces, one ruled directly from Pylos, the other from an unidentified location. Each province was divided into at least 16 districts, each with its own governor, called a *korete*, and a deputy. Some *koretes* held religious offices, and some were women. The districts paid taxes to the king in the form of produce, including ox-hides and woollen cloth. The king of Pylos employed 400 bronzesmiths, who had a special status and were exempt from many taxes. The king also owned about 750 female slaves, most of whom were weavers. These women came from Anatolia and were probably war captives. Records show that the women were given annual rations of 526 bushels of wheat and an equivalent amount of figs. Pylos itself had a population of around 3,000 and the whole kingdom around 50,000.

Greek hero
This scene from a sixth century BC painted pot shows Thetis giving arms to her son Achilles, the greatest Greek warrior of the Trojan War. The weapons are those of the sixth century BC. The real Achilles, if there was one, would have used a much larger ox-hide shield.

Warfare played a central role in Mycenaean society and was the major subject of art. Mycenaean warriors used horse-drawn chariots as battlefield transport, but usually dismounted to fight on foot with spear, sword and dagger. For protection, warriors carried 'figure-of-eight' shaped shields of ox-hide that were large enough to cover most of the body and legs. On their heads they wore distinctive helmets covered with boars' teeth. Some warriors wore suits of segmented bronze body armour and bronze greaves to protect the shins. Little is known about Mycenaean military organization or tactics. Warriors were ranked by birth or ability, while weapons were supplied by the palace.

MYCENAEANS OVERSEAS

During the Classical age, the Greeks were the most widespread people of the Mediterranean world. Classical Greece comprised not only all modern Greece but the whole Aegean coastline of Anatolia and Cyprus, and also southern Italy and western Sicily, which were known as 'Greater Greece'. In addition, Greek colonies could be found all around the Black Sea coast, in Libya, in Spain and southern France. This movement of Greek colonization began during the Mycenaean period. Around 1450 BC, Mycenaeans colonized the Cyclades islands in the Aegean, and it was also around this time that they conquered Crete. They divided Crete into two kingdoms: the larger, comprising about 75 per cent of the island, ruled from Knossos; the smaller, comprising the western quarter of the island, from Khania. A palace, with a typical Mycenaean *megaron*, has been discovered on the island of Melos, indicating the Cyclades also formed a maritime kingdom. Later in the 15th century BC, the Mycenaeans established fortified

THE ARGONAUTS

To win the throne of Iolkos, Jason was set the task of bringing the Golden Fleece from Colchis. To help him, Jason recruited a band of heroes, including mighty Heracles, the musician Orpheus and the woman warrior Atalanta. They were known as the Argonauts, after their ship the *Argo*. After an eventful voyage, Jason reached Colchis, but found its king Aeëtes unwilling to part with the fleece. Fortunately, Aeetes' daughter, the sorceress Medea, fell in love with Jason and helped him steal the fleece by giving him a magic potion to put the dragon who guarded it to sleep. On his return home, Jason claimed his throne but rejected Medea, for which he was punished by Zeus' wife Hera, dying when the stern of the *Argo* fell on him.

Mycenaean export
This 13th–14th century BC Mycenaean stirrup jar, used for storing liquids, was discovered during excavations of the Phoenician city of Ugarit in modern Syria.

colonies at Ephesus, Miletos and other places on the southwest coast of Anatolia. Greeks continued to live on the Anatolian coast until the 1920s, when they were expelled by Turkish nationalists.

MYCENAEAN TRADE

Mycenaean merchant ships sailed around the eastern Mediterranean, south to Egypt, and as far west as Italy and Malta, trading perfumed oil (a valuable Mycenaean speciality) and textiles for luxuries. Occasionally, Mycenaeans also entered the Black Sea. It may have been such a pioneering voyage that inspired the story of Jason and the Argonauts, who sailed to Colchis (modern Georgia) to steal the Golden Fleece. Colchis was an important gold producer in the region. Fleeces placed in rivers by miners to trap gold dust washing out of alluvial deposits may have been the original golden fleeces. Mycenaean-period shipwrecks have been found off the southern Anatolian coast at Uluburun (dated to c.1300 BC), near Kas, and off Cape Gelidonya (c.1200 BC). The primary cargo of both ships was Cypriot copper, much of it in the form of 'ox-hide'-shaped ingots – about 10 tonnes of it in the case of the Uluburun ship. The Uluburun ship also carried 1 tonne of tin ingots, which probably came from Afghanistan, while the Cape Gelidonya ship carried hundreds of worn-out and broken bronze tools and other scrap metal from Canaan or Syria. In addition to metals, the Uluburun ship carried 145 Canaanite amphorae filled with terebinth resin (burned as incense), 175 ingots of cobalt blue glass, and over a hundred pieces of fine Cypriot pottery. The ship also carried many high-value manufactured objects, including Baltic amber beads, gold and silver jewellery, a collection of Mesopotamian cylinder seals, thousands of ostrich egg beads from Libya, an ivory trumpet, Egyptian faience drinking cups and an Egyptian gold scarab inscribed with the name of Nefertiti, wife of the 'heretic' pharaoh Akhenaten. These probably formed an official offering of gifts from one king to another as such collections are mentioned in contemporary diplomatic letters. Archaeologists believe that the Uluburun ship was Syrian or Canaanite, but personal artifacts found in the wreck suggest that it carried two Mycenaean passengers, possibly merchants or officials returning to Greece from a successful diplomatic mission.

Mycenaeans also went on plundering raids. Egyptian sources record raids by a people called the *Akhaiwashi* in the years around 1400 BC, while slightly later documents from the Hittite empire of Anatolia refer to attacks from *Ahhiyava*. Both names may be derivatives of *Akhaivoi* (Achaeans). Was it also during the Mycenaean period that the Trojan War was fought? The Greeks of the Classical age had no doubts that the Trojan War was a real historical event, which they believed had ended with the fall of Troy in 1184 BC. Though it was never as magnificent as Homer's descriptions of it, Troy, or Ilios, as the Greeks also called it, was an important city during the Bronze Age. Near modern Hisarlik (Turkey), Troy commanded the entrance to the Dardanelles, the narrow straits at the beginning of the sea route from the Aegean

Sea, via the Sea of Marmara and the Bosphorus Straits, into the Black Sea. Troy also commanded a land route from western Anatolia to southeast Europe, which crossed the Dardanelles, here at their narrowest point less than a mile wide. The Trojans could have used this position to exact tolls on merchant ships and overland travellers alike. They could also have denied passage to anyone they saw as a commercial competitor. This could explain why there is little evidence of regular Mycenaean voyages to the Black Sea.

TROY

Troy was founded c.3000 BC in the early Bronze Age and was destroyed, usually by fire or earthquakes, and rebuilt at least nine times before it was abandoned for good in the fourth century AD. After each episode of destruction, the residents simply levelled the site and built on top of the ruins of the old city. In time this built up a layered *tell*-like mound which stands 32 metres (105 ft) high. By the dawn of the Mycenaean civilization, Troy was in its sixth incarnation. Troy VI consisted of a citadel measuring 200 metres (220 yds) by 140 metres (150 yds) and an extensive lower town. The citadel was protected by limestone walls, 4.6 metres (15 ft) thick and 5.2 metres (17 ft) high. Inside the citadel, the large houses and palaces of the Trojan elite were laid out in ascending concentric circles. The identity of the Trojans is uncertain, but it is thought most likely that they were Luvians, a people related to the Hittites.

Gold earring
A gold earring from a grave pit at Mycenae (16th century BC).

Troy VI was destroyed by an earthquake c.1300 BC, but a new city, known as Troy VIIa, was quickly built over the ruins. Everything about Troy VIIa speaks of insecurity. Houses were crammed together within the fortifications and almost all were provided with measures for storing food in the shape of one or two huge *pithoi* buried up to their necks in the floor. The Trojans were prepared to withstand a siege if necessary. Troy VIIa lasted two generations at most. Between 1260 BC and 1240 BC, the city was destroyed by fire. Human bones found in the ruins create a strong impression that the city was stormed, plundered and deliberately burned by invaders. The date of Troy VIIa makes it very likely that this was the city destroyed by Agamemnon's army. A letter written by an unnamed Hittite king, thought to be Hattusili III (ruled 1265–1240 BC), to an unnamed king of the Ahhiyava referring to hostilities between the Ahhiyava and Wilusa (Ilios) may be a reference to the Trojan War. Troy (VIIb) was partially rebuilt after the attack, but on a less impressive scale. The city never regained its former importance and was abandoned c.1100 BC. Greek settlers reoccupied Troy c.700 BC, giving it the name Ilion. Alexander the Great visited to pay homage to his legendary ancestor Achilles, one of the heroes of the Trojan War, before setting out to conquer the Persian empire in 334 BC. The Greek city was destroyed by the Romans in 85 BC, who began to rebuild Troy for the last time later in the same year. After its abandonment in the fourth century AD, Troy's location was forgotten until its rediscovery by Heinrich Schliemann in the 1870s.

TROJAN WAR

The legends associated with the Trojan War were already well developed by the time Homer composed his epics, the *Iliad* and the *Odyssey*, in the eighth century BC, and they continued to develop for several centuries afterwards. The war was a favourite subject for Greek dramatists in the fifth century BC and for chroniclers in Roman times.

The war between the Greeks and the Trojans was caused by the abduction by Paris of Helen, the wife of king Menelaus of Sparta. Paris was one of the 50 sons and 12 daughters of Priam, the rich and powerful king of Troy. Zeus asked Paris to decide which of the three goddesses – Hera (Zeus' wife), Aphrodite and Athena – deserved to receive the golden apple, which was reserved by Eris, the goddess of discord, for the one who was the most beautiful. Aphrodite bribed Paris by offering him Helen, the most beautiful woman in the world, so he awarded the apple to her. Paris went to Sparta, won Helen's love and abducted her to Troy.

Paris' sister Cassandra, who possessed the gift of prophecy but was cursed so that no one would believe her, implored their father to return Helen, but Priam refused, so dooming Troy. Menelaus' brother, Agamemnon, the king of Mycenae (or Argos in some versions), led the Greeks on a great expedition to recover Helen, laying siege to the city for ten weary years. The war divided the gods; Athena, Hera and Poseidon siding with the Greeks; Aphrodite, Apollo and Ares with the Trojans. Homer's *Iliad* is set in the tenth year of the war and tells of a quarrel between Achilles and Agamemnon over a slave girl, the death in battle of Achilles' friend Patroclus, and of the slaying by Achilles of Priam's eldest son Hector. The *Iliad* ends with a description of Hector's funeral and burial.

Greek victory was finally secured only by the cunning of Odysseus, the king of Ithaca. Odysseus persuaded the Greeks to build a huge wooden horse and conceal within it a small party of hand-picked warriors. After burning their camp, the Greeks set sail, leaving the horse by the shore. Cassandra warned that the horse was full of warriors, but no one believed her and Priam ordered it to be taken into the city. During the night, the warriors climbed out of the horse and opened the city gates to the Greek army, which had returned to Troy under cover of darkness. The surprised Trojans offered little resistance and the Greeks plundered the city for three days, enslaving the surviving Trojans. One of the few Trojans of rank to escape was Hector's cousin Aeneas. According to later legends, Aeneas

Legendary warriors
This scene from a sixth century BC painted Attic vase shows Achilles tending to wounds received by his comrade Patroclus in battle beneath the walls of Troy.

settled with his followers in Italy. It was his descendents Romulus and Remus who founded the city of Rome. After so long an absence, most of the Greeks did not enjoy a happy homecoming but Helen, the cause of all the trouble, was meekly accepted back by her husband. Homer's *Odyssey* tells the story of Odysseus' adventures during his long journey home.

The appeal of the story of the Trojan War has never faded. Medieval Europeans admired the Trojans, described by Homer as patriotic, brave and truthful, much more than the tricky Greeks. By the time of the Enlightenment in the 18th century, sceptical, rationalist scholars had dismissed the Trojan War as an entirely legendary event. The archaeological discoveries of the late 19th century, however, forced historians to take seriously the possibility that the stories are, after all, based on historical events.

There are many signs that the Mycenaeans were feeling increasingly insecure by the later 13th century BC. At the city of Mycenae, many of the outlying buildings were burned, following which the city walls were extended and a new, strongly fortified gateway, known as the Lion Gate for its decorative reliefs, was built. The walls of Tiryns were also strengthened after buildings in the unprotected lower area of the town were burned. These walls were constructed of blocks of stone so huge that later generations of Greeks believed that they must have been built by the giant Cyclops rather than by mere humans. New defences were built on the Acropolis at Athens and a wall was built across the narrow isthmus of Corinth to control access to the Peloponnese. Tunnels leading to underground springs provided secure water supplies during sieges at Mycenae, Athens and Tiryns. Texts from Pylos describe the setting up of a coast watch system, perhaps indicating a rise in piracy. There is also evidence of economic problems. The quantity of imported goods declined, investment in rich burials by the elite ceased, and texts refer to problems with the grain harvests.

> 'At Troy, Alexander [the Great] laid a wreath on the tomb of Achilles, calling him a lucky man in having had Homer to proclaim his deeds and preserve his memory.'

Arrian *The Campaigns of Alexander* (c. AD 140)

Strong walls did not save the Mycenaeans. By around 1200 BC, all of the main Mycenaean cities had been destroyed by fire, along with many smaller settlements too. Texts from Pylos describe the city's frantic last days. Orders were sent to the coast watchers in expectation of an attack from the sea. Bronze ornaments were collected to be melted down and recast as weapons, extra taxes were levied and, in a last desperate attempt to win over the gods, human sacrifices were performed. The clay writing tablets noting these events were dutifully filed in the palace archive. Before the clay tablets had time to dry, the palace was destroyed by a fire which baked the tablets hard as brick, ensuring their survival to the present day.

DESCENT INTO THE DARK AGE

Once the wave of destruction had passed, the Mycenaeans attempted unsuccessfully to rebuild their civilization. The citadels at Mycenae and Tiryns were reoccupied, but rebuilding was on a modest scale. Overseas contacts were renewed. Fine bronzework, especially weapons, and painted pottery continued to be produced, but other crafts seem to have withered. There is no evidence of the organized, large-scale, palace-controlled craft production of earlier times. Writing fell out of use — another sign that economic life had reverted to a simpler level. There is evidence of continuing insecurity. Many settlements show signs of repeated destruction. Settlements in exposed locations were abandoned in favour of more easily defended hilltops and some of the smaller Cyclades islands seem to have been abandoned altogether. Some Mycenaeans migrated to Cyprus, founding settlements around the coast. Shortly after 1100 BC, Greece experienced another spasm of destruction, following which the last remnants of Mycenaean civilization disappeared and Greece entered a 300-year-long 'dark age'.

The causes of the Mycenaean collapse are unknown. The 12th and 13th centuries BC was a time of widespread disorder and social collapse throughout the eastern Mediterranean world. The Hittite empire of Anatolia collapsed abruptly c. 1205 BC and dozens of cities in Anatolia, Cyprus, Syria and Canaan were destroyed. Suspicion has often fallen on the so-called 'Sea Peoples', a mysterious migrating coalition of unrelated peoples from around the Mediterranean who attacked Syria and Egypt around 1200 BC. However, the Sea Peoples certainly included Greeks among their numbers. The people described in Egyptian sources as the *Ekwesh* are probably Achaeans, while the *Peleset* (the Biblical Philistines), who settled in Canaan after their repulse from Egypt in 1180 BC, had a material culture that shows strong links to Mycenaean Greece. This makes it unclear

THE CYCLOPS

In Greek mythology, the Cyclopes were an ancient race of powerful giants who had only a single eye in the middle of their foreheads. According to the best known version of the myth, the Cyclopes were the sons of the sky god Uranus and the earth goddess Gaia. The Cyclopes may have originated as minor deities associated with metalworking, as they were believed to make thunderbolts for the high god Zeus to hurl and help the blacksmith god Hephaestus at his forge. The most famous cyclops was Polyphemus, who, in Homer's *Odyssey*, captured Odysseus and his men and began to eat them one by one. Odysseus made good his escape by tricking Polyphemus into getting drunk, then blinding him by driving a sharpened olive-wood stake into his single eye.

whether the Sea Peoples were the direct cause of the troubles in the eastern Mediterranean or were simply peoples displaced by them, looking for new homes.

THE GREEK DARK AGES

The dark ages were a time of major migrations, as new Greek-speaking peoples migrated into Greece from the Balkan region. The most important of these were the Dorians, who arrived in the 11th century BC and were perhaps responsible for the wave of destructions that finally finished the Mycenaeans off. The Dorians quickly took over most of mainland Greece, along with Crete and Rhodes. It was probably the Dorians who introduced ironworking to Greece, bringing the Bronze Age to a close. At first, iron was used only to edge bronze weapons and tools, but by the time the dark ages began to come to an end around 800 BC it had become the principal material for weapons and tools. The other major Greek people to emerge from the dark ages were the Ionians. These were the descendants of Mycenaeans who managed to hold out against the Dorians in Attica (the region around Athens) and Euboea. During the dark ages, many Ionians migrated across the Aegean Sea to the coast of Anatolia, which became known after them as Ionia. The dialect spoken by Homer, Ionian Greek, eventually came to form the basis of Classical Greek.

Homer composed his epic poems in the eighth century BC, drawing on oral traditions dating back hundreds of years. The events on which Homer based the *Iliad* and the *Odyssey* took place in Mycenaean times, but the values, beliefs and social structures that motivate his heroes belong to the society of the late dark ages. Dark age society was much simpler than that of Mycenaean times. The Greeks lived in tribal communities under chiefs or petty kings who ruled with a council of elders. Chiefs and kings acted

Death mask
Gold foil death mask discovered in royal shaft grave at Mycenae. Commonly known as the Mask of Agamemnon, after the leader of the Greeks in the Trojan War, the mask was made c. 1550–1500 BC, several centuries before the war is likely to have happened.

WHO WAS HOMER?

Homer was the single greatest influence on the development of Greek civilization. His Trojan war epics, the *Iliad* and the *Odyssey*, were the basis of Greek education until Christian times. Many ancient Greeks knew them by heart and valued them not only as great literature but also as symbols of Greek unity and heroism, and as a source of moral instruction. Ironically, Homer himself is a shadowy figure. Greek traditions, dating from the seventh century BC, hold that Homer was a blind poet who lived in Chios in Ionia in the eighth or ninth century BC. Homer's poems were remembered and transmitted orally by his descendants, known as the *Homeridae*, until they were written down towards the end of the seventh century BC. Modern scholars are sceptical about the Greek traditions and, because they are such different works, many even doubt that the *Iliad* and the *Odyssey* were composed by the same person. The ancient Greeks were aware of these differences and generally believed the *Iliad* was a work of Homer's youth, while the *Odyssey* was composed in his old age. Because its language is more archaic than the *Odyssey's*, it is agreed that the *Iliad* was composed first, probably around the middle of the eighth century BC. The *Odyssey* was probably composed towards the end of the same century.

as war leader and chief priest, performing sacrifices and rituals on behalf of the community. The king and his warriors lived off private estates worked by slaves and hired labourers. Writing had no place in this world: in Homer's *Odyssey,* Odysseus' swineherd Eumaios simply keeps the tally of his master's herds in his head. Rivalry between chiefs led to wars, but also found expression in lavish hospitality and feasting. Battles were preceded, and sometimes even settled, by set-piece duels between champion aristocratic warriors. A man's most important possession was his honour. Skill in war and hunting, magnanimity and compassion were the most admired virtues. By Homer's time, stability and prosperity were returning to Greece and a new and brilliant Greek civilization was about to be born.

Mycenaean lady
Fresco of a priestess or goddess from the cult centre in the acropolis of Mycenae, 13th century BC. The painting shows the influence of Minoan art styles.

ANCIENT CHINA

CHINA rivals ancient Egypt for the longevity of its civilization. Despite periods of division and occupation, Chinese civilization has evolved without any major discontinuities from its origins around 3,500 years ago to the present day. For much of that time, China was culturally, technologically and economically the world leader. The history of ancient China culminated in 221 BC with its unification by the first emperor Shi Huangdi and the establishment of imperial traditions of government which survived until 1911. Chinese civilization began around 1600 BC with the emergence of the Shang dynasty in the valley of the Yellow river in northern China. This was the homeland of the Han (ethnic Chinese), who now make up over 90 per cent of the population of the People's Republic of China and, at over a billion strong, are the world's largest ethnic group.

Previous page:
Terracotta army
This army of 7,000 life-size terracotta soldiers was created to guard the tomb of Shi Huangdi (ruled 221–210 BC), the first emperor of China. The figures were individually made and were probably modelled on living soldiers.

Deep deposits of loess made the Yellow River valley a very favourable area for Stone Age farmers. Formed from wind-blown sediments at the end of the last Ice Age, loess is an extremely fertile, yellow-coloured soil that is light enough to be worked easily with simple stone hand-tools, such as hoes. The farming way of life became established here around 6500 BC, following the domestication of millet, a small-grained cereal. Millet is nutritionally inferior to other cereals like wheat, barley and rice because it is deficient in essential amino acids and proteins. As a result, early Chinese farmers were frail-boned and around a foot shorter than their hunter–gatherer ancestors. The farmers bred chickens and pigs and hunted to supplement their food supply.

EARLY COMMUNITIES

The early farmers of the Yellow river valley lived in small kinship-based communities. The development of more complex and hierarchical society began with the appearance of the Longshan culture (3200–1800 BC). What seems to have kick-started this process was the rapid rise in population following the introduction of rice farming from the Yangtze river basin in central China. Rice has a much higher yield than millet, and is more nutritious, but northern China has a

Longshan pottery
This goblet, made from a particularly thin material known as 'eggshell pottery', was made in separate parts – stem and body were produced independently and then fitted together. Wet firewood was added to the kiln during firing at a relatively low tempurature. This meant that carbon from the resulting smoke permeated the pottery and turned it black.

TIMELINE

6500 BC
Farming settlement begins in the Yellow river valley

1800–1600 BC
Erlitou culture: the first cities develop in the Yellow river valley

1766 BC
Traditional date for the foundation of the Shang dynasty by king Tang

1500 BC
Pictographic writing comes into use in China

1046 BC
The Shang dynasty is overthrown by king Wu, founder of the Zhou dynasty

770–481 BC
The Springs and Autumns period: China breaks up into feudal states

551–479 BC
Life of the sage Confucius

480–221 BC
The Warring States period: period of intense warfare between Chinese states

c.350 BC
Qin becomes the strongest of the Warring States

230–221 BC
King Zheng of Qin unifies China

221 BC
King Zheng adopts the title Shi Huangdi, 'First Emperor'

213 BC
Shi Huangdi orders the destruction of Chinese historical records

210 BC
Death of Shi Huangdi

206 BC
The Qin dynasty is overthrown by Gaodi, founder of the Han dynasty

relatively low rainfall so rice could only be grown with the aid of irrigation (in dry fields, not paddies). The need to organize the communal effort required to build irrigation canals and flood defences was probably a major factor in the emergence of a more hierarchical society, as it was in Mesopotamia.

LONGSHAN CULTURE

The Longshan culture developed many of the features that characterized the civilization of China's first historical dynasty, the Bronze Age Shang dynasty. Finely carved ritual vessels and tools made of jade, a very hard translucent green stone that was highly prized in China in historical times, provide evidence for craft specialization. Copper tools and ornaments appear for the first time. Regional trade networks promoted cultural homogeneity over a wide area. There is considerable evidence for organized warfare, such as increased numbers of weapons and the proliferation of fortifications built using the distinctive Chinese *hangtu* or pounded earth technique. Mass graves have been found, which may be evidence of massacres or sacrifices of prisoners of war. Elite burials appear, where chiefs have been buried with valuable grave goods and animal and human sacrificial victims. Powdered cinnabar, a reddish mercury ore known to have been associated with immortality in China in historical times, has been found placed in graves. Elegant pottery was produced using the potter's wheel. Symbols cut into many pots are seen by some archaeologists as a precursor to writing, though others consider them simply to be marks of ownership or clan identity. A system of divination using oracle bones also came into use.

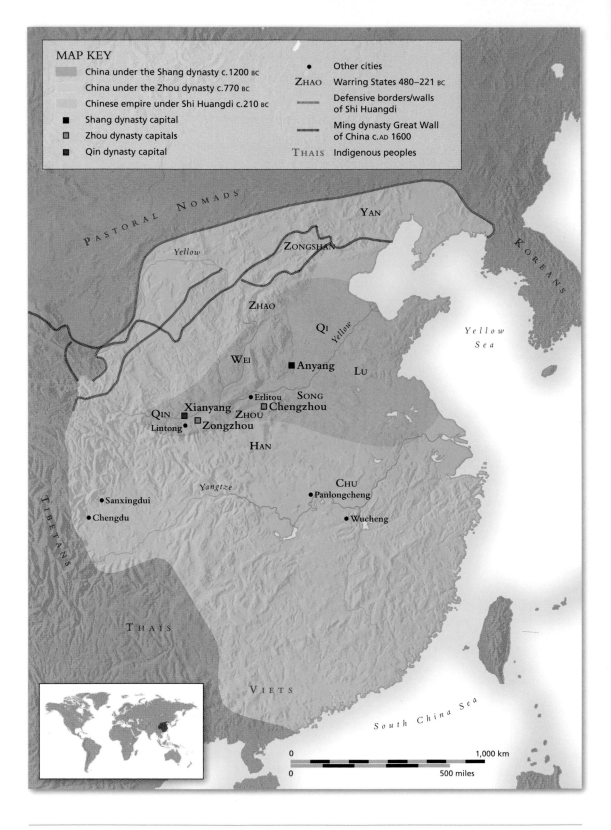

MAP KEY

China under the Shang dynasty c.1200 BC

China under the Zhou dynasty c.770 BC

Chinese empire under Shi Huangdi c.210 BC

■ Shang dynasty capital

□ Zhou dynasty capitals

▣ Qin dynasty capital

• Other cities

ZHAO Warring States 480–221 BC

┅┅┅ Defensive borders/walls of Shi Huangdi

┅┅┅ Ming dynasty Great Wall of China c.AD 1600

THAIS Indigenous peoples

PASTORAL NOMADS

YAN

ZONGSHAN

KOREANS

Yellow

ZHAO

QI

Yellow

Yellow Sea

WEI

■ Anyang

LU

QIN

•Erlitou

SONG

Xianyang

□Chengzhou

▣

ZHOU

Lintong•

□Zongzhou

HAN

TIBETANS

Yangtze

CHU

•Panlongcheng

•Sanxingdui

•Chengdu

•Wucheng

THAIS

VIETS

South China Sea

0   1,000 km

0   500 miles

In Chinese historical legend, civilization was founded by Huangdi, the Yellow Emperor, who is believed to have reigned from 2697 BC to 2597 BC. According to the legend, Huangdi was a chief who defeated a barbarian invasion. His victory won him the leadership of all the tribes of the Yellow river valley. An all-round genius, Huangdi is credited with the invention of farming, writing, government, medicine, wheeled vehicles, boats, houses, the bow and arrow, coinage and the Chinese calendar. Huangdi's wife discovered how to breed silkworms and weave silk cloth. After reigning for a hundred years, a dragon took Huangdi to Heaven, where he became an immortal. The significance of Huangdi's name is that yellow is the colour traditionally associated with earth in China.

Huangdi was the first of the Five Emperors, morally perfect sage-emperors who ruled over a golden age. The last of the emperors, Shun, was succeeded by Yu the Great (said to have ruled 2205–2197 BC), known as the Tamer of the Flood. Yu engineered the draining of a great flood by constructing outlets to the sea with the aid of dragons. On his death, he was deified and became lord of the harvest. Yu made rulership hereditary in his own family and so founded the Xia dynasty, China's first imperial dynasty. The last Xia ruler was Jie, whose wife so outraged the people by her cruel behaviour that they rebelled under the leadership of Tang and overthrew him in 1766 BC. Tang became the first king of the Shang dynasty.

Huangdi is generally regarded as a mythical character, but the Xia dynasty is widely accepted as being historically authentic in China. Many Chinese archaeologists identify the Xia dynasty with the Erlitou culture (c.1800–1600 BC), or even the earlier Longshan culture. Most western archaeologists remain sceptical, however. No archaeological evidence has ever been found for the existence of states in China before the emergence of the Erlitou culture. No documentary evidence links the Xia to the Erlitou culture, and the earliest histories to mention the Xia were written over 1,500 years after the dynasty is supposed to have ruled. The writing of history in China has always been controlled by the state and used to validate the status quo. The Xia may be an early product of this tradition: an invention of the Zhou dynasty (1046–256 BC) to help them legitimize their seizure of power from the corrupt Shang, just as the Shang had once seized power from the supposedly corrupt Xia.

The extent to which wealth and power had become concentrated in the hands of a small elite by the end of the third millennium BC is clearly demonstrated by a very large Longshan cemetery discovered at Taosi, which contains thousands of graves. The highest status individuals were buried in large graves in wooden coffins with up to 200 offerings, including jade rings and axes, furniture, drums and fine pottery. Individuals of middle rank had smaller graves with similar but fewer offerings than the elite graves. Low status individuals were buried in small graves with few or no offerings. Middle rank graves made up 11.4 per cent of the total, while elite graves made up just 1.3 per cent.

THE BEGINNING OF URBANISM

The final period of Chinese prehistory is represented by the Erlitou culture (c.1800–1600 BC) of southern Shanxi and northern Henan provinces. The culture is named after Erlitou, the largest known settlement of the period, a city covering a substantial 300 hectares (740 acres). The remains of two palaces, the earliest in China, set within a walled compound, have been discovered at the site. The palaces were large but architecturally simple timber-framed buildings with walls of wattle and daub and thatched roofs. The appearance of the palaces was made more imposing by building on pounded earth platforms which were

'The Yellow Emperor gained the power of earth, and a yellow dragon and an earthworm appeared. The Xia gained the power of wood, and a green dragon appeared, and grass and trees grew luxuriantly. The Shang gained the power of metal and silver flowed forth out of the mountains.'

Sima Qian, *Historical Records* (c.100 BC)

approached by flights of stone steps. This concept remained characteristic of Chinese palace architecture throughout imperial times. Because of the perishable building materials used, ancient Chinese cities have not left impressive ruins.

Associated with the palace complex was the earliest known bronze foundry in China. Bronze casters used a piece-mould technique in which the vessels were cast in sections, which were then assembled using mortises and tenons. This technique was constantly refined over the following centuries until the Chinese became the most accomplished bronze-casters of the ancient world, able to cast shapes of astonishing complexity. It is possible that the rulers of Erlitou exercised a monopoly over bronze production, using it to enhance their power and wealth. Members of Erlitou's elite were buried in painted wooden coffins, accompanied by bronze ritual vessels and weapons, and ceremonial jade objects. Symbols painted on pottery excavated at Erlitou may be early examples of pictographic writing. Erlitou declined quickly in the 16th century BC and was abandoned by the 15th century BC.

THE SHANG DYNASTY

Tradition dates the accession of China's first historically attested dynasty, the Shang dynasty, to 1766 BC, around the time of the emergence of the Erlitou culture. Accounts of the reign of the first king of the Shang dynasty, Tang, describe a legendary character – he is supposed to have been over 3 metres (9 ft) tall and had six-jointed arms, for example – and there are no contemporary written records of the dynasty until around 1500 BC, when a system of pictographic writing came into use. The system was already highly developed, with over 2,000 different symbols, suggesting that it had begun to be developed some time earlier using a perishable medium, such as bamboo strips.

King Tang of Shang
Painting on a silk scroll of king Tang, the semi-legendary founder of the Shang dynasty, as imagined by the Song dynasty (AD 960–1279) court painter Ma Lin. Ma Lin was also renowned for his landscape paintings.

As the symbols are directly ancestral to modern Chinese characters, the script was readily deciphered. Examples of pictographic writing have been found inscribed on oracle bones and on bronze ritual vessels, which were used to celebrate the ancestors. The pictograms found on oracle bones were simpler and more abstract than those found on bronze vessels.

CONSULTING WITH THE ANCESTORS

Most inscriptions on bronze vessels are short dedications to ancestors. Oracle bones (mostly shoulder blades of oxen and turtle shells) were used for divination. The Shang kings would make no important decision without first consulting their ancestors who, they believed, resided in Heaven where they could intercede on their behalf with the creator god Shang Di. Questions were inscribed onto the bone, which was then struck with a hot implement. This created a pattern of cracks which was interpreted by diviners. The answer was recorded on the bone, and this was stored in an archive for a time before being buried in pits in batches of hundreds or even thousands. The most common questions concerned war, hunting, weather and agriculture, but others reveal details of private life, such as a king's concern for his pregnant wife, or a request for

Axe head
This Shang dynasty bronze axe head was excavated from a richly furnished tomb at Yidu in Shandong province. Though similar axes were used in combat, this axe was probably a ritual object symbolizing power and authority. The tomb also contained the remains of 48 human sacrificial victims.

advice on how to cure a royal toothache. Oracle bones frequently mention human sacrifices. The bones also provide evidence that the traditional Chinese calendar, based on a sexagenary (60–year) cycle, was used in Shang times. Over 100,000 oracle bones have been found and that must represent only a fraction of those that were used. For centuries, oracle bones dug up by farmers were sold as dragon bones to be ground up and used as medicine.

The vast majority of oracle bones have been found at Anyang, the capital of the Shang dynasty in the 12th and 13th centuries BC. Anyang covered an area of 10 square miles (25 sq km) and consisted of a palace precinct, temple complexes, specialized craft quarters, residential quarters and cemeteries, including a royal necropolis with 12 burials in elaborate shaft tombs. The royal burials were all robbed in ancient times except for that of queen Fu Hao, which was furnished with 468 ritual bronze vessels, some containing food and wine, 755 jade carvings, 7,000 cowrie shells, which were used as a form of currency, and hundreds of other objects, including 16 human sacrifices. Inscriptions found in her tomb record that Fu Hao was the wife of king Wu Ding, who died in 1189 BC. Hundreds of graves around the royal necropolis contained the skeletons of beheaded young men and children. Some pits contained chariots, which first came into use in China in this period, together with their teams of horses and drivers.

UNCERTAIN BOUNDARIES

The size and extent of the Shang kingdom is not known for certain. From its heartland in southern Shanxi and northern Henan provinces, the influence of Shang material culture extended as far south as the Yangtze lakes and about as far north as Beijing and east into Shaanxi province. However, identifiable place names on oracle bones suggest that the Shang kings only controlled about half of this area. Oracle bone texts make it clear that the Shang fought

'The early kings of Xia earnestly cultivated their virtue, and there were no calamities from Heaven. But their descendants did not follow their example, and great Heaven sent down calamities.'

The Classic of History (sixth century BC)

frequent wars with their neighbours. Until recently, little was known about these peoples but spectacular archaeological discoveries at Chengdu, Sanxingdui, Panlongcheng and Wucheng in the Yangtze basin have uncovered evidence for states that must have rivalled the Shang in power and wealth. It is possible that the people of these states were not Han, but may instead have been related to the modern Thai and Viet peoples who still live in isolated pockets in southern China.

OUTSIDE INFLUENCES

One of the major themes of China's history has been its relationship with the steppe nomads of Central Asia. Not without good reason, the Chinese have always regarded the nomads as dangerous barbarians and over the centuries they have poured enormous resources into protecting their northern and eastern frontiers against their raids. Despite this, nomads have overrun northern China several times and in the 13th century AD the Mongols conquered the whole country. However, the nomads have also played a positive role as intermediaries on the Central Asian 'Silk Road' which linked China and the West until the development of direct shipping routes in the 16th century. Largely for patriotic reasons, Chinese historians have always stressed that Chinese civilization developed in isolation from other civilizations, but this is true only up to a point. There can be no doubt that the emergence of Chinese civilization was directly connected to the intensification of farming in the Yellow river valley and the resulting rise in population, rather than any outside influence or pressure. It is now clear, however, that much of the new technology that appeared in the Shang period was not invented independently by the Chinese, as once thought, but was ultimately acquired from the West as a result of contacts with the Indo-European nomads who dominated the steppes in the Bronze and Iron Ages.

Bronze ding
A three-legged bronze *ding* (vessel) from the late Shang period. *Dings* were used both for ritual and practical purposes and could be placed over a fire. Many contain inscriptions relating to family ancestry.

GODS OF THE SHANG

The Shang worshipped two types of gods; universal gods in Heaven, who did not receive sacrifices, and lesser earthbound deities associated with particular places and activities, who did. The main focus of Shang religion was, however, deified ancestor spirits, who were believed to be able to help or harm the living. The afterlife was seen as being an extension of this life, and for this reason the dead were buried with grave goods and animal and human sacrifices to meet their needs. Great attention was paid to providing food and drink for the dead from ritual vessels, without which their souls could not survive. A person without descendants to make these offerings had little chance of an afterlife.

SOUTHERN RIVALS TO THE SHANG

The wealth, power and sophistication of the early kingdoms of the Yangtze were completely unsuspected until construction workers discovered two ritual pits at Sanxingdui (Sichuan province) in 1986. The first pit contained layers of burnt animal bones, elephant tusks, ceremonial jade axes and daggers, and in the lowest layers hundreds of objects of bronze, jade, stone and gold, as well as pottery and cowrie shells. The contents of the second pit were even more remarkable and included a bronze casting of a tree with bronze birds on its branches, a 2.6 metre (8.6 ft) tall bronze casting of a king or god, and dozens of giant bronze heads. The style of the bronzes is unique and shows that the people who made them had a very different system of beliefs from the Shang. The objects were made around 1200–1000 BC. The pits are thought to be connected to burials of the kings of Shu, a kingdom mentioned on Shang oracle bones, but, so far, no royal tombs have been discovered. Excavations have revealed that Sanxingdui was a walled city rivalling the Shang capital Anyang in size. As no evidence for the use of writing has yet been discovered at Sanxingdui, the identity of its inhabitants is likely to remain a mystery.

Bronze statues
Bronze head and 2.6 metre (8.6 ft) tall bronze statue of a king or god. The bronze statue originally held a curved object, most probably an elephant's tusk. The patterns on the figure's dress are thought to represent intricate embroidery. Some of the Sanxingdui bronzes show traces of paint, while others were covered in gold leaf.

This technology included bronze casting, as it was practised on the eastern steppes 200 years before it was known in China. The Chinese words for the wheel, spokes, axles and the chariot are derived from Indo-European languages, suggesting that this technology arrived by the same route. Shang chariots are very similar to earlier chariots discovered in burials at Lchashen in Armenia. Many Chinese words associated with divination and magic, architecture and medicine also have Indo-European origins.

THE 'MANDATE OF HEAVEN'

The Shang dynasty came to an end in 1046 BC (some sources place it nearly a century earlier), when its last king Di Xin was overthrown by king Wu of Zhou, a vassal state to the east of the Shang kingdom in present-day Shaanxi province. The Zhou dynasty (1027–256 BC) became the most long-lived in Chinese history, surviving for nearly 800 years. By the time Nan, the 36th and last Zhou king, died in 256 BC, classical Chinese civilization had fully emerged.

Shang kings legitimized their rule by claiming descent from the creator god Shang Di from whom the dynasty takes its name. Wu was a usurper and needed to justify his overthrow of the ruling dynasty. His answer, the 'Mandate of Heaven', became the basic philosophy underpinning the legitimacy of all future Chinese dynasties. According to the 'Mandate of Heaven', the king (later emperor) was the 'Son of Heaven' (Tian, the supreme deity of the Zhou) appointed to rule 'All under Heaven', meaning the entire world. Heaven would only support the king so long as he was a just ruler and showed proper concern for the welfare of his people. If he became unjust, Heaven would send a warning to the ruler to reform. This could be a natural disaster, an eclipse of the sun, or a peasant rebellion. If he did not mend his ways, Heaven would withdraw its mandate and pass it to someone else. Di Xin had been a cruel and immoral king who supposedly invented sadistic new tortures. This was why, despite his divine ancestry, Heaven had withdrawn its mandate from Di Xin and called on Wu to overthrow him. The 'Mandate of Heaven' proved to be a conveniently flexible doctrine. Rebellion against the ruler became rebellion against the will of Heaven and so had to be punished severely. However, the mandate could be used equally well to justify a successful rebellion: its success proved that the ruling dynasty had lost the 'Mandate of Heaven' and so was no longer legitimate.

THE ZHOU KINGDOM

Historians divide the Zhou dynasty into two periods, before and after 770 BC. During the first period, known as Western Zhou, the kings had real power. During the second period, known as Eastern Zhou, royal authority collapsed and the kings became little more than the nominal overlords of a group of independent feudal states. No major cultural changes marked the accession of the Zhou dynasty. Oracle bones remained in use for divination. Ritual vessels and burial customs remained the same as they had been under the Shang. It was only later, when the declining authority of the dynasty destroyed faith in them, that these features of Shang culture were abandoned. The Zhou kingdom was based on feudalism. The kings divided the kingdom into fiefs,

JADE

Jade, a hard green or white mineral, has played an important part in Chinese culture since prehistoric times. More valuable even than gold, Jade was seen as 'the essence of the mountains' with the power to act as an intermediary between Heaven and Earth. Because of its durability and beauty, it was also associated with purity and nobility. During the Neolithic, jade *bi* discs and other jade artefacts were placed in burials, but their ritual significance at this time is unknown. In historic times *bi* discs came to symbolize status and morality.

Because of its hardness, jade is extremely difficult to carve. The introduction of bronze tools led to an increase in jade carving during the Erlitou culture. Under the Shang, jade carving was centralized in royal capitals. The grave of the Shang queen Fu Hao, who died c.1200 BC, contained over 750 jade artefacts. The use of jade as a symbol of status reached a peak under the Zhou dynasty, when six different types of *bi* discs were used, each indicating a different rank of nobility. A complex system of jade pendants developed which symbolized the values of the wearer. Under the Han dynasty (206 BC–AD 220) the dead were buried with jade objects, or even wearing jade suits, because of a belief that it conferred immortality.

which were granted to junior members of the royal family or important retainers in return for payments of tribute. A small, centralized bureaucracy served the Zhou kings at their capital at Zongzhou, near Xi'an (Shaanxi). The kings maintained standing armies on the kingdom's borders. The standing armies were augmented by troops levied from the fiefs during wartime. The Western Zhou kingdom was expansionist. Peripheral states were conquered and given to junior members of the royal family to rule as fiefs. The Zhou founded new settlements of Chinese peasants to help consolidate their control.

By the eighth century BC, the Zhou kingdom extended south of the Yangtze and as far north as modern Beijing.

PERIODS OF UNREST

Fiefs were in theory revocable, but there was an inevitable tendency for them to become hereditary and so fall out of the king's direct control. This gradually eroded royal power. Zongzhou was close to the eastern frontier of the kingdom and was vulnerable to attack by nomad raiders. After the city was sacked by the Xianyun nomads in the early eighth century BC, king Ping moved the Zhou capital east to Chengzhou, near Luoyang (Henan province) in 770 BC, marking the beginning of the Eastern Zhou period. Chengzhou was more secure, but, removed from its traditional family lands, the last of the dynasty's authority withered away and the feudal lords became, to all intents and purposes, independent rulers. It is usual to subdivide the Eastern Zhou period into the Springs and Autumns period (770–481 BC), and the Warring States period (480–221 BC). The Springs and Autumns period was one of political dissolution when China was divided into around 20 minor feudal states. The Warring States period saw the minor states consolidated into larger kingdoms which fought each other for supremacy. The period ended when the kingdom of Qin conquered the remaining kingdoms to unify China.

SPRINGS AND AUTUMNS

The Springs and Autumns period is named after the earliest surviving Chinese historical work, *The Spring and Autumn Annals*. Covering the period 722 BC to 481 BC, these were the official annals of the state of Lu. Events were recorded in the annals by year and season, hence their name. Because of the alienation of fiefs, the territory now directly controlled by the Zhou was much smaller than those controlled by most of the feudal lords, who continually made war on one another. The feudal lords continued to recognize the sovereignty of the king, partly because he was a nominal source of legitimacy for their own authority, and partly because he was too weak to interfere in their affairs anyway. The feudal lords also respected real power and recognized the strongest of their number as hegemon, who exercised primacy over the other states in the king's name. Each state had its own government, laws, religious rituals, art styles and hierarchy of ranks and social classes. The rulers had civic, military and religious duties and professed a concern for the welfare of their people (though their constant wars caused immense suffering). There was no common Chinese identity: people identified with their state.

Bronze pot
Bronze food container belonging to duke Shi You. The lid and body of this container are both decorated with tile and ring patterns. They feature engraved inscriptions, which record that the king of Zhou gave a fiefdom to Shi You, ordering that he inherit the title as well as the land and people living there.

Despite, or perhaps because of, the constant conflicts, the Springs and Autumns period was a time of great creativity in literature and in political, religious and philosophical thought. The most important intellectual figures of the age were undoubtedly the sage Confucius (551–479 BC), whose ethical system remains central to Chinese thought today, and his contemporary Laozi (who lived during the sixth century BC), whose religious teachings inspired Daoism (or, as it is also known, 'Taoism'). Confucius (Kongfuzi) was born in the state of Lu to a down-at-heel family of aristocratic descent. A diligent student who mastered a wide range of subjects, Confucius held a number of minor government posts before starting a career teaching humanities when he was in his thirties. Confucius believed that the true purpose of education was to train exemplary individuals. The end of learning was self-knowledge, but public service was also an integral part of education. Confucius wanted education to be as widely available as possible because all people, he believed, were capable of self-improvement. In his late forties, Confucius returned to government service, rising to become justice minister for the state of Lu. Realizing that his superiors were not interested in putting his ideas into practice, Confucius went into voluntary exile aged 56 and spent most of the rest of his life travelling. By the time of his death, aged 73, he had acquired about 3,000 disciples.

'In his teaching, Confucius laid emphasis on four things: culture, conduct, loyalty and honesty. Four things he avoided: foregone conclusions, arbitrary views, obstinacy and egoism.'

Sima Qian, *Historical Records* (c. 100 BC)

THE TEACHINGS OF CONFUCIUS

Confucius never wrote down his teachings. After his death, Confucius' disciples compiled a collection of his sayings, known as the *Analects* (Chinese *Lunyu*), which eventually became the basis of Chinese social, religious and philosophical thought. Because the *Analects* was not written as a systematic philosophy, it is frequently

Jade dragons
A white jade *bi* disc. *Bi* discs were associated with the sky and were symbols of social status and moral rectitude. The decorations of the disc symbolized qualities that the owner aspired to possess.

contradictory, ambiguous or opaque. Confucius was essentially a conservative thinker. His teachings emphasized respect for legitimate authority and social order, the family and ancestors, tradition and education. Confucius' political thought was based on the 'Mandate of Heaven'. Rulers have the duty of providing for the welfare of their people and maintaining peace and order. The people in return have the duty of obedience and respect for the ruler. By extension, these mutual obligations apply to other levels in society, for example, between parents and children – parents have the duty of care to their children, children have the duty of obedience to their parents – or between teacher and pupil, and master and disciple. Confucius believed that people have a natural inclination to imitate others' behaviour, so it was important for superior people, including rulers, to set a virtuous example for the common people to follow and to ensure that only virtuous people were appointed to positions of responsibility and power. This would create a social hierarchy based on true merit. The common people would, therefore, trust and respect the superior morality and wisdom of their superiors and emulate their behaviour. In principle, everyone would behave like a sage and there would be peace, order and happiness.

Sayings of Confucius
The *Analects* was a collection of Confucius' sayings compiled by his disciples after his death.

Confucian thought was systematized by later sages, the most important of whom was Mencius (Mengzi) (c.371–289 BC), who amplified Confucius' teaching on the ruler's responsibility to his people and established the orthodox Confucian doctrine that human nature is essentially good. Confucian thought was also influenced by Daoism. Very little is known about Laozi, but he was probably an older contemporary of Confucius, who he is said to have met. He is said to have been an archivist at the court of the Zhou kings, but most of the stories about his later life are legendary. Laozi is traditionally credited with writing the *Daodejing* ('The Way of Power', better known in the west as the *Tao-te Ching*), the founding text of Daoism, but it is now thought to be the product of several authors who lived between the eighth and third centuries BC. The *Daodejing* is a short work – only about 5,000 words – intended as advice to rulers. It advocates simplicity, balance, restraint and the avoidance of activity and desire as a way to achieve harmony with the *Dao* ('Way'), a metaphysical concept of fundamental reality that can only be understood intuitively or mystically. Daoism developed as both a philosophy and a religion. Religious Daoists worship Laozi as a manifestation of the Dao. One of the ends of religious Daoism was to find the secret of long life, through breathing exercises, meditation, hygiene and alchemy. Religious Daoism absorbed many of the practices of traditional Chinese folk religion and ancestor worship, and became partially assimilated with Buddhism after it was introduced to China in the first century AD.

TECHNOLOGICAL IMPROVEMENTS

The Springs and Autumns period was also a period of significant technological change. The plough, cast bronze swords, crossbows, horseback riding (adopted from the steppe nomads), coinage and eating with chopsticks all appeared in China for the first time. Iron came into use towards the end of the period. The earliest evidence for the use of iron, dating from around 500 BC, comes from the south-eastern state of Wu. Iron production first began in the Middle East c.1500 BC, spreading to India by 1400 BC, and to Europe and sub-Saharan Africa by 800 BC. The Chinese may have acquired knowledge of ironworking from India or the Middle East via the Central Asian trade routes, but major differences in the processes used mean that it is much more likely that they discovered it independently. Iron has a much higher melting point than the copper and tin used to make bronze. Furnaces used by ironworkers in the West could not achieve these temperatures. Instead, iron ore was heated in a furnace with charcoal to produce a spongy 'bloom' of iron and slag. While still hot, the bloom was worked (wrought) with a hammer to remove the slag and weld the iron into a single mass. Chinese furnaces, however, could achieve much higher temperatures and completely melt the iron. This allowed it to be cast in moulds, like bronze, and was much less labour intensive than individually forging pieces of iron from blooms. However, cast iron has a high carbon content, making it brittle and less suited to making tools and weapons than malleable wrought iron. It was only c.300 BC, when the Chinese discovered how to decarbonize cast iron by heating it in air for several days to make wrought iron, that China truly entered the Iron Age and iron tools replaced bronze tools in everyday use.

Laozi
Massive stone sculpture of the philosopher Laozi, dating to the Song dynasty (AD 960–1279) on Mount Qingyuan in Fujian, southern China. Laozi was probably a contemporary of Confucius, but his life is shrouded in legend.

THE GREAT WALL OF CHINA

The Great Wall, snaking its way along the mountain ridges north of Beijing, has become an iconic image of the might of ancient China. The truth is that the Great Wall is not really very ancient at all. Most of the wall that still stands was built by the Ming dynasty in the 16th century AD and belongs no more to ancient history than do Columbus' voyages to America.

The Ming Great Wall was the ultimate expression of a tradition of building defensive walls that goes back to pre-imperial times. China lacks natural frontiers in the north and was always exposed to raids by nomads, such as the Xiongnu (Huns), Mongols and Manchus. During the Warring States period, the states of Qin, Zhao and Yan built walls along their northern frontiers as defences against the Xiongnu. These walls were simple constructions, made by packing earth and gravel between wooden retaining walls. Nomad raiders could easily scale these walls, but their horses could not so they proved an effective obstacle. After his unification of China, Shi Huangdi ordered these walls to be linked up and extended to form a continuous barrier along the whole northern frontier. This was the first Great Wall. Under the Han dynasty, Shi Huangdi's wall was extended west to the Turfan depression to protect the Silk Road.

After the Han dynasty fell in AD 220, China broke up again into separate kingdoms, and the wall was neglected for 200 years. New sections of wall were built by the Northern Wei (AD 386–534) and the Sui dynasties (AD 581–618), but the following Tang dynasty (AD 618–907) preferred to seek security through military expansion in Central Asia. As a result of this, they felt that the wall was unnecessary and they allowed it to fall into

Longest graveyard
A restored section of the Ming Great Wall north of Beijing. Tens of thousands of conscripted labourers died building the wall and were buried inside it, earning it the nickname 'the longest graveyard on Earth'.

disrepair. Being made mostly of earth and timber, most
sections of the first Great Wall now survive as little
more than a low bank.

The concept of the Great Wall was revived by the Ming
dynasty (1368–1644) after the failure of campaigns to
suppress the Mongols and the Manchus in the 15th
century. Work on a new Great Wall of stone and brick
began in the reign of the emperor Hongzhi (ruled
1487–1505) and continued until the early 17th century.
Estimated at around 5,500 miles (8,000 km) long, this
wall was in no sense a rebuilding of Shi Huangdi's wall,
as it followed a different course, reaching far to the
south. The enormous costs of building and maintaining
the wall caused peasant unrest and civil war. In 1644, a
disgruntled general opened a gate in the Great Wall to
the Manchus, who overthrew the Ming and founded
the last dynasty of imperial China, the Qing dynasty
(1644–1912). The Great Wall was now irrelevant and
the Qing left it to decay. The theory that the Great Wall
can be seen from the Moon first surfaced in the 18th
century. In fact, no human structure can be seen from
the Moon and it is questionable whether the Great
Wall can be seen by the unaided eye even from orbit.

> 'The means whereby a ruler of men encourages the people are office and rank: the means whereby a country is made prosperous are agriculture and war.'

The Book of Lord Shang
(early third century BC)

The Warring States period saw the process of decentralization of the Springs and Autumns period go into reverse. This was not an achievement of the Zhou dynasty, which continued to decline into irrelevance as the feudal lords gave up the pretence of subservience and began to call themselves kings. Conflicts became more intense as the stronger states began to conquer the weaker. Many states began to build border walls to defend themselves from their neighbours and from steppe nomads who sought to take advantage of China's endless wars. The 17 states which existed in 480 BC had been reduced to 11 by 300 BC, and by 256 BC, when the last Zhou king was deposed, there were just seven left.

Art of War
A Chinese bamboo book, a copy of *The Art of War* by the general Sunzi (Sun Tzu) who lived sometime during the Warring States period (480–221 BC). Sunzi's insights into the nature of war and the means to attain victory have made it a classic of military theory.

KINGDOM OF QIN

The strongest of the survivors was the kingdom of Qin in western China. Geography gave Qin some important geographical advantages over its rivals. Mountainous frontiers provided some natural protection from invasion, while its frontier position gave it opportunities for expansion at the expense of non-Chinese states, such as Shu, conquered in 316 BC. Qin's rise to prominence was begun by Shang Yang, better known as Lord Shang, the capable and cynical prime minister to king Xiao (ruled 361–338 BC). Shang was a follower of a school of philosophy known as Legalism, which had developed as a response to the troubled times. Quite the opposite of Confucianism, Legalism was founded on the doctrine that people are inherently wicked and only behave themselves through fear of punishment. Where Confucius sought to restrain rulers by appealing to their enlightened self-interest, Legalism was a doctrine of royal absolutism. Rulers do not have any obligations to their subjects because their subjects would not respect their obligations to rulers if given the chance. Order can only be assured by strong government, a legal system with strictly prescribed punishments and rewards, and obedience to authority. Shang had little time for social idealism. 'A state that uses good people to rule the wicked will always suffer from disorder' he wrote, but 'a state that uses the wicked to rule the good will always enjoy order.'

Shang put the principles of Legalism into practice in Qin, turning it into a centralized, absolutist state. A principle of Legalism was that the law should be applied impartially to all, irrespective of rank. This was revolutionary, as under feudalism rank and kinship were always taken into account when deciding punishment. Another revolutionary principle was that appointment to office should be by merit alone. Shang broke the power of the hereditary aristocracy by making military service the basis of noble status. Aristocrats who failed to win military glory suddenly found themselves reduced to the rank of commoner, or even slave. To prevent nepotism, the extended family was abolished. Meritocratic reforms made it possible for commoners with ability to rise through the hierarchy and achieve noble status.

Legalism brought with it a strong anti-cultural agenda. The only activities that mattered were those that made the state stronger – agriculture, trade and military service. Far-reaching reforms in land tenure increased agricultural productivity and further weakened the aristocracy. Peasant families worked land belonging to the aristocracy under conditions approximating to serfdom. Shang gave these lands to the peasants as private property which could be bought and sold. Instead of performing labour services for their landlords, the peasants now owed labour services to the state, but those who produced harvests above a specified level were exempted. Families were formed into groups, who were held mutually responsible to the authorities for the good behaviour of their members. Travel was only allowed by permit and vagrants were enslaved. Weights and measures were standardized to encourage trade. People who made a living by cultural activities were regarded as non-productive parasites who set a bad example to the peasants. History was considered irrelevant – the people did not need to look to the past for exemplars of good leadership and virtuous behaviour, their only teacher should be the law.

THE FIRST EMPEROR

King Zhu Ji of Wei condemned Qin, saying 'it has the morality of a tiger or a wolf', but, despite recognizing the danger it posed to their independence, the other states failed to unite against it. Qin waged war against its neighbours with unprecedented ruthlessness and the defeated could expect no mercy. After the battle of Gaoping in 260 BC, the victorious Qin reputedly buried 400,000 prisoners alive. King Zheng (ruled 246–210 BC) achieved the final unification in a series of lightning campaigns lasting just nine years, from 230 to 221 BC. Zheng marked his triumph by adopting the name Shi Huangdi or 'First Emperor'.

To consolidate his victory, Shi Huangdi methodically destroyed all vestiges of the old states. He killed or deported their royal families and aristocracies, abolished feudalism and divided China into 48 commanderies whose borders were not based on those of the old states. Qin laws and institutions were extended to all of China. A professional non-hereditary bureaucracy was introduced and kept under close centralized control. Cultural and economic unity was imposed by standardizing the coinage, weights and measures, scripts, and even the axle size of wagons. Huge numbers of peasants were conscripted into the army and to work on construction projects, such as road building and irrigation schemes, and the emperor's city-sized underground tomb. Shi Huangdi linked up the border

Epang Palace
Painting of Shi Huangdi's palace at Epang, near the Qin dynasty capital at Xi'an. The vast palace was still incomplete when he died and it was burned down during the rebellion that broke out afterwards.

walls built by the Warring States to create a continuous barrier to defend China's northern frontier against nomad raids. This was the inspiration for the stone and brick Great Wall built by the Ming dynasty (AD 1368–1644). Military campaigns extended the empire in the south into present-day Fujian and Guangdong provinces, then inhabited mainly by Viet peoples. Entire communities were transplanted into newly conquered areas to ensure control. In 213 BC, Shi Huangdi ordered the destruction of all historical records, so that Chinese history would begin with him. A few texts survived, hidden by scholars at great risk to their lives: 460 dissenting scholars were buried alive.

It was Shi Huangdi's intention that his successors would be called simply 'Second Emperor', 'Third Emperor', and so on in perpetuity. In the event, his Qin dynasty did not survive its Second Emperor. The cost of Shi Huangdi's reforms ruined the economy and his brutal implementation of Legalism caused such discontent that a civil war broke out after his death in 210 BC. In 206 BC, rebels captured the Qin capital at Xianyang and massacred the entire Qin royal family. However, Shi Huangdi had done his work of destruction so thoroughly that a half-hearted attempt to restore the old China of independent kingdoms quickly failed. The empire created by Shi Huangdi passed intact under the rule of Gaodi (ruled 206–195 BC), a commoner and former bandit, who became the first emperor of the Han dynasty (206 BC–AD 220). Adopting the Confucian principle that good government depended on the fulfilment of mutual responsibilities, Gaodi relaxed Shi Huangdi's savage penal code, which imposed the death penalty even for minor offences, reduced taxes on the peasantry, and ended foreign wars. However, Gaodi did not significantly change the pattern of centralized absolutist government that Shi Huangdi had created and which became the ideal model to which all future Chinese dynasties aspired, with varying degrees of success. Shi Huangdi's anti-intellectualism and hostility to Confucian values ensured that for the remainder of imperial times he was regarded officially as a hideous tyrant. Since the creation of the People's Republic of China in 1949, Shi Huangdi's reputation has gradually been rehabilitated and today he is regarded in China as a far-sighted ruler who defeated the forces of separatism to create the first unified Chinese state. There is, of course, truth in both assessments. Not the least of Shi Huangdi's achievements was that it was from his short-lived Qin dynasty that China gets its modern name.

'Blood flowed forth upon the plains as it had since antiquity ... None could make it stop. Until now. Until this, our emperor has made the world one family and weapons of warfare are lifted up no longer.'

Inscription of Shi Huangdi, carved on Mount Yi c.221 BC

THE TOMB OF SHI HUANGDI

Shi Huangdi prepared for death by constructing an enormous mortuary complex at Lintong, near the Qin capital at Xianyang. The complex covers more than a square mile and appears to have been laid out as an idealized city, with the emperor's tomb, which lies under a huge earth mound, representing a 'forbidden city' at its centre. The tomb has never been excavated, but, according to the Han dynasty historian Sima Qian (c.145–86 BC), it was designed as a huge model of China, with rivers of mercury, and model cities and palaces made of bronze. Every imaginable luxury was placed there. The tomb had a domed copper roof to represent the sky, studded with pearls to represent the stars and planets. It was lit by huge candles of whale blubber that were intended to burn for hundreds of years. To keep out tomb robbers, automatic crossbows were placed in the tomb. When Shi Huangdi finally died, aged 49, all his concubines and all the people who had worked on the tomb and knew its secrets, said to be 700,000 people in all, were buried alive with him.

Sima Qian's description was thought to be exaggerated until the accidental discovery of the famous army of 7,000 life-size terracotta soldiers in pits adjacent to the tomb in 1974. The soldiers were originally armed, but their weapons were looted soon after they were buried. The army, which Sima Qian does not mention, was intended to defend the emperor in the afterlife against the vengeful spirits of the millions of people he had killed. More recently, soil samples taken from the mound above the emperor's tomb proved to contain high levels of mercury, lending further credibility to Sima Qian's account. Shi Huangdi was not left to rest in peace. According to Sima Qian, the tomb was wrecked during the anti-Qin rebellion in 206 BC.

Terracotta warriors
The warriors were buried in four pits. Pit 1 (pictured) represents an infantry division. Other pits represent cavalry units and the command unit.

PERSIAN EMPIRE

THE Persian empire was both the last and greatest of the empires of the ancient Near East and the world's first real superpower. Extending 2,500 miles (4,025 km), from the Indus river in the East to the Aegean Sea in the west, this vast realm was created in little more than a decade by Cyrus the Great. Less than 250 years later, it was destroyed just as quickly by Alexander the Great. Persia became a by-word for oriental despotism, but it was in many ways a tolerant empire that respected local religions and customs, and was careful not to over-tax its subjects. The empire brought together elements from all of the major Old World civilizations of the time, except the Chinese, promoting the diffusion and mixing of cultures on a scale never before possible: it was one of the greatest melting pots in history.

Persia – modern Iran – derives its name from the Parsa, an Iranian nomad people whose homeland lay somewhere in Central Asia. At some point in the ninth century BC, if not before, they began to migrate south into modern-day Iran with another Iranian people called the Medes. While the Medes settled on the Iranian plateau, the main body of the Parsa continued migrating south, finally settling between the southern edge of the Zagros mountains and the Persian Gulf. This area became known after them as Parsa or Persia (now the province of Fars in southern Iran). The indigenous population of the area was Elamite, and from them the Persians adopted many customs, including fashions in dress and writing in the cuneiform script.

PERSIAN ORIGINS

The founder of the Persian monarchy was Achaemenes, who is believed to have reigned around 700 BC. To begin with, the Persians were dominated by their neighbours, the Medes, whose king Phraortes (ruled 675–653 BC) made Persia a vassal state. Under Cyaxares (ruled 625–585 BC) the Medes allied with king Nabopolassar (ruled 626–605 BC) of Babylon against the Assyrian empire, which had dominated the Near East since around 900 BC. The alliance was sealed by the betrothal of Cyaxares' granddaughter to the Babylonian crown prince Nebuchadnezzar. After destroying the Assyrian capital at Nineveh in 612 BC, the allies shared the Assyrian empire between them. Subsequently, the Medes extended their control over eastern Anatolia, creating a border with the kingdom of Lydia, which controlled most of western Anatolia. Lydia has an important place in history as the first state to mint coins of gold and silver for use as currency, sometime around 650 BC.

CYRUS THE EMPIRE BUILDER

In 553 BC, the Persian king Cyrus II ('the Great') (ruled 559–530 BC), a descendant of Achaemenes, rebelled against Cyaxares' son Astyages (ruled 585–550 BC). Astyages invaded Persia in great strength, besieging Cyrus in his capital at Pasargadae in 550 BC. For reasons that are unknown, Astyages' army mutinied and handed him over to Cyrus.

Previous page:
Hunting scene
A stone relief carved during the fifth century BC from a stairway at the Persian capital of Persepolis shows a lion attacking a bull.

After this bloodless victory – Astyages was spared – Cyrus seized the Median capital and treasury at Hamadan and the whole Median empire tamely submitted to his rule. Cyrus' coup alarmed the proverbially wealthy Lydian king Croesus (ruled 560–546 BC). Croesus sought the advice of the famous oracle of the Greek Sun-god Apollo at Delphi, asking if he should go to war against Persia. The oracle assured him, with typical ambiguity, that if he did go to war, he would destroy a great empire. Taking this as encouragement, Croesus set out to invade the Persian empire in 547 BC. Cyrus had also prepared for war and intercepted Croesus' army near Pteria in Cappadocia (central Anatolia). The kings fought a fierce but indecisive battle before disengaging. Winter was approaching and Croesus withdrew to his capital at Sardis and disbanded his army, presumably expecting that Cyrus would do the same, as was normal in those days. Cyrus had no objection to campaigning in winter, however, and when he and his army unexpectedly arrived outside the walls of Sardis, Croesus was caught completely unprepared. Sardis fell after a siege of only 14 days. The empire whose destruction was foretold by the oracle was

A detail of the Ishtar Gate of Babylon
Named for the Mesopotamian goddess of war and sex, the great gate, covered entirely with glazed brick reliefs of real and mythological animals, was built by Nebuchadnezzar II (ruled 604–562 BC). Babylon's power declined quickly after his death and it fell easily to Cyrus of Persia.

Croesus' own. Distraught, Croesus tried to burn himself alive on a funeral pyre, but a rainstorm doused the flames and he was captured. Cyrus spared his life and later made him governor of Barene in Media.

THE FALL OF BABYLON

Cyrus delegated to his generals the task of conquering the Greek colonies on the Ionian coast of Anatolia and took the bulk of his forces east to push the borders of his empire across the Iranian plateau to the Hindu Kush mountains. In 544 BC, he founded the fortress city of Cyreschata (modern Istaravshan, Tajikistan) to protect the frontier from nomad incursions. The climax of Cyrus' career was the conquest of Babylon in 539 BC. Babylon reached the peak of its power and splendour under Nebuchadnezzar (ruled 604–562 BC). It was at this time that Nebuchadnezzar built the legendary Hanging Gardens, supposedly to please his Median wife who was pining for her mountainous homeland. Nebuchadnezzar's successor was overthrown by a palace revolution in 556 BC, which placed an official called Nabonidus (ruled 555–539 BC) on the throne. Nabonidus was a religious eccentric who spent much of his reign in Arabia, leaving his son Bel-shar-usur (the Belshazzar of the Bible) in charge of Babylon. The king's absence created deep discontent because, without his personal participation, the Babylonian New Year festival could not be celebrated. Nabonidus also alienated the priesthood of Marduk, the city's chief god, by favouring the Moon-goddess Sin instead. When he invaded the Babylonian empire in summer 539 BC, Cyrus presented himself as the servant of Marduk and the restorer of religious orthodoxy. After he defeated the Babylonian army at the battle of Opis in September, Cyrus destroyed the ancient city of Akkad, once the capital of the empire of Sargon the Great. This show of strength ended all resistance, and on 16 October, Cyrus entered Babylon without a battle. Nabonidus was captured and exiled. Cyrus' victory was especially celebrated by the Jews. The Babylonians resettled thousands of Jews in Mesopotamia after they destroyed Jerusalem in 587 BC: Cyrus gave them leave to return home.

In only 14 years, and with remarkably little fighting, Cyrus had built the largest empire that the world had yet seen. The close cultural and linguistic relationship between the Persians and the Medes certainly helped Cyrus. If it is true, as some legends claim, that Cyrus was Astyages' grandson (through his mother), then it was more of a dynastic takeover of Media than a conquest. Cyrus conciliated the Medes by appointing a Mede as his chief adviser, a practice which seems to have been followed by his successors. Hamadan, the Median capital, became joint capital of the empire, with Pasargadae and Babylon. In Mesopotamia, Cyrus established his rule so easily because of the region's 1,800 year long tradition of imperial government. The Babylonian and Assyrian empires mixed peoples and cultures, weakening local and national identities and accustoming people to rule by outsiders. Because of this, there was no spirit of popular resistance among the Mesopotamians to what was, in effect, nothing more than the succession of a new imperial dynasty. Cyrus was a much greater diplomat than a warrior and the consolidation of his empire owed much to his moderation and toleration. He showed mercy to his defeated enemies and his demands for tribute were modest. No attempts were made to interfere with local religious practices, customs and laws, and local government institutions were left intact.

Cyrus' life was so remarkable that many legends became attached to his memory and he was admired not only by the Persians but also by their enemies the Greeks. The Greek historian Herodotus (c.484–c.420 BC) recorded the legend of Cyrus' birth and upbringing. According to this, king Astyages of Media married his daughter Mandane to Cambyses, the vassal king of Persia. From their union, Cyrus was born. A prophetic dream forewarned Astyages that Cyrus would supplant him, so he brought Mandane home and ordered his adviser Harpagos to take the boy away and kill him. Instead, Harpagos gave the boy to a shepherd to bring up. When he was ten years old, Astyages recognized Cyrus as his grandson from his looks and noble bearing. Against his better judgement, he allowed the boy to live and inherit his father's throne. Astyages punished Harpagos for disobeying his orders by tricking him into eating his own cooked and minced up son. Seeking vengeance for the murder of his son, Harpagos persuaded Cyrus to rebel against Astyages. Harpagos defected to Cyrus with the best of the Median troops, leaving Astyages with an army of old men and boys. Cyrus easily defeated him and fulfilled the prophecy. In his *Cyropaedia*, another Greek author, Xenophon (c.420–350 BC), made Cyrus the epitome of the virtues expected of an ideal ruler in the ancient world. Xenophon's view of Cyrus made a great impression on the young Alexander the Great.

At the age of 70, Cyrus was killed in battle in summer 530 BC, while campaigning against Tomyris, the Amazonian queen of a nomadic tribe, somewhere in Central Asia.

THE CONQUEST OF EGYPT

Cyrus was succeeded by his ambitious son Cambyses (ruled 529–522 BC). Cambyses' main achievement was the conquest of Egypt in 525 BC. Egyptian power was much reduced since the glory days of the New Kingdom and its pharaoh Psamtek III (ruled 526–525 BC) had only just come to the throne and was very inexperienced. Cambyses also benefited from the advice of Phanes, a Greek mercenary general who had defected from the Egyptian army. Cambyses crossed the Sinai desert with the aid of Bedouin guides and fought a fierce battle against Psamtek at Pelusium in the Delta. The Egyptians wrought a savage vengeance on Phanes. His sons, who he had left behind in Egypt, were paraded in front of the army in full view of their father. The Egyptians cut the boys' throats over a bowl, mixing their blood with wine and water to make a drink, which they all shared before joining battle. Despite the savage prelude, the Egyptians were routed and resistance quickly collapsed. Psamtek was captured and later executed, allegedly for plotting a rebellion. Cambyses lacked his father's magnanimous nature.

Croesus on the pyre
This Greek vase shows king Croesus of Lydia preparing to immolate himself on a funeral pyre following his defeat by Cyrus the Great. Croesus' proverbial wealth made him the subject of many legends.

Cambyses hoped to legitimize his rule in Egypt by winning the endorsement of the Oracle of Amun at Siwa Oasis, deep in the Libyan Desert. However, the expedition he sent was engulfed in a sandstorm and disappeared. While in Egypt, Cambyses campaigned in Nubia and considered an expedition against the great Phoenician trading city of Carthage in modern-day Tunisia. Before he could do so, his brother Bardiya (also

The Cyrus Cylinder
This inscribed clay cylinder is a propaganda document issued by Cyrus the Great in 539 BC to establish the legitimacy of his conquest of Babylon by declaring his respect for his new subjects' gods and traditions.

known as Smerdis) seized the throne, forcing Cambyses to return to Persia. On the way, somewhere in Syria in summer 522 BC, he died – whether by natural causes, suicide or by murder is unclear. After Cambyses' death, Darius, a member of a junior branch of the Achaemenid family, who was with the king, hurried on to Media. Aided by six Persian nobles, Darius murdered Bardiya and claimed the throne for himself. In an inscription he had made at Bisitun, Darius later claimed that Cambyses ordered Bardiya to be killed secretly before leaving for Egypt and that the Bardiya who seized the throne was really an impostor called Gaumata. Many historians believe that Darius invented this story so that he could claim to be restoring the legitimate Achaemenid line. Many of Darius' subjects certainly did doubt his legitimacy, and he spent the first three years of his reign (522–486 BC) suppressing rebellions throughout the empire.

THE LIMITS OF EMPIRE

By 519 BC, Darius felt safe enough to secure the empire's northern border against raids by the nomadic Scythians. The following year, he crossed the Hindu Kush and descended into the Indus river valley, which was annexed to the empire. Darius then turned his attention to the western frontiers. In 513 BC, he crossed into Europe, conquering eastern Thrace (roughly modern Bulgaria), forcing Macedon to become a vassal state, conquering the Greek Aegean islands of Lemnos and Imbros. However, he failed in his main objective, which was to seize the gold mines north of the Danube, which were controlled by the Scythians. The logical next step was for Darius to conquer Greece: at least that was how it looked to the Greeks. When the Greek cities in Ionia rebelled against Persian rule in 499 BC, Athens and Eretria decided to send help. Darius crushed the rebellion in 494 BC, but treated the defeated cities leniently. To discourage further meddling by the mainland Greeks, Darius sent a naval expedition to Greece in 492 BC, but it was wrecked in a storm on the way. Darius was running out of luck. In 490 BC, he sent a second expedition, but this was defeated with very heavy casualties at the battle of Marathon by the Athenians. Undeterred, Darius began

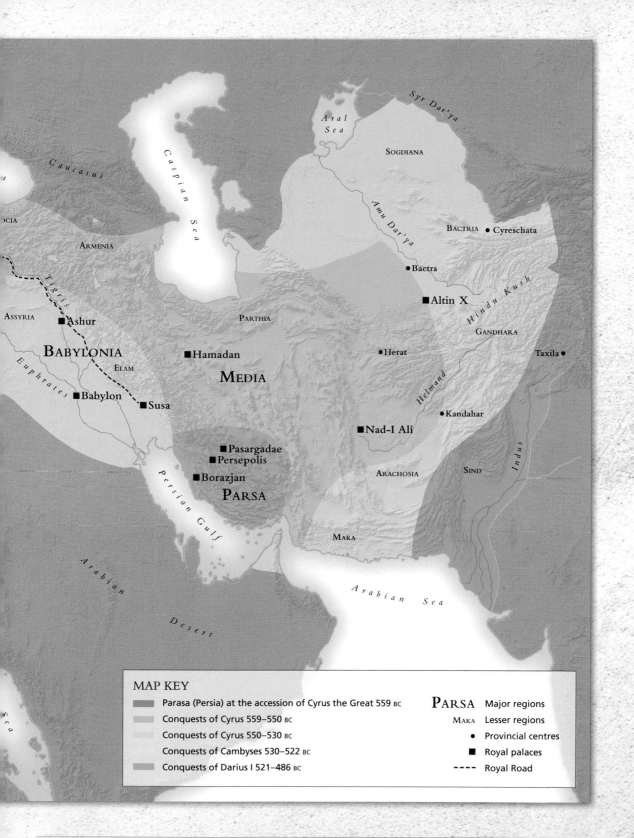

Caucasus

Caspian Sea

Aral Sea

Syr Dar'ya

SOGDIANA

Amu Dar'ya

BACTRIA ● Cyreschata

OCIA

ARMENIA

● Bactra

Tigris

■Ashur

ASSYRIA

BABYLONIA

ELAM

Euphrates

■Babylon

■Susa

PARTHIA

Altin X

Hindu Kush

GANDHARA

■Hamadan

● Herat

Taxila ●

MEDIA

Helmand

● Kandahar

Indus

■Nad-I Ali

■Pasargadae

■Persepolis

■Borazjan

PARSA

Persian Gulf

ARACHOSIA

SIND

MAKA

Arabian Desert

Arabian Sea

Sea

MAP KEY

Parasa (Persia) at the accession of Cyrus the Great 559 BC

Conquests of Cyrus 559–550 BC

Conquests of Cyrus 550–530 BC

Conquests of Cambyses 530–522 BC

Conquests of Darius I 521–486 BC

PARSA Major regions

MAKA Lesser regions

● Provincial centres

■ Royal palaces

---- Royal Road

The ancient Persian language (and Farsi, its modern Iranian descendent) belongs to the widespread Indo-European language family, to which most modern European languages, including English, also belong. Spoken today on every continent and by around half the world's people, the Indo-European languages are all descended from a common ancestor spoken by a single people who lived on the western Asian steppes around 5,000 years ago. The Indo-Europeans were successful nomadic pastoralists who gradually migrated out of their original homeland, spreading west into Europe, east into Central Asia and south into the Middle East and South Asia. As groups of Indo-Europeans spread out and lost contact with one another, their languages began to diversify and evolve into their modern daughter languages. The Persian language is most closely related to Indian languages, such as ancient Sanskrit, and modern Hindi and Urdu. Modern Farsi includes many Arabic words, a result of the Islamic conquest in the seventh century AD.

The relief at Bisitun
The relief is a propaganda work, commissioned by Darius I to establish the legitimacy of his rule. The relief shows Darius passing judgement on Gaumata and his bound followers, while Faravahar, the winged symbol of Ahura Mazda hovers above giving its blessing to the king.

to plan a third expedition, but he was diverted by a rebellion in Egypt and preparations were still not complete when he died in 486 BC.

THE INVASION OF GREECE

It was left to Darius' son Xerxes (ruled 485–465 BC) to deal with the Greeks once and for all. Xerxes' expedition was on a massive scale, designed to awe the Greeks into submission. According to some reports, the expedition which set out in 480 BC was half a million strong and was supported by a fleet of 1,000 ships. The army marched into Europe without getting its feet wet, across a mile-long bridge of boats built over the Hellespont. Xerxes was expecting an easy victory, but the sheer size of his army created enormous problems of supply and made it impossible to control effectively in battle. Most of his soldiers were poorly armed and unenthusiastic conscripts who had already spent months on the road just travelling to join the army. Although they were greatly outnumbered, the Greeks were well-trained, highly disciplined, heavily armoured citizen soldiers fighting for their homes.
The Spartans under king Leonidas fought a holding action at Thermopylai, which bought the Greeks enough time to organize their defences. At Salamis, Xerxes watched horrified from the shore as the Athenian navy destroyed his fleet. Humiliated, Xerxes returned to Asia leaving his general Mardonius to complete the campaign, but he fared no better. The following summer, the Greeks, led by the Spartans, routed the Persian army at Plataea. The aura of Persian invincibility was shattered.

KING OF KINGS

In commemorative inscriptions, Darius described himself as 'the great king, king of kings, king in Persia, king of the countries containing all races, son of Hystaspes, grandson of Arsames, an Achaemenid'. The title 'king of kings' (*shahanshah*) reveals the original tribal basis of Persian society. The Persians were divided into patrilineal tribes or clans that were ranked by seniority. The leader of each tribe was originally regarded as a king in his own right, but they were all outranked by the king of the senior tribe, who was, therefore, the king of kings. Even in Darius' day, tribal identities survived, forming the foundation of the Persian social hierarchy, the tribe of the ruling Achaemenid family enjoying the highest status. It was probably because he was from a junior line of that family that Darius stressed his Achaemenid ancestry: it was his main claim to legitimacy. Each tribe was divided into four classes of nobles, priests, farmers and artisans. This class division was probably shared by the Medes, but no attempt was made to impose it on conquered peoples.

Darius' greatest achievement was giving the Persian empire an effective administrative structure. While Cyrus had been content to govern the conquered peoples through their existing institutions, Darius reorganized the Persian empire into some 20 provinces called *satrapies*, under governors called *satraps*. *Satraps* were usually members of the royal family or the highest nobility who the king appointed directly for life. The *satrap* collected the taxes of his province and was the supreme judicial authority. The *satrap* was also responsible for internal security and for raising his province's levy of troops for the Persian army. The levies fought in national units, with their national weapons, but under Persian officers. The king personally commanded the elite 'immortals', a standing army of 10,000 professional troops recruited only from the Persians and Medes.

CONTROLLING THE REGIONS

To prevent the *satraps* abusing their considerable powers, fixed taxes and tributes were introduced, and these were based on the wealth of each province. They were usually set at about half the level each province was thought able to pay. Great trouble was taken to establish this amount, for example, by taking account of fluctuations in the harvest and careful surveying of agricultural land. Persia was exempt from paying tribute as it was not a conquered province. As a further check on the *satraps'* powers, the local garrison commanders were appointed by the king and were directly responsible to him. Finally, the *satraps* were subject to periodic inspection of royal officials, known as 'the king's eyes'. Despite these measures, when royal authority began to decline in the fourth century BC, many *satraps* enjoyed virtual autonomy. However, popular rebellions against Achaemenid rule were rare, except in the west, where the Egyptians and Ionian Greeks had strong traditions of self determination.

Darius was the greatest builder of his dynasty. He founded a new ceremonial capital for the empire at Persepolis ('City of Persia'), 25 miles (40 km) southwest of Pasargadae, and moved the administrative capital from Hamadan to Susa. Darius' official buildings deliberately emphasized the ethnic and cultural diversity of his empire, so as to showcase its vast resources. The labyrinthine new palace at Persepolis was built in an eclectic mixture of styles borrowed from Assyria, Babylon, Media, Lydia, Greece and Egypt. The achievement of the architects was to blend these disparate influences into a harmonious style that was distinctively Persian. To make sure that no visitor could miss the building's imperial message, its grand entrance staircase was decorated with low-relief sculpted friezes showing delegates from the provinces, each in his national dress, queuing to present exotic gifts to the king. Darius' palace at Susa was equally eclectic. In the palace's foundation inscription, Darius recorded all the peoples and places that had contributed

Oxus treasure
A stunning Persian gold bracelet decorated with winged griffons, part of a treasure hoard discovered next to the Oxus river (Amu Darya) in Afghanistan in 1880.

to its construction. These included craftsmen from Egypt, Ionia, Lydia and Media working under Persian supervisors and drawing rations from the royal treasury. The eclecticism of Persian architecture was equally evident in decorative arts, such as gold and silver tableware, prestige weapons, jewellery and pottery. Herodotus noted that of all peoples, the Persians were the most willing to adopt foreign fashions, though to a chauvinistic Greek such multiculturalism was hardly a virtue.

THE ROYAL ROAD

To secure good communications between Susa and the provinces, Darius created an imperial postal service and improved the roads. The main trunk road of the empire was the 1,600-mile (2,575-km) long Royal Road that linked Susa with Sardis in Lydia. Over 100 relay stations along the route provided overnight accommodation and fresh horses for official travellers. The journey usually took 90 days, but the fastest couriers made it in a week. Similar roads linked Susa with Memphis in Egypt, and with Bactra on the Central Asian frontier. In Egypt, Darius completed a canal to link the Nile with the Red Sea, begun by one of the later pharaohs. To promote internal trade, Darius introduced coinage (an idea he borrowed from the Lydians), and standardized weights and measures. For records, the imperial administration continued to use local languages transcribed into cuneiform script and written on clay tablets. In Persia itself, administrators used Elamite: the Old Persian language was never used for administrative purposes and was rarely written down except for commemorative inscriptions. Darius' successors did away with this cumbersome system, adopting the Aramaic language and alphabet for administrative purposes. Clay tablets were also abandoned in favour of parchment.

PERSIAN RELIGION

Darius and his successors continued Cyrus' policy of religious tolerance. Darius built or repaired several temples in Egypt, and allowed the Jews to rebuild the Temple in Jerusalem, which the Babylonians had destroyed in 586 BC. The traditional Iranian religion practised by the Persians and Medes shared a common

Immortals
Glazed brick reliefs from the temple of Inshushinak, the patron deity of Susa, Iran, showing two Immortals, the elite guards of the Persian kings.

origin with the early form of Hinduism practised by the *arya* who settled in India in the second millennium BC. The Iranian pantheon was divided into two categories of gods, the *ahuras* (lords) and lesser deities called *daivas*. The most important of the *ahuras* were the creator god Ahura Mazda, the Wise Lord who maintains the cosmic order; Anahiti, a river goddess who brings fresh water to the earth; and Mithra, a Sun god, whose cult later became popular in the Roman empire. The Persians did not make idols of their gods, as they believed that it was futile for humans to attempt to portray the appearance of their gods, but Faravahar, the winged symbol of Ahura Mazda, regularly appeared in portrayals of the Achaemenid kings. Royal authority derived from Ahura Mazda. He protected the Achaemenid kings and conferred on them something like the 'divine right of kings' later claimed by Christian kings in medieval Europe.

Iranian religion had strong animist elements and both fire and water were held to be sacred. The religion's most important ritual was the *yazna*, a festive meal at which a god was 'invited' to attend, in which fire and a sacred drink called *houma* were involved.

In return for the hospitality, the god was expected to give his host a 'present'. All rituals and worship were performed in the open air; the Persians did not build temples. A powerful Median hereditary priestly clan, the *Magi*, played a prominent role in religious rituals in Achaemenid times. Although Darius tried to break their power, the *Magi* later became the empire's official priesthood. The *Magi* may have played a key role in spreading Zoroastrianism, a dualist religion based on the teachings of the prophet Zoroaster, in which the universe is believed to be a battleground between forces of truth (good), represented by Ahura Mazda, and the lie (evil), represented by the evil spirit Ahriman. Zoroastrianism became the Persian state religion under the Sasanian dynasty (AD 224–651) but the extent and nature of its influence throughout the Achaemenid period is very uncertain.

AN EMPIRE IN DECLINE

Despite the disastrous failure of Xerxes' expedition to Greece in 480–479 BC, the Persian empire remained the world's largest, richest and most powerful state. The Athenians were eager to continue the war against Persia and secure the freedom of the Ionian Greeks, but most of the Greek states were simply relieved to have survived the invasion and wanted none of it. Athens continued the war alone. Xerxes paid it little attention. The failure in Greece left him demoralized and he withdrew in to his harem and its family intrigues and feuds. It seems to have been as a result of one of these that Xerxes was murdered by his uncle Artabanus and one of the harem eunuchs. Artabanus blamed the crown prince Darius for the crime, prompting the prince's brother Artaxerxes to kill him. Artabanus then tried to murder Artaxerxes to secure the throne for himself, but he inflicted only a flesh wound before he was himself killed.

Artaxerxes (ruled 465–425 BC) quickly established his authority, putting down rebellions in Bactria and Egypt. A defeat by the Athenians in Cyprus in 450 BC, persuaded him to recognize Ionia's independence by the Treaty of Kallias in 448 BC and for the remainder

Tribute bearers
Part of a relief from the Apadana (audience chamber) at the Persian royal capital at Persepolis showing a procession of provincials in their national costumes queuing to offer gifts of tribute to the king. The deputation shown here is from Lydia.

of his reign the empire was at peace. Artaxerxes was the last Achaemenid to provide effective military leadership. Harem intrigues plagued his last years, and after his death they exploded into family bloodshed. Artaxerxes' only legitimate son, Xerxes II, succeeded him. After a reign of only 45 days, Xerxes was murdered by his half-brother Sogdianus, who lasted all of six months before he was overthrown and executed by another of Artaxerxes' illegitimate sons, Darius II (ruled 423–405 BC). Darius was a weak character who was dominated by his ambitious wife, his half-sister Parysitis, and by the harem eunuchs. Darius' main success was the recovery of Ionia. When war broke out between Athens and its former ally Sparta in 431 BC, Darius decided to finance Sparta's war effort. Darius appointed his younger son Cyrus *satrap* of Lydia to help the Spartans build a fleet to challenge Athenian control of the seas. After the Spartans destroyed the Athenian fleet at Aegospotami in 405 BC, Persia reoccupied Ionia.

FAMILY INTRIGUE

Cyrus was his mother's favourite and she hoped he would inherit the throne. However, Darius appointed their elder son Artaxerxes II (ruled 404–359 BC) as heir and it was he who succeeded when Darius died in 404 BC. Cyrus was accused, probably rightly, of plotting his brother's murder, but his mother's intervention saved him from punishment and he was allowed to return to Lydia. There, he secretly recruited an army of 13,000 Greek mercenaries to fight for him. In spring 401 BC, Cyrus invaded Mesopotamia, facing no resistance until he unexpectedly blundered into an army led by Artaxerxes at Cunaxa near Babylon. Cyrus succeeded in wounding his brother in combat, but was himself killed. The Greek force, itself undefeated in the battle, refused calls to surrender and began an epic march from the heart of the Persian empire, through Anatolia, to the Black Sea where it sailed for Greece. The Greeks were opposed only by local forces, revealing Persia's military weakness. Xenophon, one of the Greek commanders, observed in his account of the expedition (known as the 'March of the Ten Thousand'), that 'whereas the Persian king's empire was strong in that it covered a vast territory with large numbers of people, it was also weak because of the need to travel great distances

THE PROPHET ZOROASTER

One of the most influential figures in the history of religion, Zoroaster, or Zarathustra, the founder of the Zoroastrian religion, is also one of the most obscure. There is even uncertainty about what his original teachings were because the Zoroastrian scriptures, the *Avesta*, were not written down until the third to seventh centuries AD. According to later tradition, Zoroaster lived 258 years before Alexander the Great conquered Persia, which would mean that he lived around 600 BC. His parents are said to have belonged the noble Median Spitama family, who lived at Rhages, near modern Tehran. However, many scholars believe that the language and the type of simple pastoral society portrayed in the *Avesta* date from a much earlier time, perhaps around 1000 BC, when the Iranians were still living a nomadic life in Central Asia.

Zoroaster was about 30 years old when Ahura Mazda revealed the truth to him in a vision. In his revelation, Zoroaster saw that the universe was a cosmic conflict between truth and the lie. Ahura Mazda is truth, creation, existence and free will. The purpose of humankind is to sustain truth through good thoughts, words and actions. Truth is constantly attacked by the evil spirit Ahriman but Ahura Mazda is supreme and will eventually triumph,

creating a new world after destroying the old one by fire. Zoroastrianism is essentially monotheistic. The other ahuras of Iranian paganism were demoted to an auxiliary role as protectors of creation and the *daivas* became equated with demons. Zoroastrianism adopted much of the ritual of Iranian paganism, such as the *yazna* sacrifice, and held fire to be a sacred manifestation of Ahura Mazda's truth. In later legend, Zoroaster was considered to be the founder of the *Magi* and the inventor of magic and astrology.

Zoroastrianism's monotheistic tendencies and dualism influenced Greek philosophy, Manichaeism and Judaism (and through it, Christianity and Islam). Despite frequent persecution in the Muslim era, Zoroastrianism survives in pockets in Iran today, and the among the Parsees in India.

Mithraeum
Fresco (second century AD) from the Mithraeum at the Roman fortress-town of Dura-Europos, Syria, believed by many scholars to show the prophet Zoroaster (right) and the influential *magus* Ostanes. Others believe that they may simply represent local followers of the cult of Mithras.

and the wide distribution of its forces, making it vulnerable to a swift attack'. The Greeks were too busy with their own quarrels to take advantage of the situation, at least for the time being.

STOPPING THE ROT

The reign of Artaxerxes II saw the gradual decline of royal authority. Taking advantage of his feud with Cyrus, the Egyptians rebelled in 404 BC and restored the rule of the pharaohs. The heavy reliance of the Egyptians on Greek mercenaries once again emphasized the superiority of the Greek way of war. Artaxerxes spent far too much time with his harem. He is reputed to have had 360 concubines and to have fathered 115 sons, only one of whom, of course, could succeed him. Harem intrigues became rife as ambitious mothers and their sons manoeuvred for position. Of Artaxerxes' three legitimate sons, the eldest was executed for treason, and the second committed suicide after the third son, Ochus, convinced him that their father suspected him of plotting to seize the throne. It was the conniving Ochus who succeeded to the throne on his father's death in 359 BC, adopting the ruling name Artaxerxes III (ruled 358–338 BC). To eliminate any possible rival claimants, Artaxerxes immediately ordered the execution of more than 80 of his closest male relatives.

Xerxes
Relief showing king Xerxes I at Persepolis. Xerxes is best remembered for the disastrous failure of his invasion of Greece in 480–479 BC.

Artaxerxes was an experienced soldier, and he put down a succession of rebellions in the western provinces. He greatly improved the effectiveness of his army by recruiting Greek mercenaries. In 343 BC, Artaxerxes even regained control of Egypt after defeating Nectanebo II (ruled 360–343 BC). The last of the pharaohs, Nectanebo fled to Nubia and vanished from history. Artaxerxes recognized the rising power of Philip II (ruled 359–336 BC) of Macedon as a potential threat to the empire and gave support to his Greek and Thracian enemies. Artaxerxes showed none of the magnanimity of earlier Achaemenids. When he sacked the rebel Phoenician city of Sidon in 345 BC, around 40,000 people were massacred. In Egypt, the temples were plundered and burned: Artaxerxes is said to have slaughtered the sacred bull of Apis with his own hands. Cyrus the Great would never have contemplated committing such a gratuitously sacrilegious act.

Credit for Artaxerxes' achievement in restoring the territorial integrity of the empire belongs mainly to his advisers – Mentor of Rhodes and the eunuch Bagoas. However, Bagoas became increasingly dominant at court and in 338 BC he murdered Artaxerxes and all of his sons except the youngest, Arses (ruled 338–336 BC), whom Bagoas made king. When Arses tried to break free of Bagoas' influence, the eunuch had Arses and his children murdered and placed Darius III (ruled 336–330 BC), a member of a junior branch of the Achaemenid family, on the throne. When Darius also tried to assert himself, Bagoas attempted to poison him. The plot was detected and Darius forced Bagoas to drink his own poison. Surviving this assassination attempt was to be the only success of Darius' disastrous reign.

TROUBLE WITH MACEDON

In 338 BC, Philip II of Macedon defeated a coalition of Athens, Thebes and other Greek cities at the battle of Chaironeia. Philip enrolled the Greeks into the Macedonian dominated League of Corinth and proclaimed an all-out war to free the Ionian Greeks from Persian domination. An advance guard was sent to northwest Anatolia in early 336 BC, but before he could follow it, Philip was murdered at a wedding feast. Philip was an exceptional soldier who revolutionized the conduct of war in Greece with his advanced siege techniques and his use of cavalry, rather than the armoured spear-carrying infantryman, as the main battle-winning arm. The fine army Philip had created now fell into the hands of one of history's greatest military geniuses, his 20-year-old son Alexander (ruled 336–323 BC), soon to be known as 'the Great'. Alexander was one of the most charismatic rulers of the ancient world, an intellectually gifted, imaginative, recklessly bold megalomaniac. Supposedly descended from Heracles (Hercules) on his father's side and Achilles on his mother's, Alexander was driven by his ambition to become a great hero and to achieve divinity. He had already shown his military ability, leading an elite cavalry unit at Chaironeia with distinction.

It is hard to imagine a man less fitted to oppose Alexander than Darius III. Darius was said to have been a courtier before his sudden elevation to the throne. He was no tyrant, but he showed no sense of purpose and no aptitude for politics or war either. His plight evoked some sympathy even from the Greeks. Arrian, the historian of Alexander's campaigns observed that 'though in other respects his conduct appears to have been moderate and decent, in military matters Darius was the feeblest of men ... His life was an unbroken series of disasters from the moment of his accession to the Persian throne.'

Van inscription
Cuneiform inscription of Xerxes I at the citadel of Van, Turkey. The inscription praises the achievements of his father Darius I and calls upon Ahura Mazda to protect the kingdom.

GREEK INVASION

Alexander invaded the Persian empire in 334 BC, landing in northwest Anatolia not far from Troy, where he went to pay homage to his legendary ancestors. Alexander brought with him about 37,000 men, consisting of 5,000 cavalry, 24,000 Greek and Macedonian infantry and 8,000 auxiliary troops, including archers, slingers, javelin throwers, surveyors, siege engineers, a secretariat and a medical corps. He was joined in Anatolia by the 10,000 men his father Philip had sent in the advance party.

Four days after visiting Troy, Alexander met his first Persian army in battle on the Granicus river (now called the Kocabas) and routed it. Alexander's march down the Ionian coast became a triumphal procession as he liberated one Greek city after another. Only at Miletos and Halikarnassos, which had strong Persian garrisons, was there resistance. By the year's end Alexander had possession of all of western Anatolia. Alexander earned a reputation as a lenient conqueror. He allowed no plundering and made no demands for tribute above what was already being paid to the Persians. He left Persian administrative structures intact and even confirmed some *satraps* in their offices if they surrendered their provinces to him voluntarily.

Darius flees
Roman mosaic from Pompeii depicting the decisive moment at the battle of Issos in 333 BC when Alexander's cavalry charge broke the Persian lines and forced Darius, shown in a chariot, to flee the battlefield.

To prevent the Persians sending naval expeditions against Greece, Alexander's next move was to cut Persia off from the Mediterranean by conquering the Levant and Egypt. By this time Darius had raised a massive army and was marching to intercept Alexander. The two kings met in battle in autumn 333 BC near Issos, on the Gulf of Iskenderun in southern Turkey. At the height of the battle, Alexander launched a headlong cavalry charge through the Persian ranks forcing Darius to flee for his life, leaving behind his mother, wife and children. Seeing their king fleeing, the rest of the Persian army broke and ran too.

Alexander began the year 332 BC by laying siege to the great port city of Tyre. This was the of the few occasions in his campaign that Alexander faced determined popular opposition. In most places, the common people passively accepted the new regime, just as they did when Cyrus created the Achaemenid empire. When Tyre finally fell in August, Alexander punished the Tyrians for their defiance by massacring 8,000 of them and selling another 30,000 into slavery. He met no more resistance as he marched south down the Mediterranean coast until he reached Gaza, which fell after a short siege. At the end of 332 BC, Alexander entered Egypt. The Egyptian *satrap* had few troops at his disposal and surrendered at once. The Egyptian people greeted Alexander as a liberator. While he was in Egypt, Alexander visited the oracle of Amun at Siwa oasis. The oracle told him that his true father was the supreme god Zeus, confirming Alexander's belief, and that of many of his contemporaries, that his amazing achievements showed him to be a living god.

Darius now sued for peace, offering Alexander all of the Persian territories west of the Euphrates river, a ransom for his family and his daughter's hand in marriage In return for an alliance with the Greek invader. Though many of his advisers thought it a good offer, Alexander contemptuously rejected it: the territories that Darius offered were no longer his to give. In 331 BC, Alexander invaded Mesopotamia and defeated Darius for a second time at the battle of Gaugamela near Nineveh on 1 October. Just as at Issos, Alexander made a direct assault on Darius' position, forcing him to flee the battlefield, and once again the Persian army broke up in panic. Demoralized by this second humiliation, Darius fled to Hamadan. Alexander hurried on to capture Babylon and the Persian treasury at Susa. The following year, Alexander destroyed another Persian army in the battle of the Persian Gates (a mountain pass) and captured Persepolis, which was sacked and burned.

Despite the succession of defeats, the Persian nobility still had the will to fight. Darius, however, did not. When Alexander left Persepolis and advanced on Hamadan, Darius fled yet again, hoping to find refuge somewhere in the eastern *satrapies*. Alexander pursued him. Near the Caspian Gates pass, Darius, full of the apathy of despair, refused to go any further. Seeing the dust of Alexander's pursuing army on the horizon, the nobles who remained with Darius murdered him and proclaimed his kinsman, Bessos, king. Alexander arrived on the scene a few hours later and ordered that Darius be given a royal burial at Persopolis. Eighteen months later, Alexander captured Bessos, the last of the Achaemenids, in Bactria and executed him.

Living god
Marble bust of a youthful Alexander the Great. Because of his remarkable achievements, Alexander was regarded as a god even in his own lifetime.

It had taken Alexander less than ten years to win complete control of the Persian empire. Alexander showed every intention of ruling through the empire's existing institutions, but he had still not consolidated his conquests when he died at Babylon in 323 BC, aged only 33 years. Alexander left as heirs only a posthumous son and a mentally retarded brother, neither of whom was capable of ruling.

COLLAPSE OF THE EMPIRE

According to the Greek historian Diodorus, Alexander's companions asked their leader on his deathbed to whom he would like to leave his empire. His reply was simply 'to the strongest'. Alexander's generals fought one another for power, carving up the empire between them during a violent campaign which lasted for 40 years before the various claims were settled. Egypt was claimed by Ptolemy, who declared himself pharaoh in 304 BC and ruled until 283 BC. The Ptolemaic kingdom lasted nearly 300 years, when it was annexed by Rome in 30 BC. To the north, the kingdom of Pergamon oversaw Asia Minor and Macedon. The kingdom expanded, reaching its peak in 188 BC before control was handed over to Rome in 133 BC by king Attalus III (ruled 138–133 BC). Persia, Media and Mesopotamia fell to Seleukos (ruled 312–281 BC) whose descendents ruled the region until the mid-second century BC when the Parthians under Mithradates I (ruled 170–138 BC) expelled them. An Indo-Iranian nomad people from Central Asia, the Parthians ruled much of the Near East until AD 224–226, when Ardashir I (ruled AD 220–240) of the Persian Sasanian family rebelled and seized power. The Sasanians consciously revived Persian identity, made Zoroastrianism the state religion, and strove in near-constant warfare with the Romans to rebuild the Achaemenid empire. In the long term, these wars weakened the Sasanian kingdom and it collapsed quickly after it was invaded by the newly Islamized Arabs in AD 637. The Persians accepted Islam, but unlike other peoples conquered by the Arabs, they resisted linguistic and cultural Arabization, retaining their language and identity. Subjected to occupation by Turks and Mongols during the Middle Ages, Persia – or Iran, as it was by then known to local peoples – re-emerged as a major regional power under the Safavid dynasty in the 16th century, a role it still plays today.

Ibex drinking horn
Rhytons, a type of drinking horn, are a distinctive Persian artefact. *Rhytons* had a wide hole at the top and a small hole at the base out of which the wine was allowed to pour directly into the drinker's mouth, as when drinking from a wineskin.

'And now may the blessing of God rest upon all men. I have told unto them the Epic of the Kings, and the Epic of the Kings is come to a close, and the tale of their deeds is ended.'

Ferdawsi, *Shahnameh* (The Book of Kings)

THE EPIC OF IRAN

The majority of our narrative sources for the history of Achaemenid Persia were written by unsympathetic Greeks. The Persians themselves had no traditions of historical writing at this time and the Achaemenid's royal archives did not survive Alexander's conquest. Official Inscriptions, such as Darius II's on the cliffs at Bisitun, were written in cuneiform. When knowledge of cuneiform died out under Alexander's successors, even Persians could not read these inscriptions. By the Sasanian period, the Persians had lost any precise knowledge of the events of the Achaemenid period and it passed from history into the realm of legend. Collections of these legends were written down during the later Sasanian period.

After the Islamic conquest, even these legendary traditions were in danger of being lost. In the tenth century, the Persian poet Daqiqi (died c.976–c.981) began to weave these traditions into a verse chronicle, beginning with the life of Zoroaster. Daqiqi was murdered before he got very far and his work was taken up by Ferdawsi (c.935–c.1020)

who spent 35 years composing the *Shahnameh* ('The Book of Kings'), a 120,000-line epic covering Persian history from legendary times down to the Islamic conquest. The best known character of the epic is Rostam, a Herculean figure who fights demons, dragons and witches. Ferdawsi wrote in pure Persian, avoiding the Arabic influences that had crept into the language since the conquest. The popularity of the *Shahnameh* did much to revive Persian language and literary forms and it is today regarded as the Iranian national epic. Ferdawsi presented the *Shahnameh* to the ruler of Persia, Sultan Mahmud of Ghazni, but was denied the reward he expected because he was a Shi'ite Muslim.

Epic poem
Illuminated page from a lavish medieval copy of Ferdawsi's *Shahnameh* depicting Jamshid, who ruled Persia wisely for 300 years until he was murdered by his rival Zahhak. Jamshid is derived from a mythological king Yima Xsaeta who features in the *Avesta*.

CLASSICAL GREECE

THE Classical civilization of ancient Greece is acknowledged as one of the most inventive and influential in world history. Greek political, philosophical and scientific ideas, as well as Greek literary, artistic and architectural forms, shaped the development of modern European civilization to an extent rivalled only by the Bible. The Romans, whose republic and empire has held Europe in thrall for centuries, borrowed most of their high culture from the Classical Greeks. Less recognized, however, is the influence that Classical Greek civilization also had on the early development of Islamic civilization throughout the Middle East. The foundations of this brilliant civilization were laid by the small city states which emerged from the 'dark ages' following the collapse of the Mycenaean civilization.

Previous page:
The Parthenon
The Parthenon temple on the fortified Acropolis rock in Athens was sacred to the city's patron deity, Athena, the goddess of wisdom. Completed in 431 BC, the Parthenon survived largely intact until AD 1687 when it was severely damaged during a war between Venice and the Ottoman Turks.

Classical Greek civilization owed little to the Mycenaeans. The Mycenaean past was vividly remembered as a heroic age, but the Greece that emerged from the dark ages was utterly changed. As stability returned to Greece in the ninth and tenth centuries BC, town life began to revive. Most towns grew up around an *acropolis*, a fortified hilltop that served as a refuge for the people of the towns and the surrounding countryside in wartime. Some of these, like Athens and Sparta – the future leaders of Greece – were reoccupied Mycenaean sites, but most of the settlements were laid on new foundations. Every town and city was an independent state or *polis* (from which our word 'politics' comes), ruled by a hereditary king or an oligarchy drawn from the aristocratic warrior class. Compared to the kingdoms of Mycenaean times, the areas controlled by most city states at the end of the dark ages was very small, but in the course of time the more successful built regional power bases for themselves.

TRADE AND LETTERS

The revival of town life was accompanied by an increase in overseas trade and agricultural production, and a rapidly rising population. Greece was indirectly benefiting from the rising power of the Assyrian empire of Mesopotamia and the appetite of its wealthy elite for imported luxuries. The needs of trade led to a revival of writing by around 730 BC, the true end of the dark ages. The Greeks did not revive the Mycenaeans' Linear B script, which was long forgotten. Instead they adapted and improved an alphabet they borrowed from their trading partners and rivals the Phoenicians. While the

Coin
A silver drachma of Athens depicting the city's patron deity, Athena. Many Greek city states began to mint coins in the sixth century BC, a sign of rising prosperity after the dark ages.

Phoenician alphabet only had letters for consonants, the Greeks added separate letters for vowels. This created a flexible writing system that was easy to learn. As a result, literacy became more widespread in Greece than in any previous ancient civilization and was an important factor in its astonishing creativity. One of the first uses that writing was put to was establishing written law codes to insure against arbitrary judgements. The earliest known was compiled for the city of Locri Epizephyri, a Greek colony in Italy, c.650 BC. The Greek legislator Drakon produced a law code for Athens c.620 BC that was so severe it has given us the word 'draconian'. Law codes were inscribed on wooden boards or carved on walls for all to see, an act which presupposes that literacy was widespread. Trade contacts with the eastern Mediterranean brought other influences to Greece, such as coinage, Babylonian mathematics and astronomy, and Egyptian architectural styles. The warriors' feast of the dark ages was replaced by the sophisticated table manners of the east, where diners reclined on couches.

OVERSEAS EXPANSION

The Greek cities coped with their rising populations by founding colonies overseas, in southern Italy and Sicily, southern Gaul, Spain, Libya and around the Black Sea. This movement started during the dark ages, was at its peak in the seventh and eight centuries BC, and came to an end in the sixth century BC, mainly because there were few remaining opportunities for colonization. There was nothing voluntary about migration: in most cities migrants were chosen by lot and faced severe penalties, even execution, if they refused to go. Greek colonies were intended to be replicas of their home communities, but they were independent city states in their own right from the outset. The colonies were important agents for spreading the influence of Greek civilization throughout the Mediterranean world and even to the Celtic lands of central Europe.

In the eighth century BC, the Greeks were still divided into different dialect groups, the Ionians and Dorians being the two largest. The Ionians were descendents of the Achaeans who dominated Greece in Mycenaean times, while the Dorians had migrated into Greece from the north during the dark ages. The Greeks' first loyalty was to their home cities. The city states were fiercely competitive and wars between them were very common. At the same time, however, the Greeks were aware that they shared a common cultural identity. All Greeks used the name *Hellenes* to describe themselves collectively, and they all worshipped the same gods. Shrines of pan-Hellenic importance, such as the Oracle of Apollo at Delphi, were protected by leagues of neighbouring cities called *amphictonies* so that they would not be violated in wartime. The Greeks also celebrated pan-Hellenic religious festivals, the most famous of which were the games held in honour of the supreme god Zeus at Olympia.

Grave pot
A large commemorative *amphora* from Athens, made c.975–950 BC. Such pots were associated with funerals and are frequently found in graves.

Oracle at Delphi
Delphi was sacred to the
Sun-god Apollo, who was
believed to speak directly
to a priestess, called the
Pythia, through a fissure
in the rocks. Greek states
frequently sought the
advice of the Oracle, but
its answers were famous
for their ambiguity.

Truces held before, during and after these festivals allowed people from all over Greece to travel to and from them in safety. All Greeks admired Homer's epics and regarded them as part of their common cultural heritage.

THE AGE OF THE TYRANTS

With their greater resources, the early city states could afford to support larger and better equipped armies than the dark-age chiefdoms. This led to the rise of a new type of citizen soldier, the *hoplite*. The *hoplite* was a heavily armoured spearman who was trained to fight in a tight, disciplined formation called a phalanx. The eighth century BC saw the first use of specialized warships, ram-equipped galleys which dominated naval warfare for the next 1,000 years. These are thought to have been an invention of the Corinthians. Galleys were rowed by free citizens, not by slaves.

Now that armies were recruited more widely from the free citizens, the power of the traditional military classes, the monarchy and the aristocracy, began to ebb away. Disciplined *hoplite* warfare promoted a strong sense of solidarity among the free citizens and the newly wealthy, in particular, resented their exclusion from power on the grounds of lowly birth. Between c.660 BC and c.480 BC, popular leaders known as tyrants, supported by the *hoplite* armies and other free citizens, overthrew the old monarchical and aristocratic order in many Greek city states.

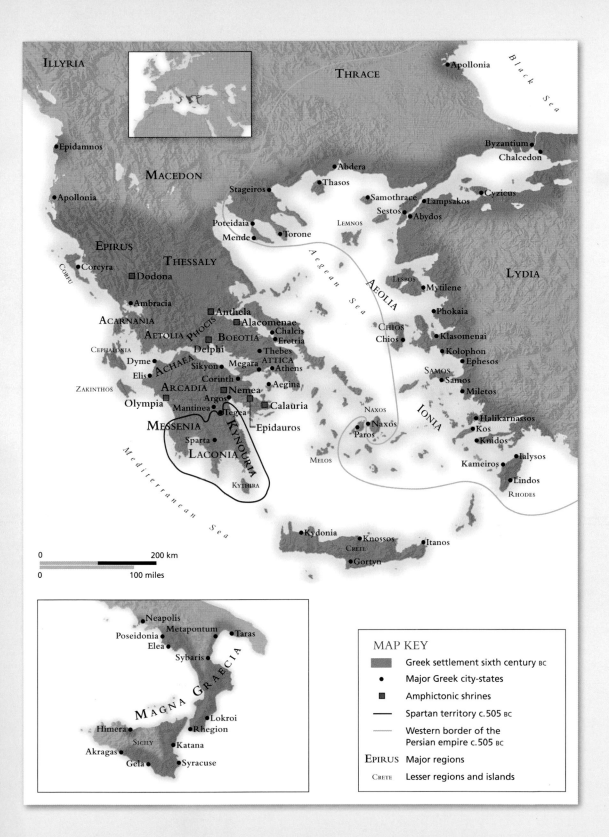

ILLYRIA

THRACE

Black Sea

● Apollonia

● Epidamnos

MACEDON

● Byzantium
Chalcedon ●

● Abdera

Stageiros ●
● Thasos

● Apollonia

● Samothrace
Sestos ●
● Lampsakos
● Cyzicus

Poteidaia ●
Mende ●
● Torone
LEMNOS
● Abydos

EPIRUS

LYDIA

CORFU
● Corcyra
THESSALY
□ Dodona

LESBOS
● Mytilene

AEOLIA
Aegean Sea

● Ambracia

ACARNANIA
□ Anthela
□ Alacomenae

● Phokaia

CHIOS
Chios ●

AETOLIA PHOCIS
□ Chalcis
□ Boeotia
Eretria ●
Delphi

● Klasomenai

● Kolophon

CEPHALONIA
Dyme ●
Sikyon ●
Megara ●
● Thebes
ATTICA ●
Athens ●

SAMOS
● Ephesos
● Samos

Elis ●
ACHAEA
Corinth ●
● Aegina

● Miletus

ZAKINTHOS
ARCADIA
□ Nemea
Argos ●

Olympia ●
Mantinea ●
Tegea ●
□ Calauria

NAXOS
● Halikarnassos
● Kos
● Knidos

MESSENIA
KYNOURIA
Epidauros

IONIA

● Naxos
Paros ●

● Kameiros
● Ialysos

Sparta ●
LACONIA

MELOS

● Lindos
RHODES

Mediterranean Sea

KYTHIRA

0   200 km
0   100 miles

● Kydonia
● Knossos
CRETE
● Itanos
● Gortyn

MAGNA GRAECIA map:

● Neapolis
Poseidonia ●
Metapontum ●
● Taras
Elea ●
● Sybaris

MAGNA GRAECIA

● Lokroi
Himera ●
● Rhegion
SICILY
● Katana
Akragas ●
Gela ●
● Syracuse

MAP KEY

Greek settlement sixth century BC

● Major Greek city-states

■ Amphictonic shrines

— Spartan territory c.505 BC

— Western border of the Persian empire c.505 BC

EPIRUS Major regions

CRETE Lesser regions and islands

In others, the fear of tyranny was by itself enough to force the extension of political rights, at least to the newly rich. By 600 BC, only two important Greek city states, Sparta and Argos, were still ruled by kings.

POPULAR RULERS

The term 'tyrant' (*tyrannos*) originally meant a ruler who had achieved power by his efforts rather than by inheritance. The association of tyranny with oppressive and violent government came later, when the limitations of the institution became apparent. Tyrants were at first genuinely popular rulers, who developed a reputation for freeing poorer citizens from debt slavery, and redistributing land from the rich to the poor. Many tyrants were model rulers. For example, Peisistratos, who ruled Athens from 546 BC to his death in 527 BC, introduced many benevolent reforms, including a property tax to subsidize poorer farmers, and travelling judges to improve the administration of justice throughout the countryside. He provided work for labourers and craftsmen with a programme of public works, including the construction of the first temples on the Acropolis. By establishing a drama festival in honour of the wine god Dionysos, Peisistratos laid the foundations for the great achievements of Athenian playwrights of the fifth century BC. He is also widely credited with establishing the first 'standard' texts of Homer's works. Peisistratos opened the marble quarries on Mount Pentelikon, and these later provided the stone for the building of the Parthenon. He also encouraged the development of the silver mines at Laurion, which contributed so much to Athens' future wealth.

Homer
Admiration of Homer's epics was one of the foundations of a common Greek cultural identity. Homer was the basis of a literary education and many Classical Greeks knew his works by heart.

The weakness of tyranny, however, was its reliance on public support. The reforms enacted by the tyrants encouraged citizens to expect greater and greater participation in political life. When this was not forthcoming, public support waned and dissent increased. The tyrants had no intention of giving away the power they had won and turned to repression to suppress opposition. In most cities, the common citizens and the aristocracy eventually buried their differences and united to overthrow the tyrants. Tyrannies rarely lasted more than two or three generations.

THE RISE OF SPARTA

The most important state to resist tyranny was Sparta, an inland city in Laconia in the southern Peloponnese. The Spartans were the descendants of Dorians who settled in Laconia c.1000 BC. By around 800 BC, the Spartans had conquered all of Laconia. Their fellow Dorians, known as the *perioikoi* ('the dwellers about'), were forced to perform military service for Sparta, but remained free. They were important to the Spartan state as craftsmen, especially as manufacturers of armour and weapons. The descendants of the original Achaean inhabitants of the land became serfs called *helots*. In 735–715 BC, the Spartans conquered the neighbouring region of Messenia. The land was divided equally between all Spartan citizens. The Messenians were allowed to stay on the land, becoming *helots*, and paying half their produce to their Spartan masters.

Spartans liked to consider themselves to be political conservatives because they remained loyal to the institution of monarchy. However, the Spartan monarchy was always a very exceptional one, having two kings and two parallel royal families. Sparta became even more exceptional after the Messenians rebelled against their oppressors in 660 BC. The Messenians outnumbered the Spartans by seven to one and it was only with great difficulty that their rebellion was defeated. The Spartans, left shaken by the rebellion, concluded that their future security could only be assured by maintaining a state of constant combat readiness. To achieve this, Sparta introduced a radical constitution that turned it into a militaristic, *hoplite* state.

According to tradition, the founder of the Spartan constitution was Lykourgos, a semi-legendary character about whom absolutely nothing certain is known. In reality, the constitution was probably not created by a single legislator, but evolved over a number of years. The constitution limited the powers of the monarchy to the right to declare war and lead the Spartan armies. As the philosopher Aristotle later said, the Spartan kingship was in effect 'a hereditary generalship for life'. In other respects, the kings' freedom of action was limited by the council of elders, the citizen assembly (which comprised the whole *hoplite* body), and the five *ephors* or 'supervisors'. The citizen assembly had the right to vote 'yes' or 'no' to all legislation, but not to debate or modify it, and to elect the *ephors*, who enjoyed wide legal powers to hold the kings to account for their actions. All citizens were eligible to become an *ephor*: they served for one year and could not be re-elected.

SPARTAN MILITARISM

Spartan society was totally geared for breeding good soldiers. At the age of seven, boys were taken from their families to begin the *agoge*, an austere, state-organized upbringing aimed towards military training and excellence. Education centred around gymnastics and training for war and involved developing loyalty to the group, increasing an individual's pain tolerance, hunting and stealth, as well as dancing and singing. The ultimate aim of the *agoge* was to mould the individual Spartan into the most efficient and terrifying fighting machine. Bullying was officially condoned and comforts were few, even shoes were forbidden. Meals were deliberately inadequate to encourage boys to use their initiative to find extra rations or even steal them from their fellow students. The boys were also encouraged to fight among themselves to find out who was the dominant leader within the group. Boys who dropped out of the *agoge*, the 'tremblers', lived with the shame for the rest of their lives and could never become a full citizen. In the final stage of the *agoge*, the *krypteia* ('concealment'), the boy hid out in the countryside to prove his manhood by hunting down and murdering a *helot*. At the age of 20, those who completed the *agoge* became full citizens and joined a dining-mess and military training unit called a *syssitia*. Though now allowed to marry, they were expected to live in the *syssitia* until the age of 30, when they were finally able to set up their own households. Even then, however, men were expected to eat daily in the *syssitia*. The common upbringing created a tough, cohesive, disciplined, conformist society, in which a man's birth counted for little. Spartans were proud to describe themselves as *homoioi*, 'the men who are equal'.

TIMELINE

c.900 BC
Revival of town life as Greece emerges from the post-Mycenaean dark ages

776 BC
Earliest recorded Olympian games

c.730 BC
Origins of the Greek alphabet

534 BC
The world's first drama festival founded at Athens

509 BC
Kleisthenes introduces a democratic constitution for Athens

490 BC
The Athenians defeat the Persians at Marathon

480 BC
The Athenian navy defeats the Persian fleet at Salamis

479 BC
A Spartan-led army defeats the Persians at Plataea

457–445 BC
The first Peloponnesian War between Athens and Sparta

448 BC
The Treaty of Kallias ends the Persian Wars

447–432 BC
Construction of the Parthenon temple at Athens

431–404 BC
Sparta defeats Athens in the Second Peloponnesian War

c.387 BC
Plato founds the Academy at Athens for teaching philosophy

338 BC
The Greek city states are conquered by Philip II of Macedon

Olympia, in the western Peloponnese, was a sanctuary dedicated to Zeus and named for the home of the gods on Mount Olympos. The athletic festival which made Olympia famous was first recorded in 776 BC, but it probably originated during the dark ages. The festival was held once every four years until it was abolished by the Christian Roman emperor Theodosius in AD 393 because of its pagan associations. Olympia became wealthy from the offerings of visitors. The gold and ivory statue of Zeus, by the Athenian sculptor Phidias (490–432 BC), which stood in the temple of Zeus, was considered to be one of the Seven Wonders of the World.

The earliest games consisted simply of a 180-metre (200-yd) foot race, but by 632 BC they had expanded to include foot races of different distances, horse racing, chariot racing, wrestling, boxing and the pentathlon (running, jumping, discus, javelin and wrestling). Later, separate events for boys were introduced. Two days before the start of the event, the athletes who had gathered to compete joined a procession to the sanctuary from the nearby city of Elis. The festival lasted for five days, attracting thousands of spectators from all over Greece. The stadium could seat 40,000 people. The festival was an exclusively male event; women were not even permitted to watch. At the end of the festival, the victors went in procession to the temple of Zeus to receive their olive wreaths. Though these were the only prizes given, successful athletes could expect to be treated as heroes by their home cities. The festival closed with the sacrifice of 100 oxen to Zeus and feasting.

Ruins of Olympia
The partially reconstructed ruins of the Philippeon at Olympia, dedicated to the Macedonian leader Philip II, father of Alexander the Great. Other buildings on the site included other temples, treasuries for each of the Greek cities and the stadium.

While the Spartan men turned themselves into a military elite, they were not allowed to take part in manual labour. Instead, all productive activity was left to the *helots* and the *perioikoi*. The *helots* were treated harshly by their Spartan overlords, often being forced to carry out degrading tasks and subjected to frequent ritualistic beatings in order to reinforce their lowly position. There are even records of *helot* massacres, where Spartans would select those *helots* most likely to rebel and kill them to prevent unrest.

SPARTAN ECONOMY AND WOMEN

Sparta deliberately did not use coinage. Instead, iron bars – the stuff of weapons – were the medium of exchange. Trade was unimportant. Because the state had taken over the role of the family, Spartan women enjoyed much greater freedom than other Greek women, who had few rights and led lives confined mainly to the homes of their fathers or husbands. Spartan women could own and inherit property, run businesses and take an active, if informal, role in politics. The women of Sparta even practised gymnastics naked, like the men. This was something that other Greeks found profoundly shocking.

Substitute jars
A painted Attic *krater* (wine jar) from the fifth century BC depicting Helen of Troy and Menelaus, the legendary king of Sparta. Though regarded today as great artworks, painted vases like this were really cheap substitutes for vessels of silver and gold. The red figures represent gold inlay, while the black background represents tarnished silver (ancient Greeks did not polish silver, so as not to wear it away).

THE GREEK HOPLITE

War was an accepted part of everyday life in ancient Greece. All able-bodied male citizens were liable for military service and had to provide their own arms and armour. Greek armies included lightly armed skirmishers and small numbers of cavalry, but most Greek soldiers fought as *hoplites*.

As many Greek city states could not afford to support a standing army, the *hoplites* and the tactics they used provided a ready solution to the near constant warfare between various states. The armour and weapons used were relatively cheap and within the means of the average citizen. The *hoplite* was a foot soldier whose main weapon was a 3-metre (9-ft) long iron-tipped spear. He also carried a short sword for use in close-quarter combat. For protection, the *hoplite* wore a bronze helmet, breastplate and greaves to protect the lower legs. He also carried a large round hardwood shield called a *hoplon* (hence the name 'hoplite').

The tactics employed by the *hoplite* troops were quite simple and could be mastered quickly. Even so, they could still be devastatingly effective. *Hoplites* trained to fight as part of a phalanx, a tight linear formation, about eight ranks deep, which bristled with spears and presented a formidable wall of shields against frontal attack. There was no place in the phalanx for individual heroics: breaking ranks threatened the security of everybody and such exhibitionism was frowned upon. Family and friends were always grouped together to give the men a strong incentive to support one another.

Corinthian helmet
Greek *hoplites* used several different styles of helmet. The Corinthian, which offered a good compromise between protection and visibility, was the most popular.

The main object in battle was to break the enemy phalanx. Phalanxes advanced at a run and, when they met, the impact could be so great that spears shattered and the front ranks on both sides were thrown to the ground. After that, the battle became a pushing match as each phalanx used its collective muscle to try to force the other phalanx back, with orders being given to push different parts of the phalanx forwards by a set number of steps or even half-steps. The aim of this was to cause fear and panic in the ranks of the opposing phalanx as they tried to counter any such moves. Only the first two ranks of each phalanx were in direct weapons contact with the enemy; the rear ranks were there to add weight to the formation and to prevent the men at the front trying to run away if they lost their nerve. If a phalanx did collapse, casualties could be very heavy as the victors aimed their spears at the exposed backs of their fleeing enemies.

Against poorly armoured or undisciplined soldiers, the phalanx was terrifyingly effective. Until the rise of the Roman legionary army in the third century BC, Greek *hoplites* were widely regarded as the finest soldiers in the Mediterranean world and were often employed as mercenaries by the Persians and Egyptians. Conflict with the Persians even led to the development of a lightly armoured *hoplite*, known as the *ekdromoi*, who was more mobile and could run out from the phalanx to engage Persian skirmish troops.

***Hoplite* combat**
Hoplites got their name from their large, round hardwood shields, called *hoplons*, shown well in this frieze from the Parthenon.

The most radical experiment in government was in Athens, where a form of direct democracy was introduced that gave every freeborn Athenian man the right to vote in the citizen assembly. The Athenians, with some justification, liked to think of themselves as the polar opposites of the Spartans: creative, intellectual individualists who also knew how to have a good time. Athens was a different sort of city from Sparta. While Sparta looked just like a big unplanned village, Athens, with its many impressive public buildings, looked like an important city. While Sparta lay inland and turned its back on international trade and colonization, Athens had founded dozens of colonies and traded with the whole Mediterranean world. Indeed, Athens relied on grain imported from the Black Sea region to feed its people. Because of this, Athens paid the same attention to its navy that Sparta did to its army. Athenians were Ionians and regarded Dorians, like the Spartans, as not quite as truly Greek as themselves.

POLITICAL LIFE

Athens suffered the same tensions between the aristocracy and the ordinary citizens as other Greek cities. Athens' monarchy was abolished in the early seventh century BC, and its religious, military and judicial powers were spread over nine magistrates called *archons*. When they left office, *archons* became lifetime members of the council of elders, called the *Areopagus*, after a hill below the Acropolis where it met. *Archons* were elected annually, but only the hereditary aristocracy was entitled to vote. The aristocracy's first response to popular demands to extend voting rights was repression, exemplified in Drakon's harsh law code. Fearing that the citizens might support a tyrant, the aristocracy gave the *archon* Solon (c.639–c.559 BC) absolute powers to draw up a new constitution in 594–593 BC.

Solon believed that social justice was essential to *eunomia*, a well-ordered society. He abolished debt slavery, cancelled debts, and ended the aristocratic monopoly of power by making wealth rather than birth the qualification for public office. Solon divided the population into four classes whose political rights were graduated according to their wealth. The richest class was the *penta kosiome dimnoi*, 'the 500-measure men', whose

Greek galley
A painted Greek cup showing a type of small galley known as a *penteconter*. Propelled by a single square sail and about 25 oarsmen on each side, a *penteconter* could reach speeds of up to 9 knots (10 mph).

> 'One might reasonably suppose that Athens lies at the centre of Greece, or, for that matter, the whole of the inhabited world.'

Xenophon c.355 BC

income exceeded 500 measures of corn a year. Next were the *hippeis*, men who were rich enough to equip themselves as cavalry. The third class were the *zeugites*, the *hoplite* class, which was mainly made of small farmers who lived in Attica (the territory of Athens). The fourth, and poorest and largest, class were the *thetes*, who were landless labourers and urban craftsmen. Men of this class fought as lightly armed skirmishers and, as Athens developed as a naval power, as oarsmen in the galleys. *Archons* could only be elected from the two richest classes. To balance the aristocracy's control of the *Areopagus*, Solon introduced a popular legislative assembly of 400 members, 100 of which were elected by each of Athens' four traditional tribes.

Solon's constitution went too far for the aristocracy and not far enough for most citizens and, when his term of office ended, he went into exile to escape the controversy he had caused. In the long term, Solon's constitution laid the foundation for Athens' most important political legacy to the world, the introduction of democracy, but its immediate impact was slight. The aristocracy refused any further concessions and in 546 BC the tyrant Peisistratos seized power. Peisistratos' tyranny survived until 510 BC, when his son Hippias was overthrown by a Spartan invasion. The Spartan invasion was engineered by Kleisthenes (c.570–c.508 BC), an Athenian aristocrat exiled by Peisistratos. Kleisthenes outmanoeuvred an aristocratic attempt to reverse the reforms of Solon and, with popular support introduced a democratic constitution.

THE RULE OF KLEISTHENES

Kleisthenes' first act was to abolish the four traditional tribes. Each tribe had its own territory and the aristocracy had been able to exploit inter-tribal rivalries to block reforms. Kleisthenes divided Attica into three regions, the interior, the coast and the city. The number of tribes was increased to ten, and each was given a division of land, called a *trittye* ('third'), in each of the three regions. By mixing together people from different areas, Kleisthenes hoped to promote the growth of a more cohesive Athenian identity. The basic unit of local government within the *trittye* was the *deme* ('village' and by extension the people who lived there, hence 'democracy', rule of the people). The new tribes became the basis of military organization. The men of each tribe formed a separate regiment under an elected commander. Each tribe elected 50 representatives to an enlarged legislative assembly of 500, which was divided into 10 committees to oversee the day-to-day business of the state. The citizen assembly met monthly on the Pnyx hill. Every major decision of state, including declarations of war, was subject to majority voting. All citizens over 30 were eligible to stand for office. Another of Kleisthenes' reforms was to allow the citizens to vote to exile over-ambitious politicians as a safeguard against any tyrannical pretensions. The system was known as ostracism

Ostrakas
As a safeguard against tyranny, Athenians could vote to exile any politician they thought was getting too powerful. Citizens voted by scratching the name of the politician they wished to see exiled on a potsherd or *ostraka*, from which the custom got its name, 'ostracism'. The *ostraka* at the top bears the name Pericles, while the other two *ostraka* below it mention Themistocles.

> 'Darius took a bow, set an arrow on the string, and shot it up into the air crying "Grant, O God, that I may punish the Athenians".'

Herodotus, *The Histories* c.440 BC

from the potsherds (*ostraka*) used to record the votes. The last bastion of entrenched aristocratic influence, the *Areopagus*, was demoted to a court for hearing cases of murder and sacrilege in 461 BC.

Democracy remains as potent an idea today as it was in sixth-century Athens. However, no Athenian would regard any modern democracy as a true democracy. No modern state has direct citizen rule like ancient Athens. Modern citizens 'rule' indirectly through elected representatives. Athenian democracy was, however, more narrowly based than any modern democracy because only freeborn males over 20 were eligible to vote. This amounted to only about 30,000 of Athens' total population of 120,000–180,000. Citizenship was restricted to free men who had been born in Athens, so immigrants were excluded, as were all women and slaves. An Athenian man would not have seen this as being at all undemocratic. Greek men believed that women were not rational beings and were therefore incapable of voting wisely, while slaves were just property.

THE PERSIAN WARS

The Greek city states faced their greatest challenge at the beginning of the fifth century BC. In 546 BC, the Persian empire had conquered the Ionian Greek city states on the coast of Anatolia. In 513 BC, the Persians crossed into Europe and conquered Thrace (roughly modern Bulgaria), bringing their empire to the northern borders of Greece. The Greeks naturally wondered where Persian ambitions would take them next. As fellow Ionians, the Athenians sympathized with the Ionians living under Persian rule. When they rebelled in 499 BC, Athens and nearby Eretria sent help. After the rebellion was crushed, the Persian king Darius II sent envoys to the mainland Greek cities to demand offerings of earth and water as tokens of their submission. Many complied, but the Athenians and Spartans executed the envoys, a sacrilegious act, which they knew made war inevitable. When the Persian envoys demanded earth and water of the Spartans, the Spartans threw them down a well, telling them that they would find plenty of both at the bottom. In late summer 490 BC, a Persian fleet of 300 ships carrying around 20,000 men landed at Marathon, 26 miles (42 km) north of Athens. After a stand off of a few days, a phalanx of 9,000 Athenian *hoplites* and 1,000 allies from Plataea charged the Persians with levelled spears. Few of the lightly armed Persians had the courage to stand against the mass of spears and armour that fell upon them. They fled to their ships, suffering 6,400 killed against the Athenians' 192.

THE BIRTH OF HISTORY

Classical Greece saw the birth of recognizably modern history writing. Most ancient civilizations recorded history in the form of annals which simply listed events with no attempt to explain or analyze them. The first historian to go further was Herodotus of Halicarnassus (c.484–420 BC) who wrote a monumental narrative history of the Persian wars. Herodotus described his work as *istoriai*, literally meaning 'inquiries', from which we get our word 'history'. Herodotus is often known as 'the father of history', but his younger contemporary, the Athenian Thucydides (c.460–395 BC) has an even better claim to the title. While Herodotus often invoked supernatural explanations for events, in his *History of the Peloponnesian War* between Athens and Sparta, Thucydides drew his conclusions only from eyewitness and written accounts and an understanding of human psychology and motives.

GREEK ARCHITECTURE

Greek architects of the Classical period used three styles or 'orders' of architecture. The Doric order, with sturdy columns and simple undecorated capitals, developed from earlier wooden architecture in the seventh century BC. This order was most common in mainland Greece and in Greek colonies in Italy and Sicily. The Ionic order developed in Ionia in the mid-sixth century BC. Its columns were taller and more slender than the Doric and its capitals were decorated with carved *volutes* (spirals). The Corinthian order developed from the Ionic in the fifth century BC. According to legend the order's ornate capitals were inspired by acanthus leaves growing from a basket set on top of a grave column. Sculptural friezes formed an important decorative element on many Greek temples.

Doric order

Ionic order

Corinthian order

In 480 BC, Darius' successor Xerxes raised an enormous army – reputed to be 500,000 strong – to deal with the Greeks once and for all. Xerxes' army crossed from Anatolia into Europe over the Dardanelles and marched through Thrace and Macedon to invade Greece from the north. Faced with this threat, the Greeks managed to bury their differences and form a grand alliance. The Greek army tried to block the Persian advance at the narrow pass of Thermopylai. When the Persians found a route through the mountains to outflank the Greeks, the Spartan king Leonidas, with 300 Spartan *hoplites* and 1,400 allies, fought to the death to buy time for the rest of the army to escape. Greek forces withdrew to the narrow Isthmus of Corinth, which was the only land access to the Peloponnese. The Peloponnese was still vulnerable to invasion from the sea, but in September the Athenian navy destroyed the Persian fleet at the battle of

Salamis. The following summer (479 BC) the Spartans led a 48,000-strong Greek army north to Plataea, where they destroyed the much larger Persian army, decisively ending the Persian threat to Greece. Sparta and most other Greek states soon withdrew from the war against Persia, but the Athenians continued to fight for the freedom of the Ionian cities. Persia finally recognized the independence of these cities by signing the Treaty of Kallias in 448 BC.

The Persian War was one of the most important in world history. Had Greece been conquered by Persia, it is likely that its culture would have been stifled, with all the consequences that would have followed for the development of European civilization. In retrospect, the war has also been seen as a defining moment in the development of the idea of a cultural opposition between 'the West', usually standing for freedom, and 'the East', standing for despotism. It is a distinction that Sparta's *helots* would probably not have appreciated.

STRAINED RELATIONS

The Greek unity inspired by the Persian threat was only temporary, and traditional rivalries were soon revived. Sparta considered itself the natural leader of Greece, but it now had a serious rival in Athens, whose fleet had played such an important part in Persia's defeat. Athens gained prestige by championing the freedom of the Ionian cities. To pursue its war aims, Athens enrolled its Ionian allies in the Delian League, so called because its treasury was on the sacred Aegean island of Delos. Through the league, which also became a powerful commercial organization, the Athenians dominated the Aegean Sea. Athens vigorously exported democracy to other city states. With its large population of oppressed *helots*, Sparta feared democracy. By 461 BC, the two states were openly hostile.

Apollo's island
Sculpted lions guarded the sacred way to the temple of the Sun-god Apollo on Delos. Because of the island's religious importance, Delos was the meeting place of the Athenian dominated Delian League and the site of its treasury.

The most influential Athenian politician at this time was Pericles (c.495–429 BC), a brilliant orator and passionate supporter of democracy. Pericles had imperial ambitions for Athens. He tightened Athenian control over the Delian League, moving its treasury to Athens in 454 BC. Through a great programme of public works, Pericles rebuilt Athens in a consciously imperial style. His finest monument is the Parthenon, the temple of Athena on the Acropolis, which displays the restraint and proportion of Classical Greek architecture at its best. The elegant naturalism of Phidias' sculptural friezes on the Parthenon are recognized as one of the greatest achievements of Classical Greek art. The pure white of the sculptures as they survive today is the result of weathering and misguided cleaning: they were, like all Classical Greek statues, originally brightly painted.

THE PELOPONNESIAN WAR

The hostility between Athens and Sparta led to the outbreak of the indecisive First Peloponnesian War in 457 BC. The war was ended by the Thirty Years' Peace in 445 BC by which both states recognized each other's spheres of influence in the Peloponnese and the Aegean. The peace did not last. When the Second Peloponnesian War broke out between Athens and Sparta in 431 BC, most of Greece was forced to take sides. The First Peloponnesian War had taught Pericles that Athens did not have the manpower to field a large army and man a large fleet at the same time. While the war was still being fought he had begun to build a fortified corridor, the 'Long Walls', linking the city to its port at Pireaus.

Pericles
Roman copy of a bronze bust if Pericles made by the Athenian sculptor Kresilas in c.440–430 BC. Pericles masterminded Athens' strategy in the Peloponnesian Wars with Sparta.

So long as Athens maintained control of the sea, the Spartans' superior army was powerless to blockade it into surrender. When the second war broke out, Pericles brought the entire population within the city walls and harnessed Athens' naval supremacy to ship in supplies from overseas and to raid Sparta and its allies from the sea.

The Athenian war effort suffered an early blow when Pericles died in 429 BC. The war dragged on indecisively for years until, in 416 BC, Athens launched an attack on Syracuse in an attempt to deprive Sparta of grain supplies from Sicily. The expedition ended in disaster in 414 BC with the loss of 45,000 men. Worse was to come in 412 BC, when Persia agreed to pay for the construction of a Spartan fleet in return for a free hand to reconquer Ionia. The Spartans destroyed the Athenian navy at the battle of Aegospotami in 405 BC: Athens surrendered in 404 BC and disbanded the Delian League. Though the war broke the power of Athens, it did not leave Sparta strong enough to impose unity on Greece. Persian support had been crucial to Sparta's victory, and that was very quickly withdrawn and transferred to Sparta's traditional rivals. The war showed that no Greek city state could by itself achieve permanent dominance over the others.

ATHENS AND CLASSICAL GREEK CIVILIZATION

Despite the constant wars, Greek civilization flourished during the fifth century BC. Nowhere was this more so than at Athens, whose status as the leading cultural centre of Greece was unchallenged. Athens did not have a monopoly on creativity, but it was only

Theatre
The fourth century BC theatre at Delphi could accommodate 5,000 spectators on its 35 rows of seats. All Greek theatres were built to a similar design, which created excellent acoustics.

there that all the elements of Classical Greek civilization flourished together. Pericles was not exaggerating when he boasted that Athens was the 'school of Greece'. Talent attracts talent, and artists, craftsmen and scholars flocked to Athens. 'Cultural tourists' were also attracted to the city by the Dionysian drama festival, and the athletic, musical and poetic competitions of the Panathenaic festival, held in honour of Athena, the city's patron goddess.

Athens' greatest contribution to Greek, and western, civilization was the invention of drama. Drama developed from choral songs about the life and death of Dionysos. In the sixth century BC, the poet Thespis (from whose name the word 'thespian' is derived) introduced a new type of performance where he impersonated a single character and engaged in dialogue with a chorus of singers and dancers. Competitors in the Dionysian drama festival, founded in 534 BC, were originally required to produce four plays: a trilogy of tragic plays followed by a burlesque satyr play (satyrs were mythological creatures, half man, half goat, who featured in the cult of Dionysos). In the fifth century BC, the satyr plays developed into a separate genre, comedy. Only one complete trilogy of tragic plays has survived, the *Oresteia* by Aeschylus (c.525–456 BC). Aeschylus introduced a second character, allowing greater development of conflicts of character. The number of characters gradually increased and the chorus became less important. Staging became more elaborate after the first theatres were built in the fifth century BC. A side-effect of this was the development of perspective painting, first used by Athenian stage painters to create optical illusions.

Aristotle
Aristotle was a key figure in the development of scientific method, writing on a wide variety of subjects from astronomy to zoology.

GREEK PHILOSOPHY

The introduction of democracy turned Athens into a major centre for studying and teaching philosophy. Democracy made skill in public speaking and debate the key to a successful political career, so demand for education soared. Initially, it was met by the sophists, itinerant teachers who travelled from city to city teaching rhetoric, logic, astronomy, mathematics and music. Sophists were relativists: they did not believe in objective truth and many were sceptical about the existence of the gods. The most famous sophist, Protagoras of Abdera (c.490–420 BC), declared that 'man is the measure of all things'. Their relativism allowed sophists to argue a case from more than one viewpoint. This led many to see them as intellectual tricksters and is why, today, sophistry is associated with clever but dishonest argument.

The first important Athenian-born philosopher was Socrates (469–399 BC). Pre-Socratic Greek philosophers were mainly interested in metaphysical questions about the nature of the universe. Socrates was interested in ethics. Socrates believed that there were objective concepts, such as 'the good', 'bravery' or 'justice', and that these could be understood by reason. Socrates made many enemies by his ability to make those arguing with him contradict themselves through the use of rational cross-questioning. He was made one of the scapegoats for Athens' defeat in the Peloponnesian War and sentenced to death for impiety and corrupting the youth of Athens.

Socrates' ideas were developed by his pupil Plato (c.429–347 BC), also an Athenian, who sought to establish an absolute basis for knowledge with his doctrine of 'Forms' in which concepts such as 'beauty' had a real existence as eternal entities. Plato presented his thought in an accessible way using a series of dramatic dialogues in which the discourse was placed in the mouths of characters, chief among whom was his hero

THE GODS OF OLYMPOS

The Greeks worshipped dozens of gods, the most important of whom were the 12 who were believed to live on Mount Olympos in northeast Greece. The king and queen of the gods were the stern sky-god Zeus and his consort Hera, the goddess of women and marriage. The other gods of the Olympian pantheon included Aphrodite, the goddess of love; Hermes, the messenger of the gods who guided souls to the underworld; Athena, the goddess of wisdom, the corn goddess Demeter; Poseidon, the sea god; Apollo, the Sun god; Artemis, the Moon goddess; Ares, the war god; Hephaestus, the god of fire, volcanoes and blacksmiths; and Hestia, the goddess of the hearth. Also of universal importance were the wine-god Dionysos and Hades, the ruler of the underworld. There were wide variations in cultic practices in Greece and every city had a special relationship with its own particular patron deity, for example Athens with Athena, and Corinth with Poseidon. The gods behaved like powerful humans, with human virtues and vices. They interacted directly with humans and even had children by them. Greek religion had no systematic theology and no consistent moral teaching: the Greeks understood that the source of law was human, not divine.

The Greeks believed in an afterlife for the soul in the underworld. The underworld was originally conceived of as a uniformly gloomy and cheerless place. Later, it came to be believed that the souls of mortals were judged after death, the good going to blissful Elysium and the wicked to suffer in hellish Tartarus. Those who had done neither great good nor great evil went to the Asphodel Meadows, a rather bland place where souls mechanically performed a ghostly version of their everyday lives on Earth. Specially favoured humans, like the hero Heracles (Hercules), could be rewarded by the gods with deification.

Below: Heracles
This painted vase shows the hero Heracles killing the Lernaean Hydra, a many-headed serpent-like monster that was terrorizing local villagers.

Socrates. In his most famous work, the *Republic*, Plato set out his vision of the ideal state ruled by an intellectual elite of 'philosopher kings' governing in accordance with the principles of reason. In 388 BC, Plato founded his own school, the Academy, which ensured that Athens continued to be a major centre for the study of philosophy well into the Christian era.

Plato's ideas were challenged by his pupil Aristotle (384–322 BC). Aristotle was born in Stageira in northern Greece. He came to Athens aged 18 to study at the Academy and stayed on to teach. In 343 BC, he went to Macedon as tutor to the young Alexander the Great. On his return to Athens in 335 BC, he founded the Lyceum, which taught a wider curriculum than the Academy. Aristotle believed that observation and experience of the physical world were essential to rational enquiry. As well as exploring ethical issues, Aristotle wrote extensively on the sciences of astronomy, biology, chemistry, physics and zoology. Aristotle's greatest achievement was his system of logic, which has still not been superseded. It is important not to be too dazzled by the achievements of the ancient Greek philosophers. Their influence at the time was confined to a small intellectual elite and their beliefs were ridiculed by comic playwrights such as Aristophanes (c.450–385 BC), who coined the expression 'cloud cuckoo land' as a metaphor for impractical Utopianism.

GREEK SCIENCE

Building on the achievements of the Mesopotamians and Egyptians, the Greeks developed the most sophisticated science and mathematics of the ancient world. The founders of the Greek scientific tradition were the mathematicians Thales of Miletos (c.624–546 BC), and Pythagoras of Samos (c.582–507), the first person known to have described himself as a philosopher ('lover of wisdom'). Pythagoras taught that numbers were the key to understanding ultimate reality. This gave Greek mathematics a religious dimension which sometimes hindered scientific understanding, especially in astronomy, where the Sun, Moon, planets and stars were believed to move in 'perfect' circles around the Earth. This led to increasingly desperate attempts to make their observed movements fit the theory. Greek science remained an almost entirely theoretical discipline, never developing a tradition of practical experimentation.

THE DECLINE OF THE CITY STATES

The interminable wars between the city states dragged on for another 60 years after the Peloponnesian War. By the middle of the fourth century BC, the city states were exhausted by warfare and more divided than ever. The main reason no Greek city state was able to achieve what Rome achieved in Italy was their attitude to citizenship. In most Greek cities, citizenship was a jealously guarded hereditary privilege. Because of emigration, casualties in war, disenfranchisement and the natural extinction of family lines, the number of citizens in the city states gradually declined. As citizenship was the basis of military service, this had serious consequences. At the time of the Persian War, Sparta could raise over 8,000 citizen *hoplites*; after the battle of Leuktra (371 BC) it could raise a mere 800. This contrasts with the practice of the Roman republic, which was successful in increasing the number of its citizens and, therefore, the manpower eligible for military service. In Rome, an immigrant or even a freed slave could become a citizen and defeated enemies became loyal allies by granting them citizenship. In the Greek world, defeated enemies simply waited for the opportunity to take their revenge.

In the end, unity was imposed from the outside, by Philip II (ruled 356–336 BC), the king of Macedon. The Macedonians were a mixture of Greeks, Thracians and Illyrians, and were thought to be rather barbaric by the Greeks. In 352 BC, Philip began a conquest of Greece. The age of the city states ended in 338 BC when Philip destroyed the armies of Athens and Thebes at the battle of Chaironeia. To unite the Greeks behind him, Philip announced a war against Persia. Philip was murdered in 336 BC before he could launch the campaign, but his son Alexander (ruled 336–323 BC) went on to conquer the Persian empire in less than ten years. The Greeks had lost their freedom, but Alexander's empire provided them with the opportunity to spread the influence of their civilization across the Middle East into Central Asia and northern India.

ROMAN REPUBLIC

ROME was the market town that took over the known world. Its rise was a result of its representative political institutions, military might and a genius for assimilating conquered enemies and turning them into loyal Roman citizens. Between 396 BC and 270 BC, the Romans conquered their Italian neighbours. Then, in the 200 years that followed, the Romans destroyed their arch-rival, the North African city of Carthage, in an epic struggle before bringing the whole Mediterranean world under their command. However, Rome's rise came at a cost. Rome's republican system of government evolved to govern a city state and proved ill suited to ruling an empire. Corruption, social unrest, civil war and dictatorship destroyed the Roman republic and led to its replacement by the absolute rule of emperors.

According to legend, the Romans traced their origins back to the Trojan prince Aeneas, who escaped the sack of Troy with a band of followers. After many adventures, Aeneas reached Italy. Settling in Latium, he married a local princess called Lavinia and founded a dynasty. Two of Aeneas' illegitimate descendents, the twin boys Romulus and Remus, were abandoned on the banks of the Tiber river. A she-wolf saved the brothers' lives by suckling them and they were later rescued and brought up by shepherds. The brothers later decided to found a city on the spot where they had been abandoned, but they could not agree which of them should become its king. Romulus killed Remus and named the city Rome after himself. The Romans believed that these events took place in 753 BC, the 'year one' of their dating system.

A VIOLENT START

Previous page:
Battle arena
One of the greatest works of Roman engineering, the Colosseum was built in AD 70–72 to hold gladiatorial contests and other public spectacles. Gladiatorial contests began as part of funeral rites around 310 BC and quickly became a popular spectator sport. Putting on free gladiator shows was an easy way for ambitious politicians to win public support in elections for office.

Rome soon found itself at war with the neighbouring Sabines. The Romans were short of marriageable women, so Romulus invited the Sabines to a feast, where the Roman men kidnapped the Sabine women. The war that inevitably followed was stopped by the intervention of the Sabine women, who flung themselves between the combatants, and a compromise was worked out that placed Rome under the joint rule of Romulus and the Sabine king Titus Tatius. Modern historians do not give much credence to this story, but it contains important truths about the way the Romans came to see themselves. The Romans of historical times continually assimilated new peoples and cultures. They were proud to be a mixture of peoples and races and saw no shame in deriving much of their culture from others. By celebrating their mixed origins in their foundation myth, the Romans showed that they recognized this as one of their greatest strengths.

The real origins of Rome go back to the foundation in the tenth century BC of several small farming communities on the low hills surrounding the marsh that would one day be the site of the Roman Forum. In the course of the eighth and seventh centuries BC, these settlements grew and amalgamated to form a small town. It is impossible to say at what point the inhabitants of Rome developed a clear sense of themselves as a distinct people. The Romans were in origin Latins, one of several groups of Italic peoples, including the Veneti, Umbrians, Apulians, Sabines, Samnites, Lucanians and Bruttians, who migrated into Italy around 1000 BC and settled mainly in the south and centre of the peninsula. The Latins settled in the region known after them as Latium (modern Lazio). The Latins shared a common language (Latin), religious beliefs and festivals, and a common myth that they were all descendents of Latinus, the father-in-law of Aeneas. Although they lived in small independent towns and cities, the Latins had a close sense of kinship and they extended common rights of residence and trade to one another.

The Italics were only one of a diverse mixture of ethnic groups who inhabited Italy before it was conquered by the Romans. Italy's most long established inhabitants were the Ligurians and Etruscans in Liguria and Tuscany; the Sicani and Siculi, who lived in Sicily; and the Shardana, who lived in Sardinia. These peoples, who all spoke languages which were unrelated to any modern European languages, are thought to have been descendants of the earliest human inhabitants of Italy who arrived during the Ice Age.

Founding fathers
This sculpture, known as the Capitoline Wolf, shows the twins Romulus and Remus suckling from a she-wolf. The same scene was commonly shown on coins and Roman writers refer to similar sculptures being displayed in Rome. Thought to have been made by an Etruscan craftsman in the fifth century BC, recent research has shown it to be a medieval forgery.

At around the same time that the Italics were spreading south, the Messapians, distant relatives of today's Albanians, crossed the Adriatic Sea from the Balkans and settled the 'heel' of Italy. A century or so later, Phoenician merchants founded trading colonies in western Sicily and Sardinia. They were soon followed by Greeks, who founded colonies in eastern Sicily and around the 'toe' of Italy. A last piece was added to this complex mosaic of peoples in the late fifth century BC, when Celtic tribes called Gauls crossed the Alps from Germany and settled the Po river valley, which became known as Cisalpine Gaul. By the first century BC, the descendants of all of these peoples would have come to regard themselves as Romans.

THE KINGS OF ROME

The first historical king of Rome was Numa Pompilius (ruled c.715–673 BC), who was traditionally regarded as a peaceful ruler. Numa was, in truth, not much more than a village chief whose kingdom could have been crossed in a leisurely afternoon's walk. Numa's successors Tullus Hostilius (ruled c.673–642 BC) and Ancus Marcius (ruled c.642–617 BC) were more aggressive and they extended Roman territory to the sea at Ostia and southwest into the hills of Latium. Rome first began to look like a place of some importance during the reign of Tarquin I (ruled c.616–579 BC). He oversaw the draining of the Forum, then a marsh, and laid it out as a public square

Heart of the city
Originally a marsh, the Roman Forum was drained and laid out as a public square by king Tarquin I (ruled c.616–579 BC). The Forum was the political, religious and commercial centre of Rome, surrounded by shops, temples, palaces and the Senate House.

with shops and public buildings. It was probably also in Tarquin's reign that the first bridge was built over the Tiber river. Rome began to benefit from its central location in Italy and, as the lowest crossing place on the Tiber, it became a natural crossroads. Rome was close enough to the sea to take part in maritime trade, but not so close that it was vulnerable to pirate raids. By the reign of Servius Tullius (ruled c.578–535 BC), Rome had become a flourishing commercial centre with a population of 20,000–40,000. Though not as large as some of the Greek cities in the south of Italy, Rome was larger than any Etruscan or Latin city, and it dominated Latium. Rome's temple of Jupiter Capitolinus was, at 64 metres (210 ft) long, 55 metres (180 ft) wide and 40 metres (130 ft) tall, one of the largest in the Mediterranean world.

ROMAN CITIZENSHIP

Servius altered the basis of Roman citizenship by making residence rather than birth the basis of membership, thereby opening citizenship to immigrants. It was even possible for a freed slave to become a citizen. This was a truly radical measure: in most Mediterranean city states, citizenship was a jealously guarded privilege, definitely not to be shared with outsiders. Servius created a popular assembly, known as the *comitia centuriata*. This placed the citizens in voting units called centuries and divided them into classes according to the amount of property they owned and the weapons and armour they could afford.

KINGS OF ROME

According to tradition, Rome was ruled by seven kings before it became a republic.

Romulus (legendary)
753–c.715 BC

Numa Pompilius (elected by the Senate)
c.715–673 BC

Tullus Hostilius (elected by the Senate)
c.673–642 BC

Ancus Marcius (grandson of Numa Pompilius) **c.642–617** BC

Tarquin I (elected by the Senate)
c.616–579 BC

Servius Tullius (son-in-law of Tarquin I)
c.578–535 BC

Tarquin II 'the Proud' (son of Tarquin I)
c.535–509 BC

THE ETRUSCANS

The founders of western Europe's first civilization, the Etruscans were the dominant people of pre-Roman Italy. Yet, despite this, they remain one of history's mysterious peoples. Most of what we know of Etruscan history was written by unsympathetic Roman and Greek authors. Their own literature, which was extensive, has all been lost, and their unique language, preserved only in short inscriptions, has never been deciphered.

The Etruscans' homeland, Etruria (roughly modern Tuscany) had the benefits of fertile soils and abundant supplies of copper and iron ores, which they exploited skilfully. The Etruscans excelled in bronze casting and produced iron on an industrial scale. Good natural harbours encouraged the Etruscans to engage in maritime trade around the western Mediterranean, exporting iron, olive oil and wine. Etruscan architects and engineers pioneered the use of the arch, which was used on a large scale in Roman architecture. Many Etruscan bridges and city walls still stand.

The Etruscan civilization flourished between c.900 BC and 400 BC. In the sixth century BC, the Etruscans founded colonies in the Po river valley and along the coast of Campania: Pompeii was originally an Etruscan city. Each Etruscan city was an independent state with its own king, but they formed a loose confederation known as the

Etruscan League. The Etruscans regarded the Greek colonies in southern Italy as a threat to their commercial interests. Despite occasional hostilities, this did not prevent the Etruscans taking a keen interest in Greek culture. By the sixth century BC, Etruscan art, writing and religion had become very Hellenized.

Most of what we know about the Etruscans' everyday lives comes from the tombs of the aristocracy. These were cut directly from the bedrock and were richly furnished and decorated with lively wall paintings of feasting, dancing and music-making, and with portraits of the deceased. Each tomb held several generations of the same family. Living relatives visited the tombs regularly to hold ritual feasts in honour of the dead.

The Etruscans greatly influenced early Rome and even provided one of their kings, Tarquin I. The Romans derived their alphabet, now the world's most widely used, from the Etruscan alphabet.

Etruscan tombs
Rock-cut tombs in the Etruscan necropolis at Populonia, Tuscany. Populonia flourished during Etruscan times as a major iron smelting centre, exploiting ores mined on the nearby island of Elba.

The assembly became the basis of a citizen army of 6,000 *hoplite*-style infantry and 600 cavalry. Servius further increased the citizen body, and, therefore, the number of potential soldiers, by granting citizenship to the conquered Latins of the surrounding countryside. So began the policy of conquest and assimilation that characterized Rome's rise to empire.

Servius was killed in a coup led by Tarquin I's grandson Tarquin II (ruled 535–509 BC). Known as Tarquin the Proud, he was to be the last king of Rome. Tarquin antagonized the Roman aristocracy by refusing to consult the Senate, the assembly of leading citizens which was appointed to advise the king. According to the historian Livy (59 BC–AD 17), who recorded Rome's early historical traditions, a group of aristocrats overthrew the monarchy after Tarquin's son Sextus raped Lucretia, the daughter of a distinguished nobleman.

THE FOUNDATION OF THE ROMAN REPUBLIC

For later Romans, the overthrow of the monarchy and the foundation of the republic was the decisive moment in their history, marking the beginning of their rise to greatness. It was traditionally presented as liberation from tyranny, but in reality it was a purely aristocratic revolution that brought no benefits to the common people of Rome. The leadership of Rome now passed to the male heads of the exclusive group of patrician families who claimed to be descended from the first senators supposedly appointed by Romulus. The patricians were determined not to lose the monopoly of power they now enjoyed as a class. To prevent any one individual gaining sole control of the state, they established a collegiate magistracy in which two men, the consuls, shared both military and civil powers. So that neither could emerge as a tyrant, each consul had the right to veto the decisions of the other. This institution was unique in the ancient world.

The *comitia centuriata* elected the consuls annually. Consuls could not stand for re-election to a second consecutive term in office, a measure aimed at preventing them from consolidating a hold on power. Although the popular assembly had the right to vote on policy, debating and deciding policy was the exclusive preserve of the Senate. This body was dominated by the patricians, whose membership was hereditary. Voting in the *comitia centuriata* was by class and was effectively rigged to ensure that the wealthier classes could always outvote the numerically much larger poorer classes. Over the next century, new elective magistracies were introduced to cope with the complexities of governing a city that was expanding rapidly. *Quaestors* were elected to oversee the city's finances, and censors to maintain the register of citizens. In times of national emergency, such as an invasion, the consuls were given the power to appoint a dictator,. This individual could wield absolute control, but only for a period of six months. The office of dictator proved dangerously attractive to ambitious and unprincipled men. The patricians competed vigorously for election and they recruited bands of dependants or clients who would support them in their political ambitions. The *plebeians* (plebs) – the mass of citizens of non-patrician birth – deeply resented their exclusion from real influence and the history of the republic was marked by frequent social conflicts as they struggled to win more rights.

TIMELINE

753 BC
Traditional date for the foundation of Rome by Romulus and Remus

509 BC
Rome becomes a republic after its monarchy is overthrown

C.450 BC
The Twelve Tables, the foundation of Roman Law, are issued

396 BC
The Romans conquer the Etruscan city of Veii, beginning their conquest of Italy

390 BC
Rome is sacked by the Gauls

272 BC
The Romans complete their conquest of the Italian peninsular

264–241 BC
Rome defeats Carthage in the First Punic War to win control of Sicily, Sardinia and Corsica

218–202 BC
Rome defeats Carthage in the Second Punic War to win control of southern Spain

149–146 BC
The Romans destroy Carthage in the Third Punic War

146 BC
Greece becomes part of the Roman Empire

58–52 BC
Julius Caesar conquers Gaul

49–46 BC
Caesar defeats his rival Pompey in a civil war and becomes dictator of Rome

44 BC
The murder of Julius Caesar leads to a renewal of civil war

30 BC
Caesar's nephew Octavian wins power, ending the civil wars

27 BC
Octavian is proclaimed Augustus, first emperor of Rome

The plebs included both rich and poor — wealthy landowners and merchants whose lack of noble birth excluded them from political life, craftsmen, unskilled urban labourers and peasant farmers.

POPULAR ASSEMBLY

In 494 BC, the plebs formed their own assembly, the *consilium plebis* (popular assembly) and elected their own officers, called tribunes. To protect the tribunes from attack by thugs employed by the patricians, the plebs declared them to be sacred and invoked curses on any who harmed them. Because of their personal inviolability, the tribunes became effective advocates for the people against arbitrary actions by the magistrates. The plebs' most effective weapon was 'secession', a form of mass civil disobedience. This was first used successfully c.450 BC, when the plebs forced the patricians to publish a written law code, the 'Twelve Tables', which became the foundation of Roman law. Another important success was the abolition in 326 BC of debt bondage, which forced many smallholders into virtual slavery if they defaulted on a loan due to a bad harvest. Power-sharing was introduced so that plebeians could hold magistracies and from 342 BC one consul was always a pleb. In 287 BC, the Senate recognized decisions of the popular assembly, known as plebiscites, as having the full force of law.

As magistracies were unpaid, these changes mainly benefited the richer plebs who could afford to stand for office. Ex-magistrates had the right to become senators, so the number of plebs in the Senate gradually increased. These plebs formed the basis of a new hereditary aristocracy known as the *nobiles* (nobles). While, in this way, the aristocracy became a more open class, the Senate did not really become any more representative of the interests of the Roman people as a whole. The only serious challenge to the Senate's authority came when the tribunes passed legislation through the popular assembly, but this rarely happened. Most tribunes were themselves wealthy and they used the office as a stepping stone towards election as a magistrate. They therefore had no interest in challenging the status quo, so Rome remained an aristocratic state. In spite of this, the combination of collective decision-making, public consultation and social mobility helped to create a community of interest between the classes. The effect of this was to provide Rome with a stable government during the years of its rise to great power status.

THE CONQUEST OF ITALY

For the first century of its existence, the Roman republic was far from secure. In 508 BC, the Romans defeated an attempt by the Etruscans to restore Tarquin II to the throne. A few years later, the Latin cities combined against Rome, but were narrowly defeated at the battle of Lake Regillus in 499 BC. Colonies of Roman citizens were founded on land conquered during the war,

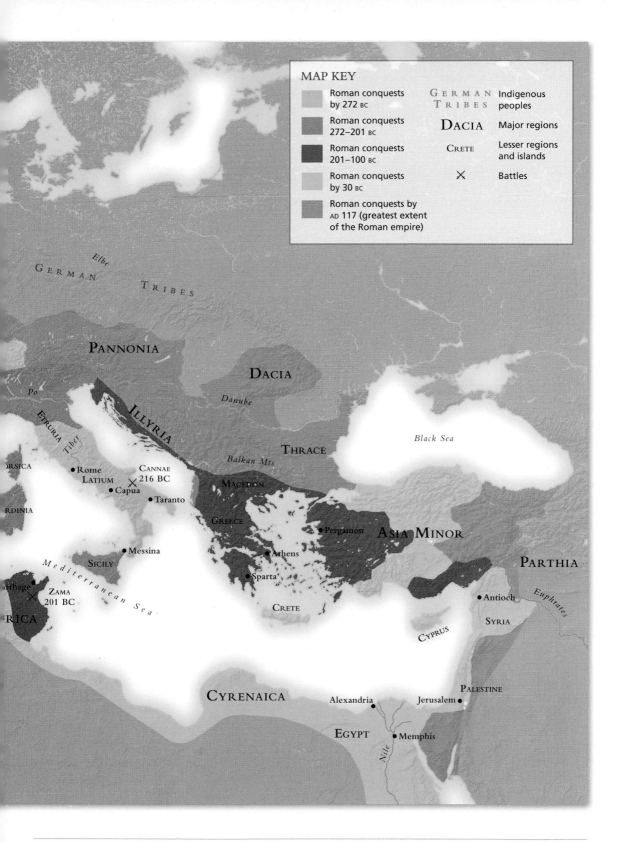

MAP KEY

Roman conquests by 272 BC

Roman conquests 272–201 BC

Roman conquests 201–100 BC

Roman conquests by 30 BC

Roman conquests by AD 117 (greatest extent of the Roman empire)

GERMAN TRIBES — Indigenous peoples

DACIA — Major regions

CRETE — Lesser regions and islands

× — Battles

GERMAN TRIBES

Elbe

PANNONIA

DACIA

Danube

Po

ETRURIA

Tiber

ILLYRIA

THRACE

Balkan Mts

Black Sea

CORSICA

Rome
LATIUM

CANNAE
216 BC

×

Capua

Taranto

MACEDON

SARDINIA

GREECE

Pergamon

ASIA MINOR

PARTHIA

Messina

SICILY

Athens

Euphrates

Mediterranean Sea

Sparta

Carthage

ZAMA
201 BC

×

CRETE

Antioch

SYRIA

AFRICA

CYPRUS

CYRENAICA

Alexandria

Jerusalem

PALESTINE

EGYPT

Memphis

Nile

beginning a policy that continued into imperial times. The policy served two purposes. It helped the Romans to consolidate their hold on newly conquered lands and it also defused social tensions in the city by providing land for its poorer citizens. No sooner was the Latin war over, than hill tribes from the Apennine mountains, the Aequi, Volsci and Sabines, began to encroach on Latium. The threat helped unite the Latins again under Roman leadership, but war with the tribes continued on and off for a century. During one attack by the Aequi, in 458 BC, the Senate decided to appoint the respected warrior Cincinnatus as dictator. Messengers sent to inform Cincinnatus of his new appointment found him behind his plough, tilling his fields. Rome was not yet so wealthy that senators did not have to work. After defeating the Aequi, Cincinnatus resigned the dictatorship before the end of his term and went back to his fields. Cincinnatus was often held up as an example of republican virtue to later, more ambitious dictators. The Romans also frequently fought the nearby Etruscan city of Veii, which was a rival for control of the Tiber valley. According to Roman traditions, which were clearly influenced by the Greek legend of the Trojan War, Veii was finally captured after a siege of ten years (405–396 BC). This, Rome's first major conquest, doubled the size of its territory.

THE GAULISH INVASION

Towards the end of the fifth century BC, the Gauls overran the Po river valley. In 390 BC, a Gaulish army crossed the Apennines, marched down the Tiber valley, routed the Roman army and sacked Rome. It was a traumatic experience which left the Romans with a lasting fear of the northern barbarians. However, Rome recovered quickly. The Gauls did far more harm to the Etruscans, who were permanently weakened by their raids. The Romans gradually tightened their control over Latium, provoking another unsuccessful rebellion in 340–338 BC. The post-war settlement provided the basis for future Roman expansion in Italy. The Latin cities were fully incorporated into the Roman state and their inhabitants became Roman citizens.

Higher calling
Messengers sent to announce to Cincinnatus his appointment of dictator in 458 BC find him at work in the fields in this painting by Juan Antonio Ribera (1779–1860). After defeating Rome's enemies, Cincinnatus resigned his year-long appointment after just 16 days. Later dictators proved less willing to surrender power.

Non-Latin communities that had supported the Latins were granted half-citizenship. This gave them most of the rights and duties of full citizens, including military service, but not the right to vote in the assemblies. In time, as they became more Romanized and proved their loyalty, half citizens could become full citizens.

EXPANSION THROUGH ITALY

Over the next 70 years, the Romans brought peninsular Italy under their control. The Romans' most determined opponents were the Samnites, whom they fought and defeated in three wars (343–341 BC, 327–304 BC, 298–290 BC). It was to help move troops quickly for the fight against the Samnites that in 312 BC, the Romans built the first of their famous all-weather roads, the Appian Way, between Rome and Capua. The last to hold out against Rome was the Greek city of Tarentum (Taranto), which called on king Pyrrhus of Epirus in Greece for help. Pyrrhus, who was considered one of the greatest generals of the time, invaded Italy in 280 BC. Pyrrhus defeated the Romans in two great battles at Heraclea and Ausculum, but suffered such heavy casualties that he withdrew in 275 BC (it is from this we get the term 'Pyrrhic victory'). Tarentum surrendered to Rome three years later. Rome's wars were fought with the full support of its citizens. For the common soldiers, conquest brought the chance of plunder and land: for their generals it brought prestige and political influence. Rome became wealthy

Roman road
Part of the Appian Way, which linked Rome to Capua. Built in 312 BC by Appius Claudius Caecus, it began a network of all-weather roads that eventually stretched to around 55,000 miles (88,500 km).

BATTLE AT CANNAE

on war booty and, with a population now of around 150,000, was one of the largest cities in the Mediterranean world. With the manpower of Italy at its command, Rome had become a power to reckon with.

THE STRUGGLE WITH CARTHAGE

The first treaty the Roman republic made with a foreign power was with the great Phoenician trading city of Carthage in North Africa. Carthage dominated the trade routes of the western Mediterranean and controlled an empire that included western Sicily, Sardinia, Corsica, the Balearic Islands and the southern coast of Spain. The treaty of friendship, signed in 509 BC, recognized mutual spheres of influence and was renewed in 348 BC and 306 BC. However, as Roman power grew, a conflict of interests was increasingly likely.

In 264 BC, the city of Messina, in eastern Sicily, appealed to Rome for protection against the nearby Greek city of Syracuse. Carthage feared allowing the Romans to get a foothold in what it regarded as its sphere of influence and allied with Syracuse against Rome. This led to the outbreak of the First Punic War (264–241 BC), which derives its name from *Poeni*, the Latin for Phoenician. The Romans won early victories in Sicily, quickly knocking Syracuse out of the war, but they soon realized that they could not win so long as Carthage controlled the sea. The Romans had no traditions of naval warfare but, using a beached Carthaginian galley as a model, they built and manned a fleet of 100 warships in a matter of months. They won their first naval battle in 260 BC. This was the kind of thing the Romans prided themselves on: learning from their enemies and beating them at their own game. In 256 BC, the Romans invaded North Africa to take the war to Carthage, but were forced to withdraw in 255 BC after suffering heavy casualties. Sicily again became the focus of the war, which now became one of grim attrition. In the end, Rome won because it had the manpower to support both a large army and a large fleet, while the Carthaginians did not. In 241 BC, the Romans destroyed the last of Carthage's navy. Cut off from supplies, the Carthaginian garrisons in Sicily were forced to surrender. In addition to Sicily, Rome gained control of Sardinia and Corsica. In 227 BC, magistrates were appointed to govern each of these new territories. The sphere of a magistrate's responsibility was called his *provincia*, or province. This did not originally have a geographical meaning, but it came to be applied to all of Rome's overseas possessions.

THE SECOND PUNIC WAR

The Carthaginians compensated themselves for their lost territories by building a new empire in Spain. At the same time, the Romans conquered the Cisalpine Gauls, completing their take-over of Italy. As Rome extended its influence west into Gaul (roughly modern France), and the Carthaginians expanded north towards the Pyrenees, a new conflict over spheres of interest became inevitable. The Carthaginian general Hannibal (247–182 BC) was eager to revenge Carthage's defeat in the First Punic War. In 219 BC, Hannibal laid siege to the Spanish city of Saguntum, a Roman ally, knowing full well the consequences. Saguntum appealed to Rome for help. When Hannibal ignored an ultimatum to withdraw, Rome declared war, beginning the Second Punic War (218–202 BC).

Secure in their command of the sea, the Romans planned to invade North Africa. They were, therefore, taken by surprise when Hannibal marched an army overland from Spain, through Gaul and across the Alps to invade Italy from the north. Hannibal hoped that the Cisalpine Gauls and the other Italian peoples would rise in rebellion against Rome and so neutralize its main advantage over Carthage, its manpower. Hannibal was to be disappointed. Despite winning brilliant victories over the Romans, culminating in his masterpiece at the battle of Cannae in 216 BC, where he enveloped and destroyed two consular armies, most of Rome's subjects remained loyal.

DEFEATING CARTHAGE

The war in Italy became a stalemate. Hannibal was too skilful a general for the Romans to defeat him battle, but Hannibal lacked the strength to capture Rome. This suited the Romans. While its best general was wasting his time in Italy, the Romans conquered Carthage's empire in Spain and, in 204 BC, finally launched the long-delayed invasion of North Africa. Hannibal was called home to defend Carthage. The commander of the Roman expeditionary force was Publius Scipio (237–183 BC), later nicknamed 'Africanus'. Scipio was a survivor of Cannae and he had made a careful study of Hannibal's tactics. At the battle of Zama in 202 BC, Scipio destroyed Hannibal's army: Carthage surrendered soon afterwards. The Romans imposed harsh peace terms. Carthage was reduced to a small territory in Tunisia. It had to pay Rome an enormous indemnity and its Spanish possessions became Roman provinces.

Counting the cost
This Renaissance statue shows Hannibal with an urn filled with the rings taken from Roman nobles killed at the battle of Cannae. As a child, Hannibal was sworn to eternal hatred of Rome. One of history's greatest battlefield tacticians, Hannibal's grand strategy in his war against Rome was fatally flawed and he led Carthage to catastrophic defeat.

THE EARLY ARMY

The army of the early republic fought in a phalanx much like contemporary Greek *hoplites*. In their campaigns against the Gauls and Italian hill tribes, the Romans found the phalanx to be clumsy and gradually evolved more flexible tactics, but infantry remained the main arm.

By the time of the Punic Wars, Roman soldiers were divided into four classes by experience and equipment. The youngest, fittest and least experienced formed the *velites*, light infantry whose main role was skirmishing ahead of the main battle line. This comprised three ranks of armoured infantry armed with javelins and a short thrusting sword (the *gladius*) for close-quarter combat. The first rank, the *hastati*, was made up of men in their 20s with some combat experience. The *principes* formed the second rank. These were battle-hardened soldiers, mostly in their early 30s. The oldest men, the *triarii*, formed the third rank of the heavy infantry, acting as a reserve and helping to steady the younger soldiers. Only property owners were permitted to serve, on the principle that only men who had a stake in the state could be relied upon to defend it. All property owners between the ages of 17 and 60 could be conscripted, but those over 47 would only be assigned garrison duty. Soldiers spent more time digging than fighting because they were expected to build a fortified camp every night when on campaign. Soldiers were theoretically supposed to buy their own arms and armour. By the time of the Punic Wars, however, the state had effectively taken over that responsibility.

The basic tactical unit of the army was the maniple, literally 'a handful'. Maniples of *velites*, *hastati* and *principes* were composed of two *centuries* of 60 to 80 men each, while maniples of *triarii* had one *century*. The smallest unit capable of independent action was the *cohort*, made up of one maniple each of *velites*, *hastati*, *principes* and *triarii*, plus a unit of 30 cavalrymen, totalling 450 to 570 men. Ten *cohorts* made up one legion. Soldiers supplied by Rome's Italian subjects were organized in exactly the same way, except they were required to supply double the number of cavalry. A normal Roman field army, known as a consular army because it was commanded by one of the two consuls, consisted of two Roman legions and two Italian legions. During the Second Punic War, Rome could raise around 750,000 soldiers from a total Italian population of nearly four million, an astonishing feat of mobilization for an ancient society. With manpower on this scale, it is easy to see how Rome could survive even defeats as severe as the battle of Cannae against Carthage.

Roman weapon
From around the time of the Punic Wars, the *gladius*, a short thrusting sword was the Roman infantryman's main weapon for close quarters fighting. The *gladius* was also popular with gladiators, who get their name ('swordsman') from the weapon.

Officers of the army
This ivory carving from Praeneste (Palestrina), made around 200 BC, shows a group of Roman officers, all with plumed helmets and oval shields.

> 'Until the destruction of Carthage, the people and Senate shared the government peacefully. When the people were relieved of their fear of Carthage, the vices of prosperity appeared.'
>
> Sallust (c.40 BC)

Rome's victory over Carthage made it the dominant power of the western Mediterranean. Over the next 200 years, the Romans steadily extended their power over the entire Mediterranean world. This was not so much the working out of an imperial master plan as a kind of imperial creep. Many wars of conquest started out to chastise troublesome neighbours and establish secure borders, but every new province that was added to the empire created a new set of border problems, drawing Rome on to yet further conquests. Roman expansion was also driven in a rather haphazard way by the power struggles within the Roman nobility. Military success offered a sure route to political influence and a general who added territory to the empire was awarded a status-enhancing 'triumph', a procession through the streets of Rome, leading his troops, chained prisoners and carts of booty, in a gilded chariot. Generals, of course, took the lion's share of war booty and prisoners, who could be sold as slaves. The Romans liked to believe that they never fought a war without provocation, but they were very easily provoked. Prayers for the expansion of the empire even formed part of the state religion.

MASTER OF THE MEDITERRANEAN

Rome's conquest of the eastern Mediterranean began as a simple punitive expedition against Philip V of Macedon, who had supported Carthage during the Second Punic War. Once sucked into the rivalries of the Greek states, the Romans were drawn inexorably on into the Balkans, and then into Asia Minor and the Levant. Roman domination of the region was completed by the annexation of Egypt in 30 BC. The powerful Parthian empire of Persia, whose fast-moving horse archers proved a match for Rome's disciplined but slow-moving armoured infantry, was a barrier to further expansion in the east. In the Third Punic War (149–146 BC), Rome finally destroyed Carthage and acquired a province in North Africa. Carthage had recovered too quickly for Roman liking after the Second Punic War. When the Carthaginians retaliated, without Roman permission, against the Numidians (a Berber people) for raiding their territory, the Romans seized the pretext to finish off their old rival once and for all. In 125–121 BC, the Romans conquered southern Gaul to create a land link between Italy and Spain. Julius Caesar conquered the rest of Gaul in 58–52 BC, taking the Roman frontier to the Rhine river. By the beginning of imperial rule in 27 BC, the Roman empire was close to its natural limits of expansion: the most significant new provinces added during the imperial period were Britain, in the mid-first century AD, and Dacia (roughly Romania), in the early second century AD.

CARTHAGE

Rome's rival, Carthage was founded in 814 BC by Phoenician settlers from Tyre, on the coast of what is now Lebanon. Thanks to its fine harbour and its position astride the main Mediterranean trade routes, the city flourished and it recovered quickly from its defeats by Rome in the First and Second Punic Wars. The Romans finally captured Carthage in the Third Punic War (149–146 BC) after a three-year siege. The entire surviving population were sold into slavery and the city was razed to the ground. Carthage's harbour was too good to waste, however, and the city was refounded by Julius Caesar as a colony for veteran soldiers.

Rome's rise from city state to world empire resulted in profound cultural and social changes. Following the conquest of Greece, plunder in the form of silver plate, sculptures, paintings, furniture, bronze ornaments and books flooded into Rome, starting a craze for all things Greek. The first Greek-style marble temple was built in Rome in 148 BC. Roman nobles commissioned Greek craftsmen to create works of art, while an influx of Greek slaves, including musicians and cooks, changed Roman tastes. Greek drama inspired the works of the first Roman playwright, Plautus (c.250–184 BC), and made theatre fashionable. Athletic competitions, inspired by the Olympic games, started to be held. Romans of the old school, such as the writer and statesman Cato the Elder (234–149 BC), feared that Greek luxury was undermining republican virtues and corrupting society.

THE IMPACT OF EXPANSION

It was certainly true that Roman society was becoming more corrupt. As war booty, tribute and taxes from its conquered provinces flooded into Rome, the potential rewards of political office multiplied, intensifying competition within the senatorial class. Bribery, corruption and the abuse of power became commonplace. The long wars also gave generals plenty of opportunities to build up their wealth and influence, and create factions within the senatorial class to support their ambitions. At the same time, the wars had disastrous consequences for the peasant smallholder class, who provided the bulk of conscripts for Rome's citizen army. The conscription system worked well enough when Rome's wars against its Italian neighbours were seasonal affairs, but during the Punic Wars armies had to be kept in the field for years. The wars of imperial expansion which followed were no less of a burden as armies were sent further and further from home. Although conscripts were paid, the absence of menfolk from a farm could be ruinous and, of course, many never came home. Families fell into debt and were dispossessed. Their farms were bought by wealthy speculators who built up large estates which were worked by slaves captured in the wars. The landless peasants drifted to Rome, where they joined the ranks of the *proletarii*, the lowest class of citizens who were ineligible for military service because they owned no property. The social consensus that had supported the republican constitution now began to break down. Many Romans feared that the decline of the smallholder class would undermine Rome's military might. The tribune Tiberius Gracchus (168–133 BC) attempted to help the dispossessed smallholders

Master of the Mediterranean
Roman control of the Mediterranean depended on fleets of galleys, such as this, shown in a mosaic depicting scenes from Homer's *Odyssey* from Tunisia (conquered 149–146 BC).

by forcing land reform through the popular assembly. On the day of the vote, he and hundreds of his supporters were murdered by a gang of senators and their clients. Tiberius' brother Gaius, who became tribune in 123 BC, attempted to push further reforms through the popular assembly but he and 3,000 of his supporters were massacred on the Senate's orders in 122 BC.

Though the Gracchi failed, the tribunate and the popular assembly had now become a focus of opposition to senatorial government. The Senate itself became divided into two factions, the reformist *populares*, and the conservative *optimates*.

'Veni, vidi, vinci!
(I came, I saw, I conquered!)'

Words written on placards carried during Caesar's triumphal procession in 46 BC, as recorded by Suetonius (C. AD 120)

THE DECLINE OF THE REPUBLIC

In 108 BC, Gaius Marius (157–86 BC) was elected consul. From a minor landowning family, Marius was popular with the plebs, and he used his position to attack the corruption of the senatorial class. In 104 BC, he was elected consul again, to lead a war against the Cimbri and Teutones, two German tribes who had already thrashed Roman armies and now threatened to invade Italy. Marius reinforced the army by recruiting landless citizens. The Germans were decisively defeated two years later. By ending the connection between property

He doth bestride the narrow world...
Julius Caesar overthrew the corrupt Roman republic when he appointed himself dictator in 46 BC. A great soldier and skilful statesman, Caesar nevertheless lacked the political vision to provide Rome with a new constitution. Fearing that he was about to restore the monarchy, a group of senators murdered him in 44 BC.

ownership and military service, Marius opened the way for the creation of Rome's professional army of infantry legions which became a devastatingly effective agent of imperial expansion. However, the professionalizing of the army also led to the rise of dictators who ultimately destroyed the republic. The state refused to grant land or pay pensions to discharged soldiers. As a result, they looked to their commanders to provide for them. This dependence effectively created client armies that power-hungry generals used to support their political ambitions.

The danger first became apparent when Marius and another successful general, Sulla (138–78 BC), an *optimate*, competed for the same command. Both called on the support of their legions and a civil war broke out. Victorious, Sulla ruled as dictator from 82 BC until his death in 78 BC. After Sulla's death, two of his chief supporters, Pompey (Gnaeus Pompeius) (106–48 BC) and Crassus (115–53 BC), a successful businessman who made a name for himself defeating Spartacus' slave rebellion in 71 BC, competed for power. In 67–63 BC, Pompey brought Pontus (in Anatolia), Syria and Palestine under Roman rule. He took so much loot that he rewarded his men with 12 and half years' pay each. When Pompey returned to Rome in 62 BC he demanded recognition for himself and land for his soldiers. Reluctant to enhance Pompey's prestige, the *optimates*, who dominated the Senate, refused. Their decision doomed the republic.

A CLASH OF GENERALS

Frustrated, Pompey allied with Gaius Julius Caesar (100–44 BC), an ambitious member of a patrician family who had aligned himself with the *populares*, and Crassus to form what became known as the First Triumvirate. Together, they passed a programme of reforms through the popular assemblies, completely sidelining the Senate. Caesar's political acumen, Pompey's prestige and Crassus' wealth made them a formidable combination. In 58–52 BC, Caesar further enhanced his status by conquering Gaul, becoming wealthy and winning the devoted loyalty of his soldiers in the process. Crassus, who tried to emulate Caesar's military successes, was killed on campaign in Parthia. Alarmed by Caesar's success, the *optimates* mended fences with Pompey by voting him in as sole consul in 52 BC. The Senate demanded that Caesar disband his army. Caesar's and Pompey's supporters started fighting in the streets of Rome.

In 49 BC, Caesar led his army across the Rubicon river, which marked the boundary of his command in Gaul, and advanced on Rome. Caesar had a greater popular following than Pompey, and was far the better general. Caesar drove Pompey out of Italy and decisively defeated his army at Pharsalus in Greece in August 48 BC. Pompey fled to Egypt. Caesar followed, arriving to find that Pompey had been murdered. Caesar intervened in a dispute between king Ptolemy XIV and his sister Cleopatra, whom he placed on the Egyptian throne and took as a lover, before returning to Rome. In 46 BC, Caesar appointed himself dictator for ten years, which he upgraded to dictator for life in 44 BC. Caesar enacted a range of reforms, alleviating debt, founding new colonies for the Roman poor and veteran soldiers, ending the abused practice of tax farming in the

YOUNG CAESAR

Gaius Julius Caesar (100–44 BC) was a member of the patrician Julian family, which claimed descent from the legendary hero Aeneas. Caesar's early years were turbulent. His father died suddenly when he was 16 years old and shortly afterwards he was stripped of his inheritance by the dictator Sulla as revenge for the Julian family's support of his rival Marius. Caesar joined the army and, after a few years of distinguished service, he entered a legal career, earning a reputation for brilliant oratory.

In 75 BC, Caesar went to study in Greece, but was kidnapped and held to ransom by pirates. Caesar promised his kidnappers that he would return and crucify them after his ransom had been paid. The pirates thought he was joking, but after his release he raised a fleet and hunted them down. Returning to Rome, Caesar was elected military tribune, the lowest formal office in Roman politics. He went on to hold successively higher offices of state, including chief priest. Because of his support for the reformist *populares*, he was often accused, but never convicted, of conspiring against the Senate. In 61 BC, Caesar became governor of the province of Outer Spain, conquering the Lusitanians of present-day Portugal. Caesar finally reached the highest office in 59 BC, when he was elected consul. He immediately allied with Pompey and Crassus to form the First Triumvirate.

The Romans were a pagan people who worshipped a pantheon of deities whose influence extended to all aspects of daily life. Roman paganism had no systematic theology and no moral teaching. Much of its mythology, and many of its gods, were borrowed from the Etruscans, Greeks and others. The main object of Roman religion was to secure the *pax deorum*, the goodwill of the gods, by performing a complex calendar of ancient ceremonies. It was the ceremonies themselves that were believed to be effective, not the depth of belief or moral qualities of those performing them. The ceremonies therefore had to be observed absolutely precisely. Any mistake made a ceremony invalid and it had to be begun again.

The chief god of the Roman pantheon was the sky-god Jupiter, called *Optimus Maximus* ('Greatest and Best') by the Romans, who stood for justice, good faith and honour. The cult of Jupiter was believed to have been founded by Romulus, who prayed to him for victory in a battle with the Sabines. Jupiter was the focus of the public ceremonies performed for the welfare of the state. The Romans had no professional priesthood. Public ceremonies to Jupiter, and other state gods such as the war-god Mars, were performed by the aristocracy on behalf of the community. The private rituals of the household gods, including Vesta (goddess of the hearth), the Penates (minor gods of the store-cupboard), and the Lares (ancestral spirits), were performed daily by the male head of the household. The temple of Vesta in the Roman Forum was the symbolic home of the Roman people. The temple contained a sacred hearth, tended by the six Vestal Virgins. The hearth's fire was kindled during the festival of Vestalia on 1 March and was kept burning all year long. If the fire was allowed to go out, as it did in 216 BC shortly before the battle of Cannae, the Romans believed it presaged some disaster. The Romans believed firmly in omens. No important decision, such as going to war, would be made without first consulting the gods. This was usually performed by a diviner, who examined the entrails of sacrificed animals or interpreted the feeding behaviour of sacred chickens. Unusual natural or astronomical events and dreams were believed to be messages from the gods.

The Romans were tolerant in matters of religion. When they encountered foreign gods with attributes similar to their own, they assumed that they were the same gods, only known by different names. In this way the Romans regarded the supreme Greek god Zeus and the Phoenician sky-god Baal as being equivalent to Jupiter. Increased contacts with the eastern Mediterranean as Rome grew led to the introduction of new cults, such as those of the Greek healing god Aesculapius and the Anatolian mother goddess Cybele. The proliferation of cults led many educated Romans, such as the orator Cicero (106–43 BC), openly to question the literal existence of the gods. In the early centuries AD, the impersonal nature of traditional paganism led many Romans to adopt eastern mystery religions, such as the cults of the Persian god Mithras, the Egyptian goddess Isis and Christianity.

The sacred fire
The Temple of Vesta in the Roman Forum, home of the sacred hearth fire of the Roman people. Temples of Vesta were always round, with the door facing east towards the rising Sun, the source of all life.

> 'Augustus seduced the army with bonuses, the citizenry with cheap corn and everyone with the sweetness of peace.'
>
> Tacitus (c. AD 100)

provinces, and completing the extension of Roman citizenship to all of Italy. Caesar's rule was popular with almost everyone but the aristocracy.

THE FIRST EMPEROR

Though Caesar had overthrown the republic, no consensus emerged about a new constitutional settlement. Caesar took to wearing the purple robes of kingship, issued coins bearing his own portrait, and, though he refused the royal title, ruled as king in all but name. Fearing that Caesar intended to restore the monarchy, a group of senators, led by Marcus Junius Brutus and Gaius Cassius Longinus, publicly stabbed Caesar to death in the Senate house on 15 March 44 BC. They had so far lost touch with public opinion that the conspirators truly expected the Roman people to celebrate the death of a tyrant. The public reaction to their announcement of Caesar's death and the restoration of republican liberty was so hostile that the bewildered conspirators were forced to flee from Rome.

The stage was set for a second civil war. Cassius and Brutus raised forces to support the senatorial cause. Against them were two of Caesar's generals, Mark Antony and Lepidus, and Caesar's young nephew and adopted son, Octavian, who together formed the Second Triumvirate. After Cassius and Brutus were defeated and killed at Philippi in Macedonia in 42 BC, the *triumvirs* divided the empire between them. Octavian got Rome and the west, Lepidus North Africa, and Mark Antony the east where, like Caesar before him, he fell under the spell of Cleopatra, becoming her lover. After Octavian forced Lepidus into retirement, relations between Octavian and Mark Antony began to deteriorate and war between them became inevitable. After their defeat at the battle of Actium in 31 BC, Mark Antony and Cleopatra committed suicide, leaving Octavian as master of the empire. By now the war-weary aristocracy was ready to accept that its monopoly of power was over. In 27 BC, Octavian forced the Senate to award him a new name – Augustus (ruled 27 BC–AD 14), meaning 'revered one'. He was also given the new title of *princeps* ('first citizen'), together with consular powers and command of the army, which allowed him to exercise absolute power. Augustus' successors adopted the title *imperator* ('commander'), from which our word 'emperor' comes. Augustus' constitution, in effect a thinly disguised monarchy, brought the Roman empire centuries of peace, political stability and prosperity.

Head of an emperor
Coin showing the head of Augustus, the first emperor of Rome. Augustus ruled for over 40 years and was nearly 80 when he died, but to the end of his reign he was always portrayed on coins and in statues as a young man.

The cult of Mithras
Statue of the Persian god Mithras. Mithraism was one of many foreign cults introduced to Rome by soldiers returning from overseas campaigns of conquest.

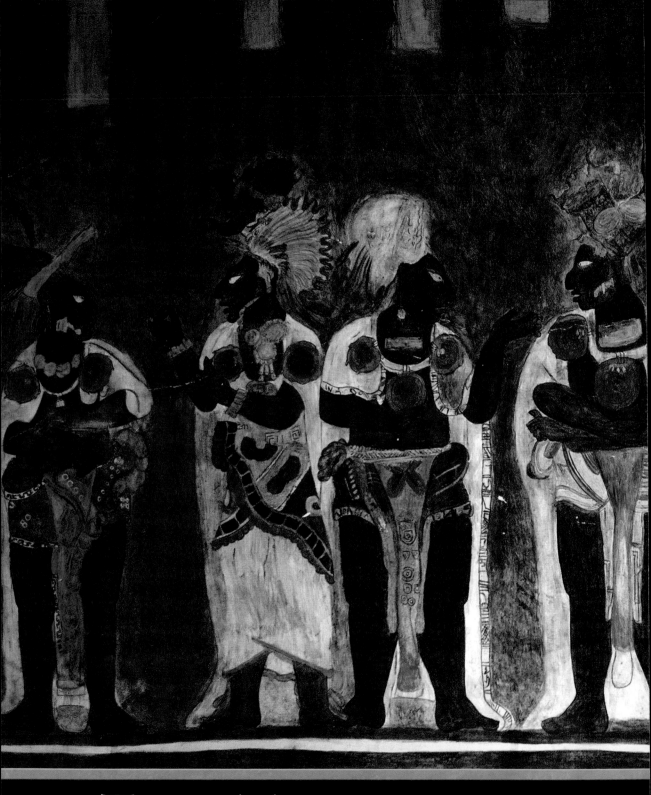

THE MAYA

IN 1839, an American diplomat, John Lloyd Stephens, and an English artist, Frederick Catherwood, became the first outsiders to explore the rainforests of Central America. What they discovered, crumbling among the twisted roots of the rainforest trees, were the remains of the Maya civilization, the most sophisticated and long-lived of the ancient Mesoamerican civilizations. Catherwood's atmospheric, yet precisely detailed, lithographs of the Maya ruins revealed to the wider world a civilization so alien that most contemporaries refused to believe that it could have been created by American Indians: Phoenicians, Egyptians, a wandering lost tribe of Israel or even survivors from Atlantis, maybe, but certainly not the local Maya Indians, who then lived as simple subsistence farmers.

The physical similarities between the Maya and the people depicted on monuments in these ruined cities had already been noted by an earlier visitor, Juan Galindo, a Guatemalan army officer. Galindo was killed in a civil war in 1839, before his own drawings of the sites were published, and he has rarely received the credit due to him for identifying the real creators of this remarkable civilization. However, it is only in the last 30 years that the ancient Maya have been truly revealed. This was the achievement not of archaeologists but of linguists whose painstaking research cracked the code of the Maya's esoteric hieroglyphic writing. The first archaeologists to study the Maya concluded that they had been a peaceful race of astronomer-priests: their texts told a very different story.

ORIGINS OF THE MAYA

The Maya originated around 4,000 years ago in the heavily forested Guatemalan highlands. Their history is conventionally divided into three periods, the Preclassic (2000 BC–AD 250), the Classic (AD 250–909) and the Postclassic (909–1697). The Preclassic period was the formative period of the Maya civilization. At the beginning of the Preclassic, the Maya lived as hunter-gatherers. By around 1200 BC, they had settled in permanent villages and adopted farming. Between 1000 BC and 800 BC, groups of Maya migrated out of the highlands, north into the lowland rainforest of Petén and the drier but still forested plains of the Yucatán peninsula. The Maya still inhabit most of this area today. The Maya population rose steadily, and by around 600 BC, towns and cities began to grow up at places like Kaminaljuyu and El Baul in the highlands and Nakbe and El Mirador in Petén. This development marks the emergence of the Maya civilization, which was to survive for nearly 2,000 years. By way of comparison, the more famous Aztec civilization of Mexico lasted barely 200 years.

The most important influence on the Maya during the Preclassic was the neighbouring Olmec civilization, with which they had strong trade links. Very much the 'mother culture' of Mesoamerica, the Olmec gave the Maya their calendar systems, writing in hieroglyphs and the practice of building ceremonial centres with temple pyramids.

Previous page: Rendition of Mayan fresco
The temple of Bonampak is renowned for its colourful murals depicting stylized figures and inscriptions. The realistic paintings of conquest and warfare found in the burial chambers are fine examples of the great surviving treasures of the Maya era.

The Maya quickly outstripped their teachers, building
larger cities and more ambitious monuments, and
producing more sophisticated art. Evidence for
writing and calendrical knowledge appear first in
the highlands, where, in the first century AD,
hereditary kings began to erect steles (upright
stone slabs) carved with portraits, glyphic texts
and dates to commemorate their deeds. With
an area of 2 square miles (5 sq km), the largest
highland centre, Kaminaljuyu, was dwarfed by
the lowland city of El Mirador, which at its
peak in the first century AD covered 10 square
miles (26 sq km) and had a population of perhaps
80,000 people. Its central pyramid rising over
72 metres (235 ft) above a massive artificial
platform is one of the most massive structures
built by any ancient civilization. Raised stone
causeways 2–6 metres (6–18 ft) high and
18–46 metres (60–150 ft) wide linked El
Mirador to the satellite cities of Nakbe and
Tintal, 7.5 and 12.5 miles (12 and 20 km)
away. Maya causeways were covered in
crushed white stone, giving them their
name *sacbe*, meaning 'white road'. Such
a city must have possessed a powerful
centralized government, but its exact
nature is elusive. This hugely impressive
city did not survive, however. For
unknown reasons, El Mirador and several
other lowland cities were abandoned in
the second century AD.

THE OLMEC

Mesoamerica is a sharply defined cultural region of Central America, extending south from central Mexico to northern Honduras and El Salvador. The ancient civilizations of the region, which included the Maya and the Aztecs, shared common cultural characteristics, including writing in hieroglyphs, the use of 260-day and 52-year ritual calendars, temple pyramids, a sacred ball game, the ritual importance of blood sacrifice and a diet based on maize, beans and squash. These characteristics were all brought together for the first time in the Olmec civilization, which originated in the swampy tropical lowlands of Veracruz around 1400 BC.

The focal points of Olmec civilization were grand ceremonial centres with populations numbering in the thousands. The earliest of these, at San Lorenzo, flourished from around 1200 BC until 1000 BC, when it was destroyed in what is thought to have been a ritual act to mark the end of a calendar cycle or a change of dynasty. San Lorenzo was succeeded by a new centre at La Venta, site of the first Mesoamerican temple pyramid, which flourished until c.400 BC, when it too was ritually destroyed. A third ceremonial centre developed at Tres Zapotes after the fall of La Venta. By this time, the Olmec civilization was in decline as newer civilizations, such as the Maya, began to overtake it and it died out early in the Christian era.

Olmec pottery
An Olmec pot in the shape of the eagle god, who was associated with the sky, the Sun and rulership.

The Olmec's most famous monuments are the giant sculpted stone heads they erected at their ceremonial centres to commemorate their rulers. So far, 17 heads have been discovered. The kings are portrayed wearing 'football helmets'. These are thought to have been protective headwear, worn during the rough sacred ballgame. Sculpted stone altars show kings emerging from the underworld. It is thought that the kings were shamans who claimed the power to travel to the underworld and mediate with their gods to secure good harvests for their people.

The identity of the Olmecs remains a mystery to this day. It is not known what language they spoke or even what they called themselves. Their modern name comes from *Olmeca* (meaning 'rubber people'), the Aztec name for the people who, in the Aztecs' own time, supplied them with rubber from Veracruz.

Big heads
This 3-metre (10-ft) tall giant stone head from San Lorenzo portrays an Olmec ruler. The head was sculpted from a 50-tonne basalt boulder transported by river rafts over 60 miles (96 km) from the volcanic Tuxtla mountains.

TIMELINE

C. 1400 BC
Emergence of the Olmec civilization in Veracruz

600 BC
The first Maya city states develop in Petén and the Guatemalan highlands. Earliest Maya temple pyramids are built

AD 36
The earliest Maya calendrical inscription

AD 100–200
Maya hieroglyphical script in use

AD 250–909
The Classic period of Maya civilization

AD 378
The Maya come under the influence of the Mexican city of Teotihuacán

AD 799–909
Collapse of the Classic Maya civilization in the Petén lowlands

AD 850–900
The Itzá Maya found Chichén Itzá in Yucatán

AD 987
Chichén Itzá comes under Toltec rule

1221
Hunac Ceel restores Maya rule at Chichén Itzá

1524
Cortés begins the Spanish conquest of the Maya

1697
Tayasal, the last surviving Maya city state is conquered by the Spanish

Mayan stele
Detail of a sculpted Maya stele from Copán showing king Waxaclajuun Ub'aah K'awiil (ruled AD 695–738). Steles are a characteristic Maya monument. Carved with hieroglyphic texts, portraits of rulers and scenes of myths and religious rituals, the Maya erected steles to commemorate important events, such as the accession of a new king or victory in war.

The beginning of the Classic period (AD 250–909) is marked by the erection of the first commemorative steles by rulers of the lowland Maya. The Classic Maya combined a common cultural identity, outstanding creativity and constant conflict in a way that invites comparison with Classical Greece or Renaissance Italy. The Maya lands were divided between more than 50 city states ruled by hereditary dynasties. These cities had populations ranging from around 5,000 to over 50,000, and they were linked and divided by a complex hierarchy of family ties, diplomatic alliances and entrenched rivalries. Only recently, following the almost complete decipherment of Maya glyphs, have historians begun to unravel these relationships. All Maya kings were not equal. The rulers of the stronger cities were 'over-kings' who maintained the kings of weaker cities as politically dependent, tribute-paying vassals.

THE RISE OF TIKAL

Palenque, Yaxchilán, Copán, Piedras Negras and Calakmul all at times achieved positions of regional domination, but for much of the Classic Tikal was the pre-eminent Maya city. Tikal was one of the lowland cities that survived the late Preclassic collapse. It entered the Classic in a strong position under a stable dynasty that had held power since around AD 90. This dynasty came to an abrupt end on 31 January 378, when the reigning king Chak Tok Ich'aak I and his entire lineage were executed by Siyaj K'ak'. Siyaj K'ak' was an invader, a general sent from the great city of Teotihuacán in the Valley of Mexico to conquer the Maya. Several other Maya cities submitted to Siyaj K'ak' and a mural from Tikal's neighbour Uaxactun graphically shows a Maya king submitting to a Mexican warrior appointed by the general to rule. Mexican influences on Maya art and architecture proliferated. Tikal itself was virtually rebuilt.

Siyaj K'ak' installed a boy called Yax Nuun Ayiin I (ruled AD 379–404) as king of Tikal. The boy's father, a ruler known as Spearthrower Owl, may have been the king of Teotihuacán. The style of Yax Nuun Ayiin's rule was entirely Mexican, but his son Siyaj Chan K'awiil II, better known as Stormy Sky (ruled AD 411–457), returned to Maya traditions. During his reign, Tikal became the pre-eminent Maya kingdom and it remained so until AD 562, when king Wak Chan K'awiil was captured and sacrificed by the ruler of Calakmul.

Calakmul remained the pre-eminent Maya kingdom for nearly 150 years, reaching its height under king Yuknoom the Great (ruled AD 636–683), who directly or indirectly controlled almost all of the Petén lowlands. By the time of Yuknoom's death, Tikal was resurgent. Yuknoom's successor Yich'aak K'ak led a campaign against Tikal in AD 695 and was crushingly defeated. Warrior kings fought for a century to restore Tikal's former glory, but only partially succeeded.

THE MAYA COSMOS

Maya civilization is best understood through its world view, which drew no clear boundaries between the natural and the supernatural. The gods were as much

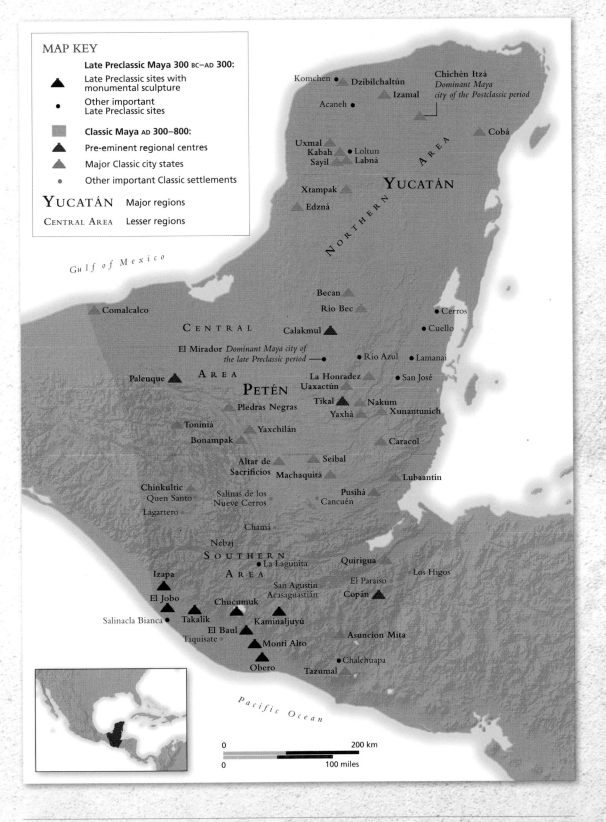

MAP KEY

Late Preclassic Maya 300 BC–AD 300:

▲ Late Preclassic sites with monumental sculpture

• Other important Late Preclassic sites

▩ **Classic Maya AD 300–800:**

▲ Pre-eminent regional centres

▲ Major Classic city states

• Other important Classic settlements

YUCATÁN Major regions

CENTRAL AREA Lesser regions

Gulf of Mexico

Komchen •   Dzibilchaltún •   **Chichén Itzá**
Dominant Maya city of the Postclassic period

Acaneh •   ▲ Izamal

• Cobá

Uxmal ▲
Kabah ▲ • Loltun   NORTHERN   AREA
Sayil ▲   Labná

Xtampak ▲   YUCATÁN

▲ Edzná

Becan ▲
Rio Bec ▲

CENTRAL   Calakmul ▲   • Cerros

• Cuello

El Mirador *Dominant Maya city of*
the late Preclassic period — •   • Rio Azul   • Lamanai

▲ Comalcalco

Palenque ▲   AREA   La Honradez ▲   • San José

PETÉN   Uaxactún ▲

Piedras Negras ▲   Tikal ▲   Nakum ▲
Yaxhá ▲   Xunantunich ▲

Toniniá ▲   Yaxchilán ▲

Bonampak ▲   Caracol ▲

Altar de ▲   Seibal ▲
Sacrificios   Machaquitá ▲   Lubaantin ▲

Chinkultic ▲
Quen Santo   Salinas de los   • Pusihá
Nueve Cerros   • Cancuén
Lagartero ▲

Chamá •

Nebaj •

SOUTHERN
AREA   • La Lagunita   Quirigua ▲   Los Higos •

Izapa ▲   San Agustin   El Paraiso •
Acasaguastián •   Copán ▲

El Jobo ▲   Chucumuk ▲

Salinacla Bianca •   Takalik ▲   Kaminaljuyú ▲

El Baul ▲
Tiquisate •   Monti Alto ▲   Asuncion Mita ▲

Obero ▲   • Chalchuapa

Tazumal ▲

Pacific Ocean

0 — 200 km
0 — 100 miles

Ball games
The ball court at Copán, dedicated to the macaw god on 6 January AD 738 by king Waxaclajuun Ub'aah K'awiil. Maya ball courts were sacred spaces, believed to be on the threshold of this world and the next.

a part of the natural order as humans. The Maya conceived of the world as the back of a giant caiman that was swimming in the primordial sea. At the centre of the world was a sacred ceiba tree whose branches held up the heavens and whose roots descended into the underworld, so uniting the three realms of the universe. The heavens and the underworld were abodes of the gods, and of spirits of dead ancestors, but living humans could also pass between realms and deal with the gods directly. The gods were neither outstandingly wise nor omnipotent and they needed the veneration and sacrifices of humans: it was for this reason that they had created them. The Maya believed that the present world was merely part of an eternal cycle of creation and destruction – every previous world was destroyed by a great flood. According to the Maya calendar, the same fate will soon overtake this world too: created on 13 August 3114 BC, it is scheduled for destruction on 21 December 2012, after which a new cycle will begin.

BALL COURT OF THE GODS

Every Maya city had a ball court. The Maya believed that the court was a threshold between this world and the underworld. The game was played by two teams using a hard rubber ball. Players wore helmets and padded clothing to protect them. Points were scored for delivering the ball to markers on the court and for passing it through a small circular stone goal set high on a wall at each end of the court. Goals were rare because players were not allowed to use their hands. Ball games formed part of the celebrations following victory in war. They were a re-enactment of battle by teams selected from the victors and from captives taken in the war. The outcome of these games was always predetermined. The captives would lose and then be sacrificed to the gods.

The Maya believed that all those who were sacrificed were guaranteed a comfortable afterlife in the underworld dwelling in the shade of a sacred ceiba tree, eating well and never having to work. Warriors who died in battle, women who died in childbirth, priests, kings and people who committed suicide by hanging also were assured a place in this paradise. The wicked were condemned to dwell in Mitnal, the lowest level of the underworld.

The Maya pantheon contained dozens of gods, most of whom were associated with forces of nature, fertility, the seasons, kingship, travel and work. Confusingly, some gods appeared in different manifestations, not unlike the avatars of Hindu gods. The lord of the heavens was Itzamná, a reptilian deity, whose body was stretched across the night sky forming the Milky Way. As Hunab Ku, Itzamná was the creator god, and he was also the Sun-god Kinich Ahau. The rain-god Chac had four aspects associated with colours and the cardinal points of the compass: the Red Chac of the east; the White Chac of the north, the Black Chac of the west; and the Yellow Chac of the south. Chac is represented with a long down-curling snout and two curved fangs projecting downwards from his mouth. For farmers, Chac was the most important of all the gods, and his intervention was often sought. The maize-god Yum Kaax was shown as a young man with a stylized maize plant growing from his head. Like maize itself, the maize god's destiny was controlled by the gods of rain, wind, drought, famine and death. K'awiil, the reptilian god of royal dynasties, had special significance for kings.

Hoop dreams
A close-up of the goal at the ball court at Chichén Itzá. Scoring a goal by passing the ball through the hoop without the use of the hands was exceptionally difficult.

The Maya had a large priestly class, but the main intermediaries between the people and their gods were their kings. Maya kings were hereditary, theocratic rulers who combined supreme political and religious authority. Kings were closely identified with the maize god whose gift of corn was the basis of Maya civilization. A king's foremost responsibility was to maintain good relations with the gods and, in doing so, secure a good harvest for his people.

THE LIFE OF A KING

Royal succession was by primogeniture: a king was usually succeeded by his eldest son. Women were acceptable as rulers only to prevent a dynasty dying out. Possession of royal blood was not enough to guarantee succession. The heir to the throne was expected to prove himself in battle by taking captives, who would be sacrificed at his investiture. Royal investitures culminated in the king's enthronement on a cushion of jaguar fur (jaguars were symbolic of royal power) and presented with the symbols of royal authority, including a spectacular headdress made of jade and shell adorned with the iridescent feathers of the quetzal bird.

CITY DESIGN

The layout of Maya cities reflected their view of the cosmos. The king's palace represented the earthly realm at the centre of the cosmos so was always built near the centre of the city. The nobility enjoyed the privilege of building their homes close to the palace, while commoners lived in suburbs away from the centre. North was associated with the heavens, where the ruler's ancestors dwelled, so it was here that the tombs, pyramids and funerary temples were built. As ball courts represented the threshold between this world and the next, they were built between the palace and the tombs and temples.

A king's life was bound by a calendar of rituals. During rituals, the king adopted the identity of the god who was being honoured by dressing in costume and wearing a mask. Dance and music accompanied many rituals. Kings, their wives (the Maya were polygamous) and other members of the royal family took hallucinogenic drinks and smoked strong tobacco to induce trances, during which they communicated with the gods. They also performed what must have been excruciatingly painful acts of self-torture, giving their own blood to nourish the gods by piercing or mutilating their tongues, ears, lips and genitals with stingray spines, thorns and bones. Even royal children were not exempted from these rituals, which began at the age of five or six.

After his ritual duties, the king's most important role was war leadership. War was constant during the Classic period because it was the best way for a king to enhance his prestige. However, Maya war was never total war. A king did not set out to conquer and destroy a rival city, but to force it to submit and pay tribute. A defeated city retained its sovereignty and its over-king rarely interfered in its internal affairs. In battle, it was more important to take prisoners than to kill. The fate of prisoners depended on their status. Low rank warriors became slaves or servants or were even adopted by families with no sons. High rank warriors were likely to be tortured and sacrificed. The most prestigious sacrifice was, of course, a captive king.

Kings gained prestige with age, and death was seen as the re-enactment of the maize god's descent to the underworld. In the underworld, the dead king underwent apotheosis before going to dwell in the heavens. In preparation for his journey, the dead king was laid out in a stone tomb, dressed with his finest jade jewellery and jaguar skins, and dusted with blood-red powder made from haematite and cinnabar. Offerings of food and drink, effigies of gods, haematite mirrors, musical instruments, exotic seashells, furniture and human sacrifices were placed in the tomb. If the king was important enough, a pyramid was built over the tomb and a temple was erected on top as a shrine for the king's veneration. It sometimes happened that tombs, and even pyramids, were themselves entombed within the pyramids built over the tombs of later kings.

Beheading
A Maya warrior carries the severed head of a sacrificial victim. Sacrifice was a privilege normally reserved only for high-ranking captives: sacrificial victims were guaranteed an honoured place in the afterlife.

The Maya's greatest intellectual achievement was their complex and precise calendar system. All the Mesoamerican civilizations used a 52-year calendar cycle based on a 260-day ritual almanac and the 365-day solar year. The working of the almanac is best imagined as two interlocking wheels, one with 20 cogs representing named days, the second with 13 notches, numbered one to 13. The system gave each day a number value. The same combination of day and number recurred once every 260 days. The almanac was used to determine whether a particular day was lucky or not. Armed with this vital knowledge, the Maya could avoid holding important ceremonies and events, such as investing a king, starting a war or inaugurating a temple, on an ill-starred day.

COUNTING THE DAYS
The solar year was divided into 18 months of 20 days and a period of five unlucky days. The same combination of dates on the two calendars recurred only once every 52 years. This calendar is thought to have originated in the Zapotec civilization of the Oaxaca Valley in Mexico. The 52-year calendar was primarily used for timing religious rituals. It was of limited use for recording historical events because there was no way to distinguish a date in one 52-year cycle from another.

The problem of accurate historical dating was solved by the 'Long Count' calendar. This may have originated with the Olmec, but was perfected by the Maya. The Long Count calendar was based on subdivisions of time called *baktuns* (ages) of 144,000 days (c. 400 years), *katuns* of 7,200 days (c. 20 years), *tuns* of 360 days, *uinals* of 20 days, and the *kin* of one day. Each cycle of the world lasted for 13 *baktuns*, that is 5,125 years. Long Count dates were calculated from the beginning of the present world, which the Maya believed had happened in 3114 BC.

Dates were recorded in bar and dot numerals. Bars had a value of five and dots one, so a bar and three dots equalled eight. The Maya independently discovered the mathematical concept of zero, which they represented with a stylized shell. The Maya number system was vigesimal, using base 20 rather than ten as in the modern decimal system.

MASTERING THE STARS

A sophisticated knowledge of astronomy underpinned the Maya calendar. Many Maya buildings are aligned to mark equinoxes and solstices, and the seasonal rising and setting points of the Moon. The best known of these, the Caracol at Chichén Itzá, was probably a purpose-built astronomical observatory. With only naked eye observations, Maya astronomers calculated the length of the lunar cycle to 29.53020 days; astonishingly, just a few seconds short of the 29.53059 days calculated by modern astronomers. The Maya also knew that the solar year is approximately six hours longer than the calendar year of 365 days, but the Maya calendar did not use leap years to compensate for this.

The planet Venus was closely observed by the Maya. The first day of the 260-day almanac, 1 Ahau, belonged to Venus and, because of its associations with battle, was a good day to start a war. Venus appears both as a morning and an evening star. The reappearance of Venus in the dawn sky after a period of invisibility was a time of great peril. The event had to be preceded by ceremonies to ward off evil. So that these ceremonies could be performed at the right time, the Maya created a third calendar cycle of 584 days.

Mayan observtory
The circular tower at Chichén Itzá, known as the Caracol ('the snail'), is thought to be a purpose-built astronomical observatory with sight-lines on movements of the Sun, Moon and Venus. The structure probably dates to the late Classic period.

Maya Writing

Knowledge of astronomy, the calendar cycles and history was controlled by a powerful caste of scribes of high social rank. Scribes enjoyed the patronage of the creator god Itzamná, who invented writing. The Maya script was the only writing system used in ancient Mesoamerica that could represent all aspects of spoken language. The Maya wrote using glyphs. The system combined ideographic and phonetic elements. Glyphs represented either syllables, which could be combined to 'spell out' words, or were ideograms (abstract representations of objects and concepts). Kingdoms had distinctive emblem glyphs which stood as claims to sovereignty. These had two parts, one representing the city or dynasty, the other representing the individual king.

The Maya wrote on a wide range of media. Glyphs were carved in stone and wood, painted on pottery and walls, and written on paper made from the inner bark of fig trees. Maya glyphs were written in double columns, to be read left to right and top to bottom. Pages of bark paper were bound to make books or codices. Thousands of codices once existed but all except four were destroyed by the Spanish following their conquest of the Maya. The most important Maya codex to have survived is the *Popol Vuh* ('The Book of the Mat'), which records Maya creation myths.

Mayan glyphs
Part of a Maya commemorative inscription from Quiriguá, in Guatemala. About 500 different Mayan glyphs are known, more than any other Mesoamerican script.

The bedrock of Maya society were the peasant farmers whose surplus food supported the craftsmen, merchants, scribes, priests, nobles and kings. The Maya civilization was unusual in that it reached the peak of its development in a rainforest environment rather than a fertile floodplain. Rainforest soils have low fertility because nutrients are leached away by heavy rainfall or are locked up in trees: as a result they cannot usually support the intensive agriculture needed to sustain large urban populations.

FARMING A RAINFOREST

In modern times, Maya farmers used the *milpa* system of agriculture, which is adapted to rainforests. *Milpa* fields are created by cutting down the natural vegetation, letting it dry and burning it off. The ash fertilizes the new field, but after only a few years of farming the soils become exhausted. The field is abandoned and returns to forest. The land may need to be left fallow for more than 20 years before it has recovered enough fertility to cultivate. *Milpa* agriculture needs a lot of land and could not by itself support the Maya cities. Farmers used various methods to intensify food production, such as using household waste to fertilize vegetable gardens and building raised fields in swamps. The Maya did not use the plough so the land was worked entirely with hand tools.

Maize was the Maya's most important crop, so important that in myth, the gods fashioned the first humans from maize dough. The life cycle of the maize plant was full of spiritual meaning, serving as a metaphor for the stages of human life from birth, through maturity to death and ultimately rebirth in new generations of children.

> 'They rejoiced over the discovery of the marvellous mountain filled with yellow corn ears, and white corn ears, and cacao and chocolate ... It was full of the sweetest foods.'

Popol Vuh, Maya creation myth

Other important staples were squash, sweet potatoes and manioc (cassava), a high-yielding starchy root vegetable. Tree crops such as avocado, cacao, guava and breadnut, were also important food sources, and they required little labour and could even be grown in the cities. Chilli and vanilla were the most important spices used by the Maya. Beans provided the Maya with most of their protein as they kept few domestic animals. Ducks, turkeys, doves and dogs were bred for meat. Fish, shellfish and wild game were also eaten. Cotton was the most important non-food crop. It was spun into thread, dyed with plant and mineral dyes, and woven into cloth. Farmland was owned by lineage groups and was worked communally. Farmers paid taxes to the king in the form of food, cloth and labour on building projects. They also worked the lands of their local lord and gave him 'gifts' of food, and made offerings to the gods through the priests.

CRAFTWORKERS

Between the farmers and the small Maya social elite were the craftworkers. Most craft production was on a household scale with a senior family-member directing production. As well as some part-time farming, such enterprises would produce pottery, stone tools, jade and turquoise ornaments, cloth, baskets and mats. Metals were not used during the Classic period. There was probably a clear division of labour in craft production, with women certainly specializing in spinning and weaving. In the late Classic period, there was industrialized mass-production of pottery in specialized workshops. Moulds were used to create standardized products.

Considerable numbers of skilled stone cutters, sculptors, plasterers and woodworkers must have been needed to build the many tombs, temples and pyramids that dominated Maya cities. Others may have worked burning lime to make plaster, and grinding pigments for paint – Maya buildings and sculptures were brightly painted in red, white, yellow and green. The chisels used by stone cutters and sculptors were produced at flint mining centres: these useful tools would have been created by specialist craftworkers.

Long-distance trade in the Maya world was in the hands of itinerant merchants and peddlers who bought and sold goods in local markets. While local trade was in necessities, long-distance trade was mostly in luxuries for the elite. The main exports from the Maya lands were jade, obsidian, salt, cacao, jaguar furs and quetzal feathers. Imports included rubber, turquoise and bitumen. The Maya understood the principle of the wheel, but did not use it for transport, probably because they lacked draught animals. Trade goods were, therefore, carried by porters in human caravans, or by canoes along rivers and along the coast.

DRINK OF THE GODS

Chocolate – *xocoatl* – was a sacred drink for the ancient Mesoamerican elite. Cacao beans were probably first used to make drinking chocolate by the Olmecs around 1200 BC, but there is evidence that the Maya cultivated cacao trees not long after this date. According to their inscriptions, chocolate was mainly drunk by the Maya during religious rituals, probably because of its mild stimulant effect. Maya drinking chocolate was a frothy, bitter drink, flavoured with chilli pepper, vanilla or annato. Cacao beans were so valuable they were widely used as a form of money in Mesoamerica: the Aztecs even went to war to conquer areas that produced them.

In the later eighth century AD, the Maya kingdoms were outwardly flourishing. Great monuments were still built and the population was rising. In AD 790, more kingdoms erected commemorative steles than at any time in Maya history. The dominance of warfare in the stele texts is the only clue that all was not well with the Maya. Yet within a decade, the Maya were in crisis. One by one, the lowland kingdoms collapsed. The population declined dramatically, new building ceased, and the tradition of erecting steles came to an end. The last monuments were erected at Palenque in AD 799, at Yaxchilan in AD 808, at Quirigua in AD 810, at Copán in AD 822, at Tikal in AD 889 and at Calakmul in AD 899 or AD 909. By AD 950, every city in the lowlands lay in ruins and was being reclaimed by the forest.

DECLINE AND FALL

Studies of sediments drilled from lake beds reveal that the Maya had become the victims of an ecological crisis brought on by their own success. The late Classic was a time of massive deforestation, soil erosion and soil exhaustion. Over-exploitation of fragile rainforest soils brought about the collapse of agriculture. Starvation followed with political disintegration not far behind. Their failure to secure good harvests undermined the legitimacy of the kings. Within a century, a population that had numbered over two million was reduced to a few tens of thousands.

The wider circumstances of the collapse seem to be related to the destruction of Teotihuacán around AD 650. The dominance of that great city had suppressed inter-state competition throughout Mesoamerica: its fall created a power vacuum that Maya rulers tried to fill through warfare and by commissioning ever more ambitious building projects. In the century after the fall of Teotihuacán, Maya civilization reached its peak, but only at a price. Pressure on the peasantry to supply food, labour and building materials increased to such an extent that agriculture was intensified beyond the point that could be sustained by the environment. The short-term gains of agricultural intensification succeeded in hiding the underlying malaise for several decades. When soil fertility finally began to fail, kingdoms fought desperately over the areas where agriculture was still viable. Once these areas too were over-exploited, the complete collapse of Maya civilization in the lowlands became inevitable.

Great city
View from the Pyramid of the Moon to the 60-metre (200-ft) tall Pyramid of the Sun. With a volume of approximately 1.2 million cubic metres (40 million cubic ft), the pyramid was the largest building of the Precolumbian Americas – by way of comparison, the Great Pyramid of Khufu has a volume of approximately 2.5 million cubic metres (90 million cubic ft). All the pyramids at Teotihuacán originally had temples on their summits.

THE PLACE OF THE GODS: TEOTIHUACÁN

Even in ruins, Teotihuacán ('the place of the gods') spoke to later generations of Mesoamericans of power. It was here, they believed, that the gods had met to create the world. Teotihuacán began modestly, around 200 BC, as one of many small market towns in the fertile Valley of Mexico. When its dominating neighbour Cuicuilco was destroyed by a volcanic eruption around 50 BC, the city began to grow rapidly. By AD 100, Teotihuacán's population was about 40,000 and by the time the city was at its height in its Classic period (AD 150–650) that had reached 150,000.

Unusually for a New World city, Teotihuacán was carefully planned on a grld pattern around a vast ceremonial centre. This centre was dominated by the huge pyramids of the Sun and the Moon. With a base measuring 210 metres (690 ft) across and a height of over 65 metres (210 ft), the Pyramid of the Sun is the largest building of the pre-Columbian Americas. Teotihuacán was also a commercial centre and it controlled much of Mexico's trade in obsidian. The influence of Teotihuacán can be seen in the art and architecture of cities across Mesoamerica. Little is known about Teotihuacán's political organization and it is not clear whether this was the result of conquest or because local elites emulated the styles of what was the most powerful city of its day. Few texts, which might shed light on this, have been discovered. For unknown reasons, Teotihuacán was violently destroyed around AD 650, sending shock waves throughout Mesoamerica.

Maya civilization survived the Classic collapse in a diminished form in the Guatemalan highlands and the Yucatán. The fall of the great cities of the Petén benefited the Maya in these areas by creating new political and commercial opportunities. This was especially true of the Putún or Itzá Maya, a seafaring people who operated a trading network along the Caribbean and Gulf coasts from their homeland on the Bay of Campeche. Sometime around AD 850–900, the Itzá founded Chichén Itzá in northern Yucatán.

THE POSTCLASSIC MAYA (909–1697)

In AD 987, Chichén Itzá was captured by Kukulcán, and was rebuilt in the Mexican Toltec style. The Toltecs were descendants of two tribal coalitions which migrated into the Valley of Mexico after the fall of Teotihuacán and quickly became the dominant power there. Little is known about their history, but their legends feature prominently in the traditions of the Aztecs, who claimed to be their descendants. The most important legend concerns Topiltzin-Quetzalcóatl, a real king born in AD 935 or AD 947, who came to be identified with the god Quetzalcóatl ('feathered serpent'). Because he opposed human sacrifice, the god Tezcatlipoca overthrew Topiltzin-Quetzalcóatl, who fled east overseas on a raft of sea serpents, promising one day to return and reclaim his kingdom. Intriguingly, Kukulcán's name means 'feathered serpent' in Maya and feathered serpent motifs are found everywhere in Chichén Itzá.

The new Toltec rulers depopulated the surrounding area, concentrating the local Maya around Chichén Itzá to make them easier to control. Toltec domination of Chichén Itzá lasted about 200 years. During that time, the city became an important religious centre, where pilgrims came to make offerings to the rain god Chaac at its sacred well. It was also around this time that the Maya first acquired metalworking skills, making ornaments and bells by casting gold and copper. In 1221, the Maya reasserted their dominance of

Yucatán, when Hunac Ceel, ruler of Mayapán, conquered Chichén Itzá. Hunac Ceel's Cocom dynasty ruled Yucatán until 1441, when their empire broke up into around 17 independent kingdoms.

Less is known about the Postclassic in the Guatemalan highlands. The Classic collapse began a series of migrations, out of which the four kingdoms of the Mam, Quiché, Cakchiquel and Pokomam Maya emerged. The Quiché were the most powerful of these until the late 15th century, when they were overtaken by the Cakchiquel. The rulers of these kingdoms claimed Toltec ancestry, but their culture was completely Maya. In the 13th century, Itzá migrants founded the city of Tayasal on an island in Lake Petén Itzá in the still depopulated Petén lowlands. This remained the sole Maya city in the region.

THE SPANISH CONQUEST
The culture shock when the Old and New Worlds met for the first time at the beginning of the 16th century was great on both sides. Unfortunately for the people of the New World, this was no meeting of equals. The Europeans who followed Columbus across the Atlantic possessed technology undreamed of in the New World. The Old World civilizations all grew up in contact with one another. Even if these contacts were indirect, through nomadic traders for example, they led to the exchange of ideas and technology. Whatever one civilization invented soon spread. In 1500, all the Old World civilizations possessed ocean-going ships, iron and steel and gunpowder weapons.

The same links that transferred technology also spread diseases. The consequences of diseases like the bubonic plague that ravaged Eurasia in the 1340s were catastrophic, but the survivors passed their natural resistance on to their descendants. In contrast, the peoples of the New World suffered from few epidemic diseases. When they first came into contact with Europeans, they had no resistance to common diseases like influenza and measles. Epidemics raged far in advance of European explorers and settlers, killing tens of millions of native Americans and softening them up for conquest.

The first contact between the Mesoamerican civilizations and Europeans took place in 1502 between Columbus and the crew of a large Maya trading canoe off the coast of Honduras. Sporadic contacts followed and, probably as a result of these, the Maya were decimated by smallpox. The Spanish conquistador Hernán Cortés briefly landed in Yucatán in 1519 on his way to invade the Aztec empire. It took Cortés only two years to conquer the Aztecs. In 1524, Cortés began the conquest of the Maya.

The Maya proved much more difficult to conquer than the Aztecs. In part, this was because the tropical environment of the Maya lands was more challenging than the uplands of Mexico. The main reason, however, was the Maya's lack of political unity. The centralized Aztec empire fell easily into Spanish hands because, once they had captured the capital and the emperor, they could control the rest. The Maya lacked any centralized institutions, and the Spanish conquest was therefore a piecemeal affair. The highland Maya were subdued by 1527, but it took another 20 years to conquer the Maya of Yucatán. The last Maya kingdom to fall was Tayasal in Petén. Secure on its island, Tayasal was not finally conquered by the Spanish until 1697.

Feathered snake
A head of the feathered serpent deity Kukulcán at Chichén Itzá. Kukulcán is the Maya equivalent of the Mexican feathered serpent god Quetzalcóatl, whose worship was central to Toltec and Aztec religion.

THE INCA

THE last and greatest of the civilizations of ancient South America was *Tawantinsuyu*, the empire of the Incas. This well-organized state united 12 million people and almost all of the Andean region under its rule. The Inca empire was also the first New World civilization fully to leave the Stone Age by bringing metal tools and weapons into everyday use. Barely a century old when it was conquered by the Spanish in 1532–1536, the empire was heir to a tradition of civilizations extending back to the third millennium BC. The Incas' own historical traditions deliberately obscured this rich past. Believing themselves to be the chosen people of the sun god Inti, they maintained that civilization had begun with them and saw their wars and conquests, like so many of history's great powers, as part of a divine mission to bring enlightenment to the barbarous.

**Previous page:
Machu Picchu**
Lying on a ridge high above the Urubamba river valley in Peru, Machu Picchu was built as an administrative and religious centre by the emperor Pachacuti.

Although the Inca empire fell in relatively recent times, our knowledge of it is in some ways more uncertain than for many far more ancient civilizations. Almost uniquely for a highly organized state, the Incas used no system of writing. Our understanding of the other ancient civilizations discussed in this book is informed by their own contemporary records. In contrast, all our accounts of Inca history, beliefs and political and economic organization were written only after their conquest by the Spanish. Some of these accounts were written by Spanish colonists, who were hostile or may not have fully grasped what their native informants were telling them. Other accounts were written by conquered Incas who had learned to write and may be presenting an idealized view.

EMPIRE OF THE SUN

Archaeologists believe that the Incas emerged from the Killke culture, which flourished in Peru's Cusco valley between c.AD 1000 and the late 15th century. They spoke Quechua, a language spoken by eight to ten million people in the Andes today. According to their legends, the first Inca was Manco Cápac. Several different stories were told about Manco and it is possible that he is a completely legendary figure, invented to give the Inca rulers a divine ancestry. In the best known story, Manco Cápac was the son of the Sun god Inti. His father sent him to earth with a gold staff called tapac-yauri, instructing him to build a temple at the place where the staff sank into the ground. Manco emerged from a cave at Pacaritambo (the 'Dawn Inn'), about 18 miles (29 km) southeast of Cusco, along with his three brothers and four sisters. From two other caves at Pacaritambo emerged the first ten *ayllus* (clans) of the Incas. After a search lasting many years, Manco finally found a place where his staff sank easily into deep, fertile soil – here he founded the city of Cusco, the capital of the Inca empire. Over the spot where his staff had sunk, Manco built the Coricancha, the Incas' most important temple, and dedicated it to Inti. The Incas believed this spot marked the centre of the universe. Manco married his sister Mama Oqlyo. They had a son, Sinchi Roca, who eventually succeeded Manco as ruler. After a reign of about 40 years, Manco turned to stone. This ancestral stone was one of the Incas' most sacred objects, or *huacas*.

If Manco Cápac was a real historical figure he must have ruled around 1200. There is less doubt about Sinchi Roca (reigned around 1230) – his mummified body was still preserved at Cusco at the time of the Spanish conquest, along with those of his

Manco Cápac
The semi-legendary founder of the Inca state, is shown in this sketch by Guamán Poma (c.1535–c.1616), a native Peruvian who became literate in Spanish. He wrote an account of Inca government, comparing it favourably with the oppressive Spanish colonial government.

Andes mountains, Peru
The Andes are the world's second highest mountain range, after the Himalayas, with peaks rising over 6,000 metres (20,000 ft). The Incas pastured large herds of llamas and alpacas on the cold high pastures below the snowline.

successors – so he may have been the real founder of the Inca state. For 200 years, the Inca state was no more than a local power, controlling just a few hundred square miles. However, this changed dramatically during the reign of Pachacuti Inca Yupanqui (ruled 1438–1471). Pachacuti gave the Incas a sense of divine mission. He claimed that the creator god Viracocha had appeared to him in a vision and directed him to perform great deeds. Armed with this 'mandate of heaven', Pachacuti created the Inca empire, *Tawantinsuyu*, the 'Land of the Four Quarters'.

A TIME OF CRISIS

Pachacuti came to the throne at a time of crisis for the Incas. Faced with an invasion by their powerful enemies, the Chankas, Pachacuti's father Inca Viracocha, and his elder brother, Urcon, fled from Cusco. Pachacuti rallied the Incas and led them to a decisive victory. At a critical moment of the battle, Pachacuti strengthened his warriors' faltering courage by crying out that the stones in the fields were turning into armed men to help them fight. As result of his victory, Pachacuti usurped the throne.

Seizing the moment, Pachacuti united the neighbouring Quechua-speaking tribes under his leadership and awarded them Inca citizenship, at a stroke securing their loyalty and greatly increasing the troops at his disposal. Now, Pachacuti began to conquer the Chankas, the Ayamarca and the Cuyo, among many others. Enemies were invited to submit, and those who refused were conquered with great brutality. Conquered tribes were required to supply warriors for the Inca armies. Once he had secured full control of the Cusco region, Pachacuti spent several years conquering the small Aymara kingdoms of the Lake Titicaca basin, the most densely populated region of the Andes. At this point, Pachacuti handed over command of his armies to his son Tupac Yupanqui, while he concentrated on building a strong government for his empire.

Through the remainder of his father's reign, and throughout his own reign (1471–1493), Tupac Yupanqui campaigned relentlessly, adding over 300,000 square miles (800,000 sq km) to the Inca empire. Tupac's first campaigns had expanded the Inca empire through the Peruvian highlands north into Ecuador. Since the ninth century AD, the Peruvian coast had been dominated by the Chimú empire. The Chimú defended their southern frontier with strong fortifications, but they were unprepared for the speed of Inca expansion. When he invaded the empire in 1470, Tupac easily outflanked the Chimú defences by attacking from the north. As the Incas closed in on his capital at Chan Chan, the Chimú emperor's courtiers persuaded him to surrender. Tupac swept on south, conquering the Nazca and other peoples of the Peruvian coast.

In 1471, Pachacuti abdicated in favour of Tupac. Early in his reign, Tupac faced a major rebellion by the Aymara around Lake Titicaca. After crushing the rebellion, Tupac began a series of campaigns which brought vast areas of modern Bolivia, Chile and Argentina into the Inca empire. By the time of his death in 1493, the Inca empire extended over 3,000 miles (4,800 km) north to south and was close to the practical limits of expansion. The Amazonian rainforest and the southern Andes were regions with sparse and mobile populations that would have proved difficult to control and had environments that were unsuited to intensive agriculture. Some modest conquests in Ecuador by Tupac's successor Huayna Capac (ruled 1493–1525) brought the empire to its greatest size.

MAP KEY

Inca heartland, 13th century

Maximum extent of the Inca empire 1525

- - - Chimú empire c.1470

■ Inca capital

● Known Inca provincial capitals

● Other Inca sites

ANTISUYU Major regions

Saraguro

Cusibamba

Sullana
Piura

Huancabamba

CHINCHASUYA

Cajamarca

Chiquitoy Viejo
Chan

Huaylas

Tamboratra

Huarás

Tunsucancha

Huánuco

Paramonga

Pumpo

Tarma Tampu

Anson

Jauja

Lima la Vieja

Pachacamac

Lurín

Incawasi

Huamunga

Machu Picchu

Vitcos

Ollantaytambo

Tambo Colorado

Pisac

Huaitará

Cusco

Abancay

Ica

Andahuaylas

Vilcashuamán

CUNTISUYU

ANTISUYU

Paredones

Raqchi

Ayaviri

Acari

Hatuncolla

Lake
Titicaca

Chigna Jota

Chucuito

Island of the Sun

Atico

Juli

Yumina

Pomata

Chuquiabo

Tiwanaku

Torata Alta

Cochabamba

Chiribaya Alto

Cotopachi

Paria

Hualla
Tampu

Porco

Pica

Tupiza

COLLASUYU

Catarpe

Peine Tampu

Meteorite Tampu

Andes

Mountains

Pacific Ocean

Atacama Desert

0   300 km

0   200 miles

Andean Origins

The Andean civilizations had surprising origins. In the rest of the world, the first complex societies developed only after the beginning of agriculture. In the Andes, complex societies first developed in fishing communities on the Pacific coast, which did not even use pottery. Thanks to the rich marine resources, these communities had labour to spare to build impressive ceremonial centres and temples as early as c.2600 BC. Farming – based on native food plants like potatoes and quinoa, and domesticated llamas and alpacas – began first in the uplands c.2000 BC. It spread to the arid coastal lowlands a few hundred years later, after irrigation techniques had been developed. Pottery came into use c.1800 BC.

Andean gold
Mochica gold headdress from a royal burial. The offerings in Moche burials reveal them to have been skilled craftsmen in gold, silver and copper metalwork, textiles and pottery.

Long-distance trade routes developed linking the coastal fishing communities and farming communities of the coastal lowlands with farming communities in the highlands and the Amazon basin. This interaction between the inhabitants of different environmental zones became a major factor in the development of the Andean civilization, as empire-building rulers sought to control the resources of as many different zones as possible.

Sophisticated monumental architecture first became widespread in the Early Horizon period (800–200 BC). The dominant culture was the Chavín style, which originated at Chavín de Huántar, a complex of masonry temples, subterranean passages and ceremonial courts with monolithic sculptures of gods and monsters, high in the eastern Andes in Peru. Chavín is thought to have been a pilgrimage centre for a religious cult which eventually spread over much of the Peruvian Andes. This period saw the first metalworking (in gold) in South America and the production of fine woven and embroidered textiles.

Huaca Pucliana
The Huaca Pucllana, an adobe (mud brick) ceremonial centre consisting of courtyards, ritual platforms, elite tombs and a 22-metre (72-ft) tall pyramid, at Lima, Peru, was built between AD 200 and AD 700. In the Inca Quechua language, 'huaca' signifies any sacred site.

The first state in South America developed in the Moche valley on the coast of northern Peru during the Early Intermediate period (200 BC–AD 750). At the heart of the Moche state were two vast adobe pyramids, the Huaca del Sol and the Huaca de la Luna. The larger of the two, the Huaca del Sol, was a stepped structure 40 metres (130 ft) tall, built of 143 million adobe bricks. Each brick bears a maker's mark, suggesting that the Moche invented the labour tax system later used by the Incas. The Moche did not use writing, but sent messages using beans painted with lines and dots. Around AD 200, the Moche began to conquer the neighbouring valleys along the coast, consolidating their conquests by building fortresses and provincial capitals. After AD 500, the Moche state went into decline as a result of repeated devastating floods and finally collapsed around AD 700. By this time, however, powerful states were also beginning to develop in the highlands, at Wari and Tiwanaku, for example. These rival empires dominated the highlands until they collapsed in a period of drought c.AD 1000.

The creation of the Inca empire was both a military and an administrative achievement. Inca armies were the largest and best organized in the history of ancient South America. Spanish sources and Inca oral traditions record that armies of over 100,000 warriors could be raised and, thanks to efficient logistics, kept in the field for long campaigns. Apart from a small elite force of imperial lifeguards, known as the *aucakpussak*, only the officers were full-time professional soldiers. The vast majority of Inca warriors were part-time conscripts. It is not clear how warriors were trained: it may be that it was a normal part of every man's upbringing.

THE MILITARY SYSTEM

Most South American Indians preferred to fight at long range with javelins and bows and arrows. Inca warriors brought a new ruthlessness to battle, fighting hand-to-hand with copper-headed clubs, battle axes and hardwood swords and spears. Engaging their enemies at close quarters like this made decisive, annihilating victories much more likely and prisoners were rarely taken. Inca armies were highly organized and tightly disciplined. Warriors were divided into regiments, and these were subdivided into smaller units based on multiples of ten, the smallest unit being ten men. Pack trains of llamas and female porters kept the army supplied when it was on campaign. Inca generals mastered sophisticated tactics, such as feigning retreat to draw unwary enemies into an ambush. They also understood the importance of holding forces in reserve to deal with unexpected situations and could exploit their superior manpower to divide their forces and attack their enemies from several different directions simultaneously. Warriors expected to be rewarded with beer, a share of plunder, gifts of cloth and decorations for bravery.

INCA HIGHWAYS

The Inca empire was unique among Andean states in building a network of strategic roads – estimated at around 12,500 miles (20,000 km) long, it was second only in size to the Roman empire's among ancient civilizations – which allowed troops to move quickly to combat threats to the borders or rebellions in the provinces. Deep gorges were spanned by rope suspension bridges and tunnels were dug to avoid lengthy detours around unscaleable cliffs. Government runners called *chasquis*, stationed every 10–12 miles (16–19 km) along the roads, relayed messages

Precarious path
Inca path and bridge at Machu Picchu. Inca roads were narrow because they were used only by pedestrians and pack animals. Many of them are still used today by the highland peoples of Peru.

to and from Cusco at an average speed of 140 miles (225 km) per day. Way stations called *tambos*, with hostels, storehouses and garrisons, were built along the roads at intervals of one day's journey. These distances were measured by the pace of a loaded pack llama. Conquests were consolidated by *mitima*, a policy of deporting rebellious populations en masse to the heart of the empire where they could be supervised, while their lands were resettled by loyal Inca subjects. The children of rulers who had submitted to Inca rule were sent to Cusco to act as hostages for their fathers' loyalty and to be educated in Inca ways.

A REGIMENTED STATE

The empire's military strength was built on the Incas' complex administrative system, which harnessed the empire's human resources with great efficiency. Inca society was rigidly hierarchical and highly centralized. At its head was the emperor or *Sapa Inca* ('the only Inca'), who was worshipped as a demi-god because of his descent from the Sun god. Below the emperor were the prefects of the Four Quarters (corresponding to the north, east, south and west), provincial governors and district officers called *karakas*. When an area was conquered by the Incas, its population was counted according to age, sex and marital status, together with its fields, pasture and livestock. The area was surveyed to make topographical models and detailed maps, which were painted on cloth. For taxation purposes, males and heads of households were graded by age and grouped into multiples of ten, rather like warriors in the army. The smallest unit was ten taxpayers, which was supervised by a foreman. In turn, ten such units were supervised by a *Pachaka Karaka* or 'chief of 100'. This continued in units of tens up to a *Hona Karaka*, or 'lord of 10,000', who was responsible to the provincial governor. It has been estimated that there were 1,331 officials per 10,000 head of the population, a number unparalleled in any other known ancient society.

THE RULING ELITE

In theory, the emperor enjoyed absolute power, but custom bound nearly all of his actions. Emperors practised polygamy, but the first and senior wife, called the *coya* ('queen'), was always a sister, so as to preserve the purity of the royal blood line. In the absence of the emperor, the *coya* acted as regent. Sister marriage was forbidden to non-royal Incas. The emperor nominated his successor, usually choosing his most capable son by the *coya*. Other royal children joined a privileged clan that lived at court.

Throughout their reigns, emperors remained deliberately remote from their subjects. Very few people had the right to meet the emperor face-to-face – usually at an audience he remained hidden from public view behind a screen. No one could approach the emperor unless he had first removed his sandals and placed a small burden on his back as a sign of humility. When he travelled around his empire, the emperor was carried in a litter. The main insignia of office were a headdress fringed with thin tubes of gold from which hung red tassels, and a war club with a gold star-shaped head. The emperor would sit on a modest cushion of red wool, which would serve as a throne.

Pack animals
A gold model of a llama. Llamas were bred mainly for meat and as pack animals; their abundant wool is too coarse to make good quality cloth.

INCA EMPERORS

HURIN DYNASTY
Manco Cápac c.1200
Sinchi Roca c.1230
Lloque Yupanqui c.1260
Mayta Cápac c.1290
Cápac Yupanqui c.1320

HANAN DYNASTY
Inca Roca c.1350
Yahuar Huacac c.1380
Viracocha c.1410–38
Pachacuti Inca Yupanqui 1438–1471
Túpac Yupanqui 1471–1493
Huayna Cápac 1493–1527
Huáscar 1527–1532
Atahuallpa 1532–1533

INCAS OF VILCABAMBA
Túpac Huallpa 1533
Manco Inca Yupanqui 1533–1545
Sayri Túpac 1545–1560
Titu Cusi 1560–1571
Túpac Amaru 1571–1572

Social security
A reconstructed Inca storehouse. The Inca state stockpiled food supplies to provide famine relief if harvests failed.

The relatively numerous Inca nobility was divided into two classes. The exclusive higher nobility shared a common ancestry with the Inca royal family. As such, they were the only true Incas. The higher nobility formed the executive decision-making class, monopolizing the highest offices of state. Provincial governors, generals and chief priests belonged to this class. The lower nobility was drawn more widely from the peoples of the Cusco valley, neighbouring Quechua-speaking peoples and the ruling classes of conquered peoples who had adopted Inca ways. As well as providing administrators, army officers and clan chiefs, the lower nobility included many technical specialists such as agronomists, architects, surveyors, hydrologists and engineers.

The nobility enjoyed many privileges. They were subsidized by the state, paid no taxes, were permitted to dress in a roughly similar way to the emperor, travel in a litter, keep servants and wear ear plugs. Because of these plugs, which set them apart from

> 'Inca Roca honoured the men of the royal family by allowing them to bore their ears where women do today, but with larger holes. This was the sign of nobility and royal caste.'

Fernando Montesinos (c.1630)

commoners, the Spanish referred to the Inca elite as the *orejones,* or 'big ears'. Though they were not considered to be noble, the state also subsidized artisans, including metalworkers, potters, weavers and jewellers, for their specialist skills. Entire colonies of artisans were transplanted from conquered provinces to settlements around Cusco.

DIVIDING THE LAND

The Inca administrative structure was superimposed onto an older Andean social structure based on the *ayllu* or clan. *Ayllus* were extended kinship groups claiming descent from a common ancestor, who was very often preserved as a mummy and displayed on special occasions. The *ayllu* was the basic land-owning unit in Inca society. No individual, even among the nobility, could own and dispose of land. For ritual and marriage purposes, each *ayllu* was divided into two groups, described as moieties by anthropologists, each with its own designated lands. Women from one moiety married men from the other moiety. Though women went to live with their husband's moiety, they remained full members of their birth moiety, so were always socially and economically independent of their husbands. *Ayllus* were ruled by two hereditary chiefs called *karakas*: the principal chief coming from the stronger moiety, and the secondary chief coming from the weaker. The chiefs managed their *ayllu*'s lands and acted as intermediaries with the gods to secure their people's well-being. If the crops failed, or any other disaster struck, the chiefs were held to be responsible and might be put to death.

For taxation purposes, the lands of an *ayllu* were divided into thirds, for the support of the community, the gods and the state respectively. Except for those in specialized occupations, all commoners paid taxes in the form of labour on the land allocated to the gods and the state. The lands of the gods had priority. The yields of these lands went to support the priesthood and to fill the temple storehouses. The state lands were given second priority. Agricultural produce was the main form of imperial wealth and it was displayed by building rows of stone storehouses in prominent locations where they could be seen from afar. The produce of the community's lands was redistributed by the local chiefs. Allotments were proportional to the number of dependants in each household.

In addition to agricultural taxes, able-bodied men also performed *mit'a*, a draft which could range from military service to labouring on civil engineering projects such as building roads, fortresses and agricultural improvements. The state had considerable discretion about the length of *mit'a* service. Government runners served 15 days a year

Inca tunic
A top-quality woven Inca tunic. The Incas considered fine textiles to be as valuable as gold.

to fulfil their *mit'a*, though they needed to train regularly to keep fit. Military service could be open-ended. Women and less able-bodied men paid taxes by producing textiles and cord. Men made cord and rope, women spun thread and wove cotton and woollen cloth from raw fibres handed out by the state officials, who also collected the finished cloth. Weaving was done on simple backstrap looms or vertical frame looms. Even the women of the royal family wove, though as a sign of femininity rather than from necessity. Different grades of cloth were produced: the highest grades, woven with intricate patterns and gold and silver thread, were highly valued.

TAKING WITH ONE HAND, GIVING WITH THE OTHER

Reciprocity was an important principle of the Inca state, and most of the taxes that were collected were eventually returned to the people. Workers and warriors performing *mit'a* expected to be supported by the state. As millions of people were performing *mit'a* at any given time, these rations used up the bulk of the royal revenues. Another major use of agricultural taxes was for famine relief. One of the purposes in building storehouses in prominent locations was to give local people reassurance that the state had the means to help them in bad times. Agricultural taxes sent to temple stores were used to provide the food and drink for the public feasts provided at religious festivals. Rulers also sponsored festivals to coincide with important periods in the agricultural year, such as planting and harvesting. People expected large quantities of *chicha* (maize beer) to be provided on these occasions. Seating at feasts was hierarchical and everyone drank from vessels appropriate for their rank: simple cups made from gourds for commoners, fine pots for minor officials and gold and silver cups for the elite.

State reciprocity to commoners mainly consisted of food and drink, but the nobility expected greater rewards appropriate to their status. Cloth, the revenue of the textile tax, was the most common reward for service. Cloth was graded according to quality, with the best cloth being given to people of the highest rank. It was mainly to provide state gifts to the elite that the artisan class laboured to produce fine pottery, woodwork and gold and silver jewellery. Stripping conquered states of their artisans deprived their elites of the means to control the production and distribution of luxuries and forced them into dependency on the gifts of the Inca emperor.

KEEPING A RECORD

Record keeping is essential for efficient government. The Inca state kept a vast amount of information relating to taxation, agricultural and census data, religious ceremonies and military organization, not in writing but on recording devices called *quipus*.
A *quipu* consisted of a long rope from which hung 48 secondary cords. Tertiary cords

'If there was a lean year, the Incas opened the storehouses and the provinces were lent what supplies they needed: then, in a year of plenty, they paid back all they had received. No one who was lazy or tried to live by the work of others was tolerated: everyone had to work.'

Pedro Cieza de Leon (1540)

could be hung from the secondary cords if needed. Knots were tied in the cords to represent single units, tens and hundreds. Different-coloured cords designated different commodities or categories of information. The *quipukamaks* (accountants) who could make and read the *quipus* were considered to be part of the lower nobility. Much of the Incas' religious and historical traditions was committed to memory by professional memorizers and was transmitted orally from generation to generation.

THE MEANS OF SUBSISTENCE

A major factor in the economy of the Inca empire (and of all previous Andean empires) was the interaction between different climate zones in the Andes. The mountains rise from the Pacific coast to an average elevation of between 3,000 metres (10,000 ft) and 4,500 metres (15,000 ft), but many peaks rise to over 6,000 metres (20,000 ft) and are heavily glaciated. The mountains are dissected by deep valleys and by high plateaus and basins, the largest of which is the Bolivian Altiplano, which averages 3,350 metres (11,000 ft) altitude. In the east, the mountains drop steeply to the rainforest of the Amazon basin. The mountains range from 400 miles (650 km) to as little as 75 miles (120 km) wide. Because of their great vertical range, the Andes contain a wide variety of environments, from rainforest at lower altitudes, through temperate forest to puna grassland above around 3,350 metres (11,000 ft). Above about 4,500 metres (15,000 ft) is mountain tundra, permafrost and snow and ice. The practical limit for agriculture is around 3,500 metres (12,000 ft), but the Incas made extensive use of the puna to pasture large herds of llamas and alpacas (both members of the camel family). The narrow coastal lowlands of Peru and northern Chile are extremely arid, but are crossed by seasonal rivers flowing out of the mountains, making agriculture possible with irrigation. The coastal waters have some of the richest fisheries in the world.

The products of the different environmental zones were exchanged vertically between communities: dried and salted fish and salt came from the coast; cotton, chillies, gourds, sweet potatoes, avocados and peanuts from the tropical lowlands and foothills; manioc (casava), fruits and exotic birds' feathers from the edge of the Amazonian rainforest; maize, quinoa (a native Andean cereal), potatoes and ulluco (a tuberous root) in the temperate zone; and meat and wool from the herds kept on the puna. Households at all altitudes bred guinea pigs for meat, feeding them on waste vegetable scraps. The desire of rulers to control the resources of as many different environmental zones as possible was a major motive for imperial expansion. The wide range of food sources available to the Incas provided considerable insurance against the failure of any individual crop. However, the Incas were vulnerable to famine as a result of El Niño events, which occur

Inca goldwork
The Incas worked gold, silver and copper by beating and casting. The Incas also made bronze, but its high tin content made it too soft to make useful tools for everyday use.

every three to seven years. Caused by unusually warm ocean temperatures off the west coast of South America, a severe El Niño causes the collapse of fish stocks, destructive flooding in the coastal lowlands and droughts in the Andean uplands. State stores provided food under these circumstances, but all aid was expected to be paid back once harvests recovered. Night frosts are common in the highlands, but daytime temperatures can still be high because of the tropical Sun. The Inca used these daily extremes of temperature to freeze-dry tubers and meat. Food preserved this way could be stored safely for many years.

FARMING, METALWORK AND MASONRY

The Incas maximized agricultural production by building irrigation canals and extending the area of cropland by building stone-faced terraces on steep mountainsides. Many of these canals and terraces are still in use today. The vast scale of Inca terraces impressed the Spanish conquistadors, and it was probably from their name in Quechua, *andenes*, that the Andes mountains were named. Although the Incas were still mainly reliant on wooden and stone tools, they were the first in the Americas to use significant quantities of metal implements, including copper and bronze crowbars, chisels, knives, axes and club heads. Inca metalworkers were expert in casting gold and silver jewellery and figurines, but little of this survived very long after the Spanish conquest: they were melted down into ingots and shipped to Europe.

The Incas are probably most famous today for their impressive polygonal masonry, spectacular examples of which survive in the 'lost city' of Machu Picchu, and at the Sacsahuaman fortress and other locations around Cusco. Using stone hammers, stonemasons shaped massive stone blocks, some of them weighing over 100 tonnes so that they fitted together with such precision that often not even a razor blade can be inserted between them. Archaeologists are still not sure how the Incas moved such heavy weights without a knowledge of pulleys and cranes.

INCA RELIGION

Inca religion centred on the official state cult of the Sun-god Inti, the divine ancestor of the Incas. Most Incas were farmers and they were particularly devoted to Inti because it was his warmth that made the earth fertile and ripened the crops. In art, he was represented by a human face on a rayed disk. Inti's wife was the Moon mother Mama Quilla, who regulated women's menstrual cycles. The Incas used the phases of the Moon to calculate their calendar. Other important gods were Pachamama, the earth mother, and Apu Illapu, the rain bringer. During droughts, the Incas made pilgrimages to Apu Illapu's temples to offer prayers and human sacrifices. In myth, Apu Illapu drew water from the Milky Way, the 'Celestial River', to pour onto the earth as rain.

The Incas' creator god, Viracocha, was rather distant from the common people's everyday concerns. The Incas believed that Viracocha created humans from clay at Tiwanaku on Lake Titicaca. He also created the Sun and Moon, and all kinds

Inca walls
The walls of Tambay Machay, a roadside inn near Cusco, are a fine example of tightly jointed Inca masonry. Inca masons used only stone tools to shape the blocks.

of animals and plants. He travelled across the face of the earth shaping the mountains and valleys. Viracocha was the Lord Instructor of the World; he taught humans how to farm and how to live in a civilized way. After completing these tasks, Viracocha disappeared across the ocean, promising to return one day. These acts of creation did not belong to a distant past: the Incas believed that the world was still newly made. Inca religion contained elements of animism and nature worship. They recognized thousands of places in the landscape, such as rocks, mountain tops and springs as *huacas* (sacred sites). *Huacas* could also be man-made objects, such as a temple, a bridge or even the mummy of a notable ancestor. The Incas built sacred cairns on high mountain passes to which passing travellers added a stone to lighten their burdens.

Terraced mountainside
The Incas extended the area of cultivable land by terracing the sides of mountains. These Inca terraces at Pisac, Peru, are still farmed today.

INCA MUMMIES

The Incas venerated their ancestors, whose spirits could still affect the well-being of the living. The bodies of important people were mummified. Their entrails were removed, then the body was dried and wrapped in fine textiles. Mummies were seen as being if

Inti Raymi, the Festival of the Sun, was the most important of the Incas' religious festivals. Held in honour of the Sun-god Inti, the nine-day festival marked the winter solstice (21 June in the southern hemisphere). The festival was marked by animal sacrifices and feasting. Large quantities of *chicha* were drunk at the festival. Beer was provided in line with the social hierarchy: Inti received the first offering, then the Sapa Inca, the nobility, and, finally, the common people. The festival was suppressed by the Spanish in 1535.

not alive, then not quite dead either. They were brought out of their tombs to participate in festivals, when they received offerings of *chicha* beer and food. Imperial mummies had living attendants to cool them with fans and brush away flies. The Incas believed that the good, which automatically included all the nobility, went to dwell with Inti after death, while the wicked went to a damp, cold underworld. Emperors' wives did not have long to wait to be reunited with their husbands in the afterlife: they were made drunk during the funeral rites and strangled.

The Incas built many temples and shrines. These were not places of public worship – the Incas performed most of their religious ceremonies outside – so much as homes for idols, sacred objects and for priests and Virgins of the Sun. The Virgins of the Sun were women who had been consecrated to the Sun and sworn to a life of chastity. Virgins of the Sun were selected from the Chosen Women, girls picked for their beauty and educated by the state in religion and domestic arts. The virgins assisted the priests, making ceremonial robes, brewing beer for festivals and performing other duties. The senior virgin was considered to be the bride of the Sun.

PRIESTS AND SACRFICES
One of a priest's most important duties was divination. No important decision could be made unless the omens were favourable. To prepare for divination priests chewed coca leaves or drank *ayahuasca*, a narcotic that affected the nervous system. It was believed this allowed the priest to communicate directly with the gods. The most important means of divination was to inflate the lungs of a sacrificed white llama and interpret the pattern of blood vessels.

Sacrifices were offered to the gods on every important occasion. Llamas, guinea pigs, maize, coca leaves and *chicha* beer were common sacrifices. The first day of the lunar month was marked by the sacrifice of 100 pure white llamas in the main plaza at Cusco. The gods were asked to eat the offerings so that they would know that the Incas were their children. The emperor made a daily sacrifice, burning the poncho he had worn on the previous day. Though not on the scale practised in Mesoamerica, human sacrifice was an important feature of Inca religion. The inauguration of a new ruler, epidemics, famines and droughts all demanded human sacrifice to propitiate the gods. Physically perfect children were chosen for sacrifice from the Chosen Women (these were considered fortunate because this guaranteed a happy afterlife) or from subject peoples as a form of taxation. The freeze-dried mummies of several sacrificial victims have been discovered on mountain tops, where they were taken and killed as offerings to the fierce *apu* mountain spirits. The most famous of these is 'Juanita', a 12–14 year-old girl discovered on the summit of 6,290-metre (20,630-ft) Mount Ampato in southern Peru. She had been killed by a blow to the head and buried with votive offerings sometime during the reign of Pachacuti.

THE CENTRE OF THE UNIVERSE
The empire's chief religious centre was Cusco, the centre of the universe. The four main roads leading to each of the Four Quarters radiated out from the city's main plaza. Cusco was little more than a village until the conqueror Pachacuti rebuilt it on a scale worthy of the capital of a great empire, with grand palaces, temples and fortresses.

TIWANAKU: THE PLACE OF CREATION

When Pachacuti Inca incorporated Tiwanaku into the Inca empire c.1445, the city had lain abandoned for nearly 500 years. Yet for the Incas, few of their acquisitions were as important as this, for Tiwanaku was the place where they believed the creator-god Viracocha had created the present world. Impressive ruins marked Tiwanaku out as an extraordinary place of power. Most prominent are its megalithic 'Gate of the Sun', sculpted from a single block of stone weighing 10 tonnes, and its enormous ceremonial platforms built from massive closely-fitted stone blocks each of which weighs upwards of 100 tonnes. Most of these huge blocks were hauled to the site from quarries lying 6 miles (10 km) away. Other building stones were shipped across Lake Titicaca. The ceremonial heart of Tiwanaku was separated from the rest of the city by a moat to create a sacred island.

Tiwanaku lies on the southern shore of Lake Titicaca in Bolivia at an altitude of over 3,800 metres (12,500 ft). Originating c.1500 BC, Tiwanaku developed into an important religious centre between 300 BC and AD 300. Around AD 400, Tiwanaku began to extend its control over the surrounding countryside. By around AD 750, its empire extended west to the Pacific Ocean and south far into Chile and Argentina. By this time, Tiwanaku's population had grown to around 30,000, with over 250,000 people in the surrounding areas. This population was sustained by intensive agriculture using raised fields separated by canals. The canals were used to irrigate the fields and to warm them in the cold highland nights as they released the heat absorbed during the day. The canals were also used for fish farming and the silt which accumulated in them was dug out and used as fertilizer. Around AD 950, the climate became drier, agriculture failed and by AD 1000 the city was deserted.

The Sun's gate
The Gate of the Sun at Tiwanaku was found lying down and cracked in two, perhaps as a result of an attempt to move it in ancient times. The original location and purpose of the gate are unknown.

Legend has it that Pachacuti used Tiwanaku, the place of creation, as his model when building Cusco. The most remarkable building at Cusco was the Coricancha temple. Built on the site of the original temple of Inti, the Coricancha was an imperial pantheon. The temple contained six chambers built around a square courtyard. One chamber, sacred to the Sun, was lined with gold and contained a golden idol of Inti. Next to it was a silver-lined chamber dedicated to the Moon and containing a silver image of Mama Quilla. Other chambers were sacred to Viracocha, the rain-god Apu Illapu, the rainbow-god Cuichu and to various celestial bodies. To represent the integration of the empire, each of the empire's subject peoples sent one of their sacred *huacas* to be placed in the temple.

INCA ASTRONOMY

The Coricancha was also the hub of a celestial sighting dial for tracking the movements of the Sun, Moon and the Milky Way. Sighting lines, called *ceques*, radiated out from the temple to sacred places in the landscape. The reference points along the 41 *ceques* helped to define community land and water rights, and to regulate the timing of agricultural tasks, religious rituals and festivals. The Incas lacked the sophisticated astronomical knowledge of the Maya and other Mesoamerican civilizations. The only heavenly body that was closely observed, apart from the Sun and Moon, was the Milky Way. Observed from the southern hemisphere this vast river of stars divides the night sky, rotating from a northeast to southwest axis to a southeast to northwest axis, and back again. It was these two axes that defined the limits of the Four Quarters, or *suyus*, of the universe. The Inca calendar was based on the lunar month rather than the solar year, and they used no formal dating system.

THE FALL OF THE INCA EMPIRE

In 1525, the Spanish conquistador Francisco Pizarro sailed from Panama to explore the northwest coast of South America. Like all conquistadors, he was interested in gold rather than geographical knowledge for its own sake. Few of his followers believed anything profitable would be found and, after many hardships and battles with hostile Indians, most turned back. Pizarro had only a dozen men with him when, in April 1528, he landed in northern Peru and discovered the Inca empire. Not daring to go further because of his small numbers, Pizarro returned to Panama to raise a stronger expedition.

The Incas were far more vulnerable than Pizarro may have realized. Spanish settlers had accidentally introduced smallpox to Argentina a few years earlier. Native Americans lacked resistance to the disease and an epidemic spread rapidly along trade routes into the Andes, striking the Inca empire in 1525. The Sapa Inca Huayna Capac was an early victim of the disease: he was with his army at Quito in Ecuador, preparing a campaign against the northern Andean tribes, when the epidemic struck. Huayna Capac's unexpected death threw the empire into chaos. The illness progressed so quickly that he did not have time to designate his successor before he died.

The legal heir was Huáscar, the eldest son of Huayna's *coya*, but Huayna had always favoured Atahuallpa, a son by a junior Ecuadorian wife. Huayna had considered separating Quito from the rest of the empire and giving it to Atahuallpa to rule as an independent kingdom. Nothing came of this proposal and after Huayna's death Atahuallpa recognized Huáscar as Sapa Inca. Huáscar, however, suspected Atahuallpa of separatism. After Huáscar executed some of his envoys, Atahuallpa rebelled. Huáscar held the capital, but Atahuallpa was popular in Ecuador and had the support of the army there. Huáscar lost no time raising an army to confront Atahuallpa, but he suffered a

Mummy
Surviving Inca mummies are sacrificial victims interred on mountain tops whose bodies have been preserved by the freezing temperatures and low humidity. The Incas also mummified the bodies of emperors and clan chiefs. These mummies were destroyed by the Spanish, so nothing is known about the methods used to preserve their bodies.

Nothing epitomized the conquistadors' greed for gold more than the search for Eldorado, 'the gilded one'. Eldorado was originally a legendary chief of the Muisca Indians of Colombia, who was believed to plaster his naked body with gold dust during religious festivals. After the ceremonies he dived into the Laguna de Guatavita, a crater lake 35 miles (56 km) northeast of Bogotá, to wash off the dust. His subjects threw offerings of gold into the water. Spanish conquistadors first heard this tale around 1530. One conquistador claimed to have been saved from a shipwreck and was carried inland to meet with Eldorado himself. Spanish expeditions into Colombia in the later 1530s found no trace of him however.

As the search spread into the basins of the Orinoco and Amazon rivers, Eldorado became not a chief but a kingdom of gold, with legendary cities called Omagua and Manoa. The Inca empire had delivered up such vast quantities of gold, that the Spanish found it easy to believe that another such kingdom existed. Gonzalo Pizarro, the half-brother of Francisco Pizarro crossed the Andes from Quito in 1541 to search for Eldorado in the Amazon basin. He soon gave up, but his lieutenant, Francisco de Orellana, pressed on, exploring the whole length of the Amazon to the Atlantic Ocean – but still found no trace of Eldorado. In 1595, Sir Walter Raleigh explored the Orinoco in search of Eldorado, and in 1603 the Portuguese explorer Pêro Coelho de Sousa searched for the fabled city north of Pernambuco in Brazil. Many adventurers bankrupted themselves, and hundreds died, in the futile quest for Eldorado, but, in the process, they opened up South America to European colonization. North America had its own elusive counterpart to Eldorado, the Seven Cities of Cíbola, the search for which opened up the desert south-west.

Gold mask
Discoveries of intricate gold work, such as this ancient Peruvian mask, helped to fuel rumours among European explorers and settlers of a fabled city made out of gold.

succession of defeats. Finally, at Cotabamba in 1532, Atahuallpa's general Chalcuchima captured Huáscar. Soon after, Cusco surrendered. Atahuallpa ordered the execution of Huáscar and 80 of his relations, including his wives and children. As Inca royals normally married their sisters, these were therefore also Atahuallpa's close relations.

REMOVING THE HEAD

Atahuallpa was still at Cajamarca, preparing for a triumphal entry into Cusco when Pizarro returned with a force of 180 men, 37 horses and two cannons. Pizarro quickly learned of the divisions within the Inca empire. Through emissaries, Atahuallpa agreed to meet Pizarro at Cajamarca. When the two parties met, the small size of Pizarro's force made Atahuallpa complacent. Legend has it that when the two leaders first met in the market square at Cajamarca, Pizarro handed the Inca ruler a Bible, which Atahuallpa threw to the ground. Some versions of the story state that the Inca ruler did this because he simply did not understand what a book was. Even so, the Spanish took this as an insult and an excuse for war. Pizarro's men attacked the Inca soldiers and captured Atahuallpa: his lightly armed bodyguard of 3,000 warriors was no match for the Spanish with their armour, steel swords and horses. Atahuallpa offered to pay an enormous ransom for his release, but even though he kept his promise – the Incas delivered some 24 tonnes of gold and silver to the Spanish, the largest ransom ever paid – Pizarro ordered his execution in August 1533. Atahuallpa's death effectively brought the Inca empire to an end. Pizarro appointed Atahuallpa's brother, Manco Inca Yupanqui, as a puppet emperor. When he rebelled in 1535, the Incas' former subjects fought for the Spanish. In 1537, Manco and his followers fled to the densely forested Apurímac region, where they built the fortified city of Vilcabamba. From this mountainous retreat, Manco and his followers held out for another 36 years, lauching raids on the Spanish and attempting to incite revolts by the indigenous population. Vilcabamba was finally captured by the Spanish in 1572, and Túpac Amaru, Manco's son and the last Inca ruler, was caught and executed.

Pizarro was fortunate that the Incas had not had time to recover from their civil war when he launched his invasion. He was fortunate, too, that smallpox had weakened them. However, Pizarro's superior technology does not by itself explain the rapid collapse of the Inca empire. Pizarro had less than 180 men with him at Cajamarca, while 30,000 fully armed Inca warriors were camped nearby. Given decisive leadership, the Inca forces could surely have overwhelmed the conquistadors by sheer weight of numbers. Unfortunately for the Incas, the efficient centralized hierarchical government that built and supported their empire was also its undoing. No important decision could be taken without the emperor, which meant that once Atahuallpa had been captured, the empire was effectively paralysed.

'The Spaniards arrived at a moment when the country was divided between two factions. But for this division it would have been impossible – or at least very difficult – to conquer it.'

Augustín de Zárate, *The Discovery and Conquest of Peru* (1555)

INDEX

METRO BOOKS
New York

An Imprint of Sterling Publishing
387 Park Avenue South
New York, NY 10016

METRO BOOKS and the distinctive
Metro Books logo are trademarks of
Sterling Publishing Co., Inc.

© 2010 by Quercus Editions Ltd

This 2013 edition published by Metro Books
by arrangement with Quercus Editions Ltd.

ISBN: 978-1-4351-5164-2

For information about custom editions,
special sales, and premium and corporate
purchases, please contact Sterling Special
Sales at 800-805-5489 or specialsales@
sterlingpublishing.com.

Manufactured in China

10 9 8 7 6 5 4 3 2 1

www.sterlingpublishing.com